T0328842

Foreign Direct Investment and Small and Medium Enterprises

Productivity and Access to Finance

Foreign Direct Investment and Small and Medium Enterprises

Productivity and Access to Finance

Khee Giap Tan • Kong Yam Tan

Lee Kuan Yew School of Public Policy, NUS, Singapore

World Scientific

NEW JERSEY • LONDON • SINGAPORE • BEIJING • SHANGHAI • HONG KONG • TAIPEI • CHENNAI

Published by

World Scientific Publishing Co. Pte. Ltd.

5 Toh Tuck Link, Singapore 596224

USA office: 27 Warren Street, Suite 401-402, Hackensack, NJ 07601

UK office: 57 Shelton Street, Covent Garden, London WC2H 9HE

British Library Cataloguing-in-Publication Data
A catalogue record for this book is available from the British Library.

FOREIGN DIRECT INVESTMENT AND SMALL AND MEDIUM ENTERPRISES
Productivity and Access to Finance

ISBN 978-981-4678-80-3

In-house Editor: Dong Lixi

Typeset by Stallion Press
Email: enquiries@stallionpress.com

Printed in Singapore

Foreign Direct Investment and Small and Medium Enterprises: Productivity and Access to Finance

CONTENTS

About the Editors

Khee Giap Tan is the Co-Director of Asia Competitiveness Institute and Associate Professor at the Lee Kuan Yew School of Public Policy. He is also the Chairman of Singapore National Committee for Pacific Economic Cooperation. Upon graduating with a PhD from University of East Anglia, England, in 1987 under the Overseas Research Scheme awarded by the Committee of Vice-Chancellors and Principals of the Universities of the United Kingdom, he joined the banking sector as a treasury manager and served as secretary to the Assets and Liabilities Committee for three years, there after he taught at the Department of Economics and Statistics, National University of Singapore, 1990–1993. Dr Tan joined Nanyang Technological University in 1993 and was Associate Dean, Graduate Studies Office, 2007–2009. He is now with Lee Kuan Yew School of Public Policy, National University of Singapore. Dr Tan has consulted extensively with the various government ministries, statutory boards and government linked companies of Singapore government on policies concerning financial, fiscal, trade, tourism, public housing, labor, telecommunication, tourism, liveable cities, creative industry, media, community development, airport and seaport activities. He has also served as a consultant to international agencies such as the Asian Development Bank, Asian Development Bank Institute, United Nations Industrial Development Group, World Gold Council, ASEAN Secretariat, Central Policy Unit of Hong Kong, Kerzner International, Las Vegas Sands, Marina Bay Sands, and other international financial institutions and multinational corporations. Dr Tan is the lead author for eight books and published in international refereed journals such as Applied Economics (UK), ASEAN Economic Bulletin (Singapore), Asian Economic Papers (US), Competitiveness Review (UK), International Journal of Business Competition and Growth (UK), International Journal of Chinese Culture and Business Management (UK), International Journal of Economics and Business Research (UK), International Journal of Indian Culture and Business Management (UK), Journal of Centrum Cathedra The Business and Economics Research Journal (Peru), Journal of International Commerce, Economics and Policy (UK), Journal of Southeast Asian Economies (Singapore), Review of Pacific Basin Financial Markets and Policies (US), and World Review of Science, Technology and Sustainable Development (Switzerland). He is the associate editor of the journal Review of Pacific Basin Financial Markets and Policies

1

(US). His current research interests include econometric forecasting, Cost of Living Index, Global Liveable Cities Index and competitiveness analysis on 31 provinces in China, 35 states in India and ASEAN-10 economies.

Kong Yam Tan is presently the Co-Director of the Asia Competitiveness Institute. He is also Professor of Economics at the Nanyang Technological University. From June 2002 to June 2005, he was a senior economist at the World Bank office in Beijing where he worked on issues of macro stabilization, integration of the fragmented domestic market, banking reform, international trade and investment, energy security as well as regional inequality. In 2004, he was a member of the World Bank expert group on the eleventh five year plan (2006–2010) for the State Council in China. The expert group provided analysis and policy recommendations on urbanization, regional inequality, innovation policy, energy and water policy as well as strategy on banking reform to the Chinese government. Prior to that, he was the chief economist of the Singapore government (1999–2002), Head, Department of Business Policy, Faculty of Business Administration at the National University of Singapore (NUS). He is a graduate of Princeton (1975–79, class of 1931 scholar, Paul Volcker Thesis prize) and Stanford University (1980–83), where he completed his Master and PhD in three years. Prior to joining NUS, he has worked at the Hoover Institution at Stanford University, World Bank, the Monetary Authority of Singapore, and was the Director of Research at the Ministry of Trade and Industry in Singapore. His research interests are in international trade and finance, economic and business trends in the Asia Pacific region and economic reforms in China. He has published ten books and numerous articles in major international journals including American Economic Review, World Bank Economic Review, Long Range Planning, Australian Journal of Management etc on economic and business issues in the Asia Pacific region. He served as board member at the Singapore Central Provident Fund Board (1984–96) and the National Productivity Board (1989–90). He has also consulted for many organizations including Temasek, GIC, Citigroup, IBM, ATT, BP, ABN-AMRO, Ikea, Bank of China, China Construction Bank, People's Bank of China, EDB, Areva, Capitaland, Guangdong provincial government, Samsung, Mauritius Government, Ministry of Trade and Industry, Mobil, Singapore Technology, etc.

Introduction

Foreign Direct Investment (FDI), Productivity Spillovers and the Role of Small and Medium Enterprises (SMEs) Financing

Khee Giap Tan and Kong Yam Tan

Asia Competitiveness Institute
Lee Kuan Yew School of Public Policy
National University Singapore, Singapore

Abstract

There is a large literature dealing with the spillover effects of foreign direct investment (FDI) flows to emerging and developing economies at the aggregate level. Beyond the aggregate impacts, a growing number of studies also examine the impact of FDI spillovers on firms of different sizes, especially small and medium enterprises (SMEs). This book features seven chapters of empirical studies dedicated to exploring issues relating to the various interactions between FDI flows, productivity spillovers and SMEs in Asia and beyond.

Keywords: Foreign direct investment; small and medium enterprises; productivity spillovers.

The surge in foreign direct investment (FDI) flows to the emerging and developing world, especially to the Asian region as it has given rise to a large body of literature examining the multi-dimensional impacts of FDI on productivity spillovers in domestic economies, both at the aggregate and firm levels. While the focus of the early related literature was mostly aggregate in nature, the development of better firm-level datasets have resulted in a growing number of studies focussing on the spillover effects of FDI on firms of varying sizes, particularly the small and medium enterprises (SMEs). Considering the important role SMEs play in several emerging and developing economies, in terms of employment generation and their contribution to output, it is important to understand the various interactions between the different dimensions of economic globalization and the opportunities and challenges faced by SMEs in these economies. More importantly, the aftermath of the global financial crisis and the resultant rise in risk aversion has resulted in choking the traditional financing channels available to SMEs. Easing credit constraints to revitalise the SMEs remains a policy priority as improved access to financing could allow financially constrained firms to increase their total factor productivity (TFP). In this context, there is a need to design effective policies that will not only address the challenges faced by SMEs, but also ensure that they are not left behind in the process of economic globalization and contribute to greater productivity improvements.

In this light, this book examines a set of important policy issues dealing with FDI, productivity spillovers and SMEs finance in Asia and beyond. It features seven chapters of empirical studies that focus on the various dimensions of economic globalization both at the aggregate and firm-level, which assume immense policy significance.

The book begins with a case study of the impact of FDI flows on regional innovation in China. Chapter 1 by Hein Roelfsema and Yi Zhang titled 'Globalization, Foreign Direct Investment and Regional Innovation in China' examines the connections between globalization, innovation, and disparities in China at the regional level, covering 29 Chinese provincial-level regions over 16 years from 1995 to 2010. In addition to finding those regions that attract inward FDI and exports that have become more innovative during this period, this chapter makes an important contribution to the literature by finding a nonlinear U-shaped relationship between globalization, regional income levels and innovation. Specifically, the empirical results suggest that both the lower middle-income and the most advanced regions gain from globalization relative to the higher middle-income regions in terms of increased innovation. They also find that differences across regions in terms of ownership structures of FDI are important factors in explaining the "within-region" effects of globalization on innovation. Specifically, the authors find that innovation is high when FDI takes the form of joint ventures, while innovation is lower in regions with dominant foreign ownership.

The other emerging growth star in the Asian region that opened up its borders significantly to FDI flows has been India. While there have been a number of studies examining the aggregate trends and implications of FDI flows into India, studies at the firm level examining the impact of liberalization policies on firm productivity have been relatively sparse. Chapter 2 "Trade and Investment Liberalization in India: Implications for Productivity Gains" by Ram Upendra Das tackles these issues by employing a firm-level panel dataset to investigate whether greater trade and FDI flows have jointly contributed to significant productivity improvements since 2000, as measured by increases in total factor productivity (TFP). One of the important contributions of the chapter is its examination of the determinants of TFP across a range of different industries as well as testing for the combined effect of trade and investment liberalization on productivity of firms between 2000 and 2008. The productivity analysis performed for all firms as well as firms with specific characteristics such as export or domestic market orientation or those with different ownership (foreign and domestic-owned) reveal the existence of significant productivity improvements since 2000 owing to trade and investment liberalization. This chapter also identifies variables such as imports of raw materials and capital goods, size of operation, quality of employment captured by wage rates, and technology imports as crucial determinants of firm productivity.

Continuing with the theme of FDI and productivity growth, Chapter 3 by Sasatra Sudsawasd and Santi Chaisrisawatsuk titled, "Foreign Direct Investment, Intellectual

Property Rights, and Productivity Growth" focuses on the crucial role played by intellectual property rights (IPRs) in facilitating productivity enhancements through FDI flows. This chapter uses panel data for 57 countries over the period 1995–2012, to investigate the impact of IPR processes on productivity growth. One of the distinguishing features of the chapter is that it decomposes the IPR processes into three different stages — innovation process, commercialization process, and protection process — and tests whether the impact of FDI on growth depends on the stage of IPR development in the particular country. The empirical analysis in this chapter suggests that better IPR protection is directly associated with productivity improvements only in developed countries, while the contribution of IPR processes on growth through FDI appears to be fairly limited. Further, one of the other important results of the chapter is that FDI inflows create better innovative capability leading to higher growth outcomes only in developed countries, whereas for developing countries, the relevant type of capital flow is FDI outflows and not inflows and that the increase in IPR protection and commercialization help to improve productivity particularly when the country acts as the investing country.

Having examined the different dimensions of FDI flows and its impacts on productivity, the rest of chapters focuses on the growing importance of small and medium enterprises (SMEs), their performance, their constraints as well as the policy priorities of governments moving forward. As Asian countries recover from the global financial crisis and continue to rebalance their economies by promoting domestic demand, SMEs have a pivotal role to play in this process. The related literature notes that SMEs have the capacity to stimulate domestic demand through job creation, innovation, and competition and those SMEs involved in global supply chains also have the potential to facilitate international trade. Considering the importance of fostering the growth and development of SMEs through productivity enhancements, especially to promote inclusive economic growth in emerging economies in Asia and beyond, there is a need to study the various challenges confronting SME growth and development.

Further, since the post global financial crisis phase has been characterized by steep risk aversion, which appears to have had a detrimental impact on providing stable access to funding for SMEs, there is an ever-growing need to focus on designing appropriate policies that would facilitate SME access to finance through alternative sources of funding (beyond conventional bank credit). In this context, Chapter 4 by Shigehiro Shinozaki on "A New Regime of SME Finance in Emerging Asia: Enhancing Access to Growth Capital and Policy Implications" assumes immense policy significance. It focusses on two important policy priorities for Asian policy makers to promote financial accessibility for SMEs in the region — enhancing bank access to credit (bankability) as well as enabling diversified financing models — that will in turn help achieve financial inclusion. This chapter also identifies areas that policies and regulations have not effectively addressed which otherwise would have reduced the impediments faced by SMEs to enter formal financial markets as well as gain access to a variety of alternative financing instruments. It provides a detailed account of the various financing options and instruments available to SMEs and those that should be harnessed effectively. It also complements this policy analysis with an empirical estimation of the financing gap for SMEs in Indonesia, the results of which indicate the limitations of traditional bank lending to SMEs during crisis periods.

It is also important to recognize and emphasize that the financing constraints of several SMEs and micro-SMEs (MSMEs) are largely structural in nature. As reiterated by Subika Farazi in Chapter 5, "Informal Firms and Financial Inclusion: Status and Determinants," a majority of these firms operate in the informal economy and the informal firms face a variety of constraints, among which lack of access to finance ranks as the most prevalent and important operational constraint these firms face. Chapter 5 describes the use of finance and financing patterns of informal firms, highlighting the differences between the use of finance among these firms as well as identifying the most significant characteristics of informal firms associated with higher use of financial services. Specifically, this chapter attempts to identify "associations" between financial inclusion of informal firms and various firm and country characteristics. While informality is not the only barrier firms face in their use of finance, it makes an important contribution to the literature by bringing out the salience of informality of firms as a growth constraint. It provides estimates of actual use of finance by informal firms, while also quantifying the differences in the use of finance between formal and informal firms. This chapter finds that firms in the informal sector are, on average, relatively younger, i.e., less than 11 years old and that a substantial proportion of informal firms finance their daily operations through informal sources, implying that the use of loans and bank accounts is very low. Further, a comparative analysis between formal and informal small-sized firms reveals that registered firms make greater use of bank accounts and loans on a comparative basis, which aligns with conventional wisdom as well. Contrary to informal firms, registered firms on average also rely relatively less on funds from informal and internal sources.

Chapter 6 in this series focusses on Singapore as a case study to understand why Singapore has lagged with respect to labor productivity, which has particularly been a far more serious concern for SMEs. Chapter 6 by Khee Giap Tan and Yan Yi Tan on "Promoting SMEs and Enhancing Labor Productivity in Singapore: A Policy Analysis" identifies the sources of growth in Singapore and simulates different scenarios pertaining to the potential growth the economy could achieve given a level of required productivity derived on the basis of some employment-growth assumptions. This chapter then moves on to address the issue of labor productivity for SMEs particularly given that it has been a relatively bigger problem for SMEs. It examines and evaluates the performance, challenges and opportunities for SMEs in the country as well as suggesting relevant policy strategies to revitalise the SMEs that they become more competitive moving forward.

The last chapter in this book winds up the discussion by focusing on entrepreneurial activities and the importance of institutions in facilitating such activities. Chapter 7 by Salman Doo on "Determinants of Entrepreneurs' Activities: New Evidence from

Cross-Country Data" undertakes an empirical investigation of the main determinants of entrepreneurial activities across three groups of countries over the period 2004–2008, by examining the importance of institutional setting and economic growth on entrepreneurial activities. By utilizing the classification of countries based on Economic Freedom Index and the World Economic Forum, this chater groups them on the basis of whether these countries are innovation-driven, efficiency-driven, or factor-driven. Subsequently, it tests for the importance of economic freedom in spurring entrepreneurial activities in these different groups of countries. The empirical results find a positive and significant role for economic freedom to facilitate entrepreneurial activities as well as economic growth in innovation and efficiency-driven countries which are in turn characterized by strong institutional systems. At the same time, it also finds that in factor-driven countries characterized by relatively less economic freedom and weak institutions, there is a significant negative relationship between economic freedom and entrepreneurial activities.

Overall, the empirical contributions in this volume ought to provide fresh insights about the interactions between FDI flows, productivity spillovers and SMEs in emerging and developing economies.

Chapter 1

Globalization, Foreign Direct Investment, and Regional Innovation in China

Yi Zhang[*] and Hein Roelfsema[†]

Jinhe Center for Economic Research
Xi'an Jiaotong University, P. R. China

†*Utrecht University School of Economics (USE)*
The Netherlands

Abstract

This chapter explores the connection between the external opening of China and differences in innovation across Chinese regions. For the period 1995–2010, we find that regions that attract inward foreign direct investment (FDI) and exports have become more innovative. Further, we show a U-shaped relation between globalization, regional income levels, and innovation, where both the lower middle-income and the most advanced regions gain from globalization in terms of increased innovation. The higher middle-income regions gain little from globalization in terms of innovation. We provide evidence that differences in ownership structures of foreign investments and outsourcing drive the results.

Keywords: Globalization; innovation; regional development; China.

1. Introduction

Over the last 20 years, China has gradually opened its market to imports and inward foreign direct investments (FDI). Since 2001, the increased outward orientation of China is cemented by its entry into the World Trade Organization (WTO), further supporting exports and outward investment flows. To date, the drivers of the strong rise of inward FDI and its effects on domestic economic and social development have received considerable academic and policy attention. Although external trade and FDI arguably have lifted hundreds of millions out of poverty, there are two major long-term concerns. First, China is still seen as the factory of the world, concentrating resources on low cost production with a strong focus on the assembly segment of the supply chain. A key concern is whether over time Chinese firms are able to upgrade their competence through innovation, enabling them to supply inputs with a higher value added, so as to capture a larger share of total revenues in consumer markets. If external

---

†Corresponding author.

opening improves the innovative capabilities of firms and workers, this is an important link between liberalization and development. Second, an oft-voiced concern in China is that external opening of the economy magnifies the income disparities across regions, as the richest regions are also benefitting most from trade and FDI. In the long run, such increased regional disparities provide pressures for unsustainable migration flows and may add to social unrest.

We take up both these issues in this chapter and study the interaction between external liberalization, longrun development through innovation, and regional income disparities. By using a panel of Chinese regions, for the period 1995–2010, we investigate the (causal) connection between external opening and innovation at the regional level. Controlling for geographical fixed effects and focussing on patterns within regions, we show that regions that engage in trade and attract more FDI indeed become more innovative. We also show that the effects differ among geographical lines and across regional income levels. We show that the effect of globalization on innovation is stronger in the eastern coastal regions and is less pronounced in other regions. Connected to this finding, we show that the effects of external opening are strong for both the richest regions and the poorest regions, while higher middle-income regions are the relative losers from globalization. Overall, our analysis shows that external liberalization in China has had a positive effect on economic development though over time it may magnify income disparities within China through scattered effects on innovation and technological upgrading across regions.

The main contribution of this chapter is that it provides a systematic analysis of the connection between globalization, innovation, and disparities in China at the regional level. Several recent papers, to be discussed in more detail in Sec. 2, also analyze innovation across regions, pointing out the importance of research and development (R&D) spending, public stimulus, and the role of universities. But most of these papers do not address the role played by globalization. In contrast, papers that discuss the role of exports and FDI on technology diffusion in general do not address the issue of the widening regional disparities as a consequence of globalization. We also complement several firm-level studies using survey data that often do not have a time component. In addition, due to the overall improvement and availability of regional data over time, we are able to use broader measures for globalization and innovation, which provides more robust results.[1]

A second contribution of the chapter is that it incorporates many novel multidisciplinary theoretical insights from business studies and economics to empirically analyze the effects of globalization on innovation in China. Although still an important channel, the older literature focuses rather exclusively on the role of regional absorptive capacity as a moderator for inward FDI and high-tech imports to result in

---

[1] Buckley *et al.* (2002) is the other landmark study of this early period. However, these authors concentrate on differences across industries of inward FDI. They show that firms in industries that attract higher levels of FDI are on average more productive.

technology spillovers (Blomstrom *et al.*, 2001).[2] Recently, several scholars have argued that entry modes matter for the transfer of technology (Antràs, 2003; Grossman and Helpman, 2005; Grossman *et al.*, 2005; Hennart and Brouthers, 2007). As we show in Sec. 3, the dominant entry mode by foreign firms differs markedly across regions, which in turn has a substantial within-region effect of globalization on innovation. We show that joint ventures are correlated with higher levels of local innovation, and that innovation is lower in regions where full foreign ownership dominates. Further, we take account of the recent theoretical arguments that differences across regions in external orientation of firms (exports and outward FDI) account for a substantial share in the variation in innovation (Cheung, 2010).

A third contribution is that the analysis caters to the shift in public policy attention towards long-term economic growth through national innovation policies and systems (see for example, Sun and Liu, 2010; Zhou and Wei, 2011; Wei and Liefner, 2012). When over time factor accumulation growth slows down, economic development will rely on increases in total factor productivity. It is well recognized that large differences in FDI driven capital accumulation initially have contributed to a widening income gap between the coastal and the interior regions. However, since 1992, the Chinese government has aggressively pursued a policy that aims to divert FDI towards the interior regions. Yu *et al.* (2008) show that such policies on average have been a success in channelling FDI to backward regions, so it is of interest to investigate whether this policy change has contributed to innovation and thus to lowering regional income inequality in the long run.

The chapter is set up as follows. In Sec. 2, we discuss related literature that address the effects of FDI on technological development, to those that connect regional development to innovation and technology adoption, ending with closely related papers that also analyze the link between globalization and innovation in a regional context. Section 3 introduces the data and provides a descriptive analysis of the variables that are of the most concern to this chapter: globalization, innovation, and economic development across regions. Section 3 also discusses the econometric methods used in the study. Section 4 presents the empirical results, where we zoom in on differences across income groups, modes of globalization, and changes in the effects of globalization over time. Section 5 concludes this chapter.

2. Related Literature

The effects of trade liberalization and globalization on economic structure and innovation are widely studied in the literature, especially in the context of the early endogenous growth models (Grossman and Helpman, 1990, 1991; Grossman *et al.*, 1993). In general, international technology transfer is widely seen as an important contributor to economic development. The early papers have a strong focus on the

---

[2] Beyond the scope of this chapter, there is also a large literature that uses China's opening as a natural experiment to study the locational determinant of FDI of western firms from the Ownership–Location–Internalization perspective.

technology diffusion in the networks of multinational corporations that engage in FDI towards developing countries and emerging markets. Key mechanisms are the demonstration effect and the mandatory sharing of technology in mergers, acquisitions and joint ventures, which allow domestic firms to upgrade quality and launch new products. Further, the increase in competition in the domestic market because of entry of foreign multinationals provides stronger incentives for local firms to innovate.

There are several papers that study the effect of inward FDI on the innovation performance of Chinese firms. Buckley *et al.* (2002) analyze the effects of FDI across sectors and firms. They find that the investment of foreign firms has a positive effect on productivity.[3] A large number of studies confirm this finding (see for example, Cheung, 2010 and the references therein). However, there is considerable dispute about the relative importance of FDI when compared to other drivers of innovation, such as public investment in R&D and science and technology policies. On the one hand, for example Tang and Hussler (2011) argue that FDI is more important for innovation than the national innovation system. By contrast, in a study of the information and communication technology (ICT) sector, Wei *et al.* (2012) argue that locational and firm-level capabilities are more important drivers for innovation than FDI. Even stronger, controlling for endogeneity by focussing on a specific sector and specific locations, they show that innovation is negatively associated with the external orientation of firms in the ICT sector.

There have been other important qualifications that concentrate on the interaction of underlying firm and region specific factors to stress the nonlinear effect of FDI on local innovation. When taking account of endogeneity by looking at subsamples of industries and firm size, Hu and Jefferson (2002) show that absorptive capacity and complementarities in capabilities are important moderators for FDI to result in technology spillovers to local firms. In this line, an upcoming issue is whether the mode of cooperation between foreign and domestic firms affects technology transfer between partners. For the ICT sector, Sun and Du (2011) investigate the effects of the nature of the relationship between domestic and foreign owned firms on technology spillovers. They show that when firms only have production linkages, there is no significant effect on technology upgrading. By contrast, their analysis reveals that in general substantial spillovers occur when firms have technology cooperation agreements. Hence, perhaps trivial, when local domestic firms predominantly have arms-length production relations such as outsourced production contracts, the effects of inward FDI on local innovation are much less when compared to joint ventures in which partners cooperate and technology is shared. All in all, there is ample evidence that local conditions such as absorptive capacity, complementarities in production structure, public support, and the nature of the contractual relationships between foreign and domestic firms all matter for the effects of FDI on local innovation.

---

[3] As pointed out by Aitken and Harrison (1999), endogeneity is an important issue, for it is likely that foreign firms may want to invest in the more productive sectors and firms.

As Chinese domestic firms over time have become major exporters, it can be expected that experience in foreign markets also results in higher levels of innovation. The role of foreign market entry on innovation has recently received considerable attention. In the seminal Melitz (2003) model, productivity differences across firms drive internationalization, where the most productive firms (i.e., the most innovative firms) within an industry are internationally active. This setup mirrors the empirical findings of Bernard and Jensen (1999) who show that productivity drives internationalization for developed economies — and not the other way around. However, De Loecker (2007) shows that for middle-income countries exporting can have a substantial effect on firm productivity and innovation. For China, Cheung (2010) argues that FDI has positive effects on innovation through increased exporting capabilities of domestic firms. Guan and Ma (2003) show that exporting has a positive impact on innovative capabilities of Chinese firms. So far, there is little analysis beyond case studies that outward FDI by Chinese firms contributes to domestic innovation.[4]

There are large regional differences in innovation, which are seen as a major reason for regional income inequality (see Chan *et al.*, 2008 and Hu and Jefferson, 2008 for surveys on spatial determinants of innovation in China). Sun (2012) studies the interaction between innovation and regional economic development and finds a strong connection. This then leads to widening income inequality (Li, 2009). Li and Wei (2010) find strong differences in innovation across regions, where high-income regions are also the most innovative.[5] In addition, Liefner and Hennemann (2011) show that strong agglomeration effects in R&D and innovation magnify regional differences.

A small body of literature deals with the contribution of globalization to innovation across regions and its effects on regional inequality. Closest to our study, both in focus and empirical method, is the seminal contribution by Cheung and Lin (2004), who analyze the effects of FDI on innovation across Chinese regions. Using pooled OLS and a random effects panel model, they also find that inward FDI magnifies the gap in innovation across regions in the short period of 1999–2004. To measure innovation, they make use of data on patent applications at the regional level. We extend their work in several ways. To start, we use a far longer time frame, which allows both for using the fixed effects model to filter out unobserved heterogeneity across regions as well as inferring the causal effects (using internal instruments) within regions of globalization on innovation.

Using empirical techniques that restrict to analyzing differences between regions, they conclude that FDI favoured developed regions. With the help of longitudinal data, we show that recent FDI flows to low-income regions have also been successful in

---

[4] This is dubbed the Link-Leverage-Learning (LLL) mechanism, popularized by the work of John Matthews, e.g, Mathews and Zander (2007). See, for example, Fan (2011) for case studies on technology upgrading by venturing abroad in the Chinese telecom industry.

[5] A contrasting view is offered in Johnson and Liu (2011), who argue that in China there are emerging cross-regional technology markets, so that innovations are not locally restricted.

raising innovation in these regions. This positive effect in low-income regions can also be observed in Yu *et al.* (2008).

Moreover, since longitudinal data allow us to use GMM fixed effects methods, we shed light on how *within* regions, internationalization has had an effect on local innovation, arguing that this within effect differs across regions. At the firm-level — although this often restricts to cross-sectional analysis — there is also some new indirect evidence in line with our findings that the effects of internationalization differ across regions. For example, Su and Jefferson (2012) find the returns on domestic capital to be higher in the coastal regions when compared to the interior regions. By contrast, foreign owned capital is more productive in the interior regions, also pointing to a more mitigating role of FDI in the widening of regional disparities in China.

3. Data and Methodology

The data cover 29 Chinese provincial-level regions over 16 years from 1995 to 2010. To test the causal impact of globalization on regional innovation, with the help of a principal component analysis we generate a regional innovation index and a globalization index.[6] The resulting innovation index consists of several innovation output indicators at the regional level, including patent filings, new product launches, and a measure for product quality. The globalization index includes aggregated imports, exports, as well as inward and outward FDI. Precise information on the construction of the indices can be found in the appendix.

3.1. *Data exploration*

To explore the data, based on the distribution of initial 1995 regional income levels measured by gross regional product per capita (GRPPC), we split the 29 regions into four income groups. For these four groups, Table 1 shows the mean values of the innovation and globalization indices and their standard deviation within the group. We observe that, when compared to the poorer first and second quartiles of the initial income distribution, the richer regions in quartiles three and four have substantially higher average levels of both globalization and innovation. Further, for all income groups we observe that there are significant changes in the levels of globalization and innovation over time. In the panel analysis that follows, these within-region dynamics serve to identify the causal effect of globalization on innovation.

Table 1 also shows the average growth rates of innovation and globalization as well as the correlations between the two indices. The average growth rates indicate that in all groupings globalization and innovation are increasing. However, there are substantial differences in dynamics. We find that the initial high-income group of regions

---

[6] As an effective tool to identify latent patterns and to help reduce highly correlated variables, principal component analysis has been widely employed in composite indexing. Applications related to this chapter include the development of the European Innovation Scoreboard (Sajeva *et al.*, 2005) and the construction of the KOF index of globalization (Dreher, 2006).

Table 1. Main descriptive statistics and correlations for income quartiles.

Variable		Nation	Q1	Q2	Q3	Q4
Innovation	Mean	0.066	0.037	0.032	0.048	0.153
	Within S.D.	0.089	0.028	0.024	0.046	0.172
	Between S.D.	0.066	0.018	0.016	0.039	0.079
	Average growth rate	14.19%	13.11%	10.83%	10.24%	23.08%
Globalization	Mean	0.142	0.079	0.080	0.125	0.288
	Within S.D.	0.113	0.010	0.011	0.047	0.152
	Between S.D.	0.072	0.023	0.016	0.038	0.139
	Average growth rate	4.5%	3.7%	2.3%	5.0%	8.4%
Correlation		0.528***	0.296***	0.404***	0.182	0.347***

Note: Q1, Q2, Q3, and Q4 represent the first, second, third, and fourth quartile of the initial income distribution, respectively. ***Significant at 1%.

over time shows a much stronger increase in both globalization and innovation than other groups. Further, innovation in the third income quartile group of regions appears not to keep pace with the increase in global orientation of these regions. In addition, with respect to innovation, the poorest regions catch up with the middle-income regions. The last row in Table 1 shows the correlation coefficients between the innovation and globalization indices for the four income quartiles. The results indicate that the two indices are correlated, except for the third quartile of regions. A tentative conclusion is that there is a (strong) connection between globalization and innovation for the poorest and the richest regions. By contrast, the connection is much weaker for the higher middle-income regions.

As there is also large disparity across regions within each income group, in Table 2 we show the results of explorative time series regressions for each region. This analysis is to shed light on the individual regional connection over time between globalization and innovation.[7] It can be observed from Table 2 that significant connections between globalization and innovation at the individual regional level over time concentrate mainly in the second and the fourth income quartiles. For most regions in the third income quartile there is little connection between globalization and innovation. As such heterogeneous time-series effects may well be related to the underlying regional characteristics, we list the mean values and average growth rates of some selected variables. Based on the literature discussed above, we restrict this explorative analysis to variables that proxy for local absorptive capacity and the influence of foreign firms.

What can be learned from comparing regions that have comparable income levels but dramatically differ in correlation between innovation and globalization? In the lowest income group, the two provinces with high innovation (Shaanxi and Henan) actually do not have strong increases in globalization. These two regions, one with

---

[7] The time series model for each region is specified as: $Innovation_t = a_0 + a_1 Globalization_{t-1} + \theta Control_t + \varepsilon_t$. For efficiency reasons, we only control for the time trend given the limited number of observations for each region.

Table 2. Data description for selected variables at the province level.

Province	Innovation		Globalization		Time series	R&D/GRP		Schooling		Foreign exp.		Share	
	Mean	AGR (%)	Mean	AGR (%)	Coefficient	Mean	ARG (%)	Mean	ARG (%)	Mean	ARG (%)	Mean	ARG (%)
Q1 Guizhou	0.022	8.4	0.065	−0.9	0.244 (0.224)	0.004	4.4	0.201	7.2	0.120	3.2	0.670	1.5
Gansu	0.019	7.4	0.078	6.3	0.216*** (0.66)	0.010	−2.3	0.215	6.1	0.111	5.6	0.601	1.6
Shaanxi	0.040	18.6	0.071	3.1	1.374 (0.846)	0.023	1.2	0.388	6.6	0.130	20.8	0.657	2.0
Jiangxi	0.026	9.4	0.074	2.7	0.316 (0.232)	0.006	6.6	0.344	7.1	0.217	18.2	0.621	2.8
Henan	0.054	13.7	0.079	2.9	0.799 (0.609)	0.005	7.4	0.579	8.8	0.183	10.0	0.618	2.6
Yunnan	0.026	17.5	0.091	7.1	0.169 (0.130)	0.005	0.4	0.228	6.2	0.066	6.0	0.624	2.0
Sichuan	0.068	16.8	0.097	4.6	1.202*** (0.135)	0.012	0.7	0.500	5.2	0.162	16.6	0.607	2.8
Average						0.009	2.6	0.351	6.7	0.141	11.5	0.628	2.2
Q2 Anhui	0.041	17.8	0.086	4.2	1.065*** (0.185)	0.007	11.2	0.436	8.2	0.210	10.7	0.626	2.1
Ningxia	0.016	3.9	0.068	0.3	0.128 (0.184)	0.006	1.8	0.061	4.1	0.143	9.7	0.635	0.7
Hunan	0.052	12.3	0.093	6.1	0.411*** (0.061)	0.006	5.7	0.482	6.2	0.124	10.1	0.676	1.5
Guangxi	0.025	7.4	0.085	1.9	0.812*** (0.137)	0.004	3.7	0.281	7.1	0.195	5.8	0.696	2.2
Shanxi	0.027	11.0	0.081	3.3	0.867*** (0.122)	0.009	37.5	0.285	8.0	0.134	7.0	0.551	2.0
Qinghai	0.014	5.8	0.062	−1.2	0.223 (0.596)	0.005	2.5	0.060	1.5	0.034	41.7	0.606	3.7
Inner Mongolia	0.022	13.4	0.075	2.2	0.700*** (0.194)	0.004	11.2	0.197	5.5	0.171	12.0	0.589	3.4
Hubei	0.057	15.1	0.092	1.3	0.783*** (0.157)	0.010	4.4	0.509	7.1	0.268	8.5	0.635	1.7
Average						0.006	9.7	0.289	6.0	0.160	13.2	0.627	2.1
Q3 Hebei	0.044	9.3	0.100	3.8	0.423 (0.309)	0.005	9.3	0.496	7.4	0.296	9.6	0.612	2.3
Jilin	0.034	10.5	0.091	4.6	−0.229 (0.205)	0.009	4.1	0.233	4.6	0.280	5.5	0.693	1.8
Xinjiang	0.021	5.4	0.090	6.2	0.337 (0.255)	0.003	3.2	0.190	3.3	0.051	−4.6	0.610	3.2
Heilongjiang	0.039	9.1	0.102	4.6	0.241 (0.151)	0.005	19.8	0.304	5.5	0.131	−5.4	0.651	2.6

Table 2. (*Continued*)

Province	Innovation		Globalization		Time series	R&D/GRP		Schooling		Foreign exp.		Share	
	Mean	AGR (%)	Mean	AGR (%)	Coefficient	Mean	ARG (%)	Mean	ARG (%)	Mean	ARG (%)	Mean	ARG (%)
Shandong	0.131	19.3	0.195	6.0	0.868*** (0.185)	0.007	21.0	0.628	7.5	0.500	4.1	0.647	2.5
Hainan	0.017	4.1	0.102	4.7	0.143 (0.081)	0.002	1.3	0.067	6.7	0.320	26.3	0.766	1.0
Fujian	0.052	14.0	0.191	5.2	0.797*** (0.248)	0.006	3.4	0.301	8.0	0.565	0.8	0.855	0.4
Average						0.005	8.9	0.317	6.1	0.306	5.2	0.691	2.0
Q4 Jiangsu	0.230	36.4	0.336	10.2	1.529*** (0.283)	0.011	10.1	0.624	6.1	0.622	6.4	0.762	2.7
Liaoning	0.073	18.6	0.172	6.7	0.235 (0.337)	0.011	35.0	0.371	5.5	0.500	3.9	0.679	2.8
Zhejiang	0.186	28.5	0.206	9.3	1.065*** (0.185)	0.008	19.8	0.384	7.1	0.300	6.7	0.669	2.3
Guangdong	0.268	22.7	0.586	6.4	0.048** (0.023)	0.009	25.4	0.597	8.8	0.578	2.2	0.782	1.0
Tianjin	0.052	15.3	0.144	5.4	0.172 (0.244)	0.016	3.3	0.161	6.8	0.722	2.8	0.784	1.2
Beijing	0.133	15.6	0.224	9.4	0.570*** (0.132)	0.063	-4.3	0.264	3.5	0.285	14.4	0.712	1.9
Shanghai	0.133	24.3	0.346	11.1	0.240* (0.128)	0.019	4.9	0.230	3.7	0.586	5.9	0.746	1.6
Average						0.020	13.4	0.376	5.9	0.513	6.0	0.733	1.9

Note: Q1, Q2, Q3, and Q4 represent the first, second, third, and fourth quartile of the initial income distribution, respectively; Provinces are listed in ascending order of the initial income level; AGR represents for the average growth rate; time trend is controlled in time series regressions; standard deviations in parentheses, ***significant at 1%, **significant at 5%, *significant at 10%. "Schooling" is a factor variable based on primary, junior high, senior high, and higher education schools and enrolment; "Foreign exp" is the ratio of exports by foreign funded firms in total exports; "Share" captures the aggregate foreign ratio in total registered capital of foreign funded firms.

many universities (Shaanxi) and the other as the cradle to Chinese culture (Henan), possibly tap internal dynamics for innovation. The connection between globalization and innovation in general is much stronger within the second income group. Within this group, provinces with stronger increases in globalization also are more innovative (see the analysis for Anhui, Hunan, and Shanxi). Hubei is the story that goes against the trend, with a low increase in globalization and a high innovation growth rate. In Table 2, we can see the potential explanation for it, as Hubei has the highest average schooling rate for this group and also has relatively high regional R&D spending.

With respect to the underlying regional characteristics, when compared to the second quartile, in the third quartile the average share of R&D expenditure is lower and grows slower. Also, except for the two "outliers" Hebei and Shandong, most third quartile provinces have relatively low levels of human capital. Further, when compared to regions in the second income group, on average the third income group regions have a larger share of exports by foreign funded enterprises as well as a larger share of capital in the hands of foreign investors. These results provide a first insight into how regional characteristics play a moderating role in the relation between globalization and regional innovation.

3.2. *Empirical model*

To perform a structured analysis of the effects of globalization on innovation at the regional level, we use differences between regions as well as regional within effects over time. As we have data for 29 regions over various years, we model several panel regressions. In contrast to the descriptive analysis above, such panels allow for the treatment of the complex causal relation between globalization and innovation. We specify the basic estimation model as:

$$\text{Innovation}_{it} = \beta_0 + \beta_1 \text{Globalization}_{it} + \delta \text{Control}_{it} + \alpha_i + \varepsilon_{it}. \tag{1}$$

The fixed effect α_i captures regional heterogeneity and ε_{it} is the random error term. As a control variable in all base specifications, we include GRPPC. To take account of multicollinearity among the various human capital variables, using principal component analysis a single *Education* factor is created (see details in the appendix). To control for internal regional innovation dynamics, we include regional R&D expenditure and the constructed education factor. As these variables change substantially over time, adding them mitigates the omitted variable bias. In all specifications, we add year dummies to capture the time trend.

Central to the analysis is the heterogeneity of the effect of globalization across several income groups. To analyze this, we use the following interaction model:

$$\text{Innovation}_{it} = \beta_0 + \beta_1 \text{Globalization}_{it} + \sum_{r=2}^{4} \beta_r (\text{Globalization}_{it} * Q_i^r)$$

$$+ \delta \text{Control}_{it} + \alpha_i + \varepsilon_{it}. \tag{2}$$

The superscript r denotes each of the four quartiles of the initial 1995 income level distribution. Q_i^r take the value of one when province i belongs to quartile r. We use the first quartile of the income distribution as the base group — the results qualitatively are not affected by the choice of the base. As regions are split on the basis of the initial income level, the income level per capita is excluded in the panel regressions that use the quartile interaction specification.

Time-invariant unobserved regional heterogeneity is purged based on the fixed effects (FE) transformation, the random effects (RE) transformation, and the first differencing (FD) transformation, respectively. Several of these estimations may potentially provide biased results when the strict exogeneity assumption fails. One plausible reason for endogeneity to arise in our story is a feedback loop from a region's current innovative capabilities to its future competences to take advantage of globalization. According to Wooldridge (2002), such reverse causation results in a negative bias in the FE and FD estimates. As is commonly argued in time series, it is reasonable to assume that innovation this year has little effect on a region's globalization in the past. Therefore, the past values of the globalization variable are uncorrelated with the current error term and can be used as internal instruments to tackle the endogeneity problem. Using this, we employ a system GMM approach to estimate panel models with unobserved effects and sequentially exogenous explanatory variables. As doing so concentrates the analysis on the differences in within-region effects across regions, the first step is to take a forward orthogonal deviation transformation, which eliminates the fixed individual heterogeneity by subtracting from each observation the mean of future values. Next, the models are estimated using lags of the level variables as instruments for the first-differenced equations and lags of the differenced variables as instruments for the level equations. We also carry out a series of tests to ensure the validity and the strength of the instruments. Compared to standard GMM estimation, this extended method introduces more instruments, so as to improve efficiency and precision in finite samples.

4. Empirical Results

Table 3 shows the impact of globalization on innovation at the regional level over time across regions in China. As a benchmark and close to the descriptive statistics in the previous section, in column 1 we report the results of a parsimonious pooled OLS model without control variables. We see that globalization overall is positively associated with innovative capacity. Accounting for individual heterogeneity, columns 2–4 present the results using the fixed effects, the random effects estimation, as well as a first-difference transformation, respectively. Across the columns, in general, we find a significant effect of globalization on innovation at the regional level in China.

Comparing the FE and FD estimates, the substantial difference between these models raises the issue of potential endogeneity. Using an F-test for the assumption of strict exogeneity, we find strong evidence to reject it, so that the FE, RE, and FD

Table 3. Main results.

Independent variable	Dependent variable: Innovation index							
	(1) POLS	(2) FE	(3) RE	(4) FD	(5) GMM	(6) GMM	(7) GMM	(8) GMM
Globalization index	0.756***	0.257***	0.396***	0.158***	0.550***	0.515***	0.502***	0.320***
	(0.087)	(0.066)	(0.065)	(0.051)	(0.139)	(0.073)	(0.099)	(0.060)
Globalization*Q2								0.168***
								(0.063)
Globalization*Q3								−0.128*
								(0.069)
Globalization*Q4								0.844***
								(0.129)
GRPPC (ln)						0.180***	−0.007	
						(0.041)	(0.102)	
Education (ln)						0.524***	0.401***	0.617***
						(0.053)	(0.042)	(0.050)
R&D expenditure (ln)						0.099***	0.116***	0.022
						(0.037)	(0.044)	(0.044)
Year dummies	no	no	no	no	no	no	yes	yes
BP test	0.000							
Hausman test			0.125					
F-test of strict exogeneity		0.000	0.000	0.000				
AR(2) test					0.126	0.186	0.187	0.223
Hansen test of over-identification					0.405	0.247	0.982	1.000
Difference-in-Hansen tests of exogeneity					0.536	0.889	1.000	1.000

Note: Q2, Q3, and Q4 represent the second, third, and fourth quartile of the initial income distribution, respectively; BP test is under the null that individual heterogeneity is absent; Hausman test is under the null that there is no systematic difference between FE and RE estimates; F-test of strict exogeneity is a regression-based test under the null that the explanatory variables are strict exogenous; AR(2) is a test of second-order serial correlation in the first-differenced residuals, under the null of no serial correlation; Hansen test of over-identification is under the null that all instruments are valid; Diff-in-Hansen tests of exogeneity is under the null that instruments used for the equations in levels are exogenous; P-values are presented for all the tests. Standard deviations in parentheses, ***significant at 1%, **significant at 5%, *significant at 10%.

estimators are only weakly informative.[8] Consequently, we estimate the models via system generalized method of moments (GMM), using internal instrumental variables and report the regression results in column 5.[9] The estimates suggest a significant causal effect of globalization on regional innovation. As expected, the magnitude of this effect is larger than those obtained from the FE, RE, and FD estimations.

Columns 6 and 7 present the model with alternative sets of control variables, for which the findings are quite similar. In column 6, gross regional product per capita is found to be a significant determinant of local innovation. However, as income levels have a strong time trend, the changes in income over time are not significant once the year dummies are incorporated, see column 7. Across panels, the internal factors R&D spending and education levels are found to positively associated with innovation.

4.1. *The effects of globalization across income groups and geographical lines*

In Table 3, we also show the impact of globalization on innovation for different groups of regional income levels based on model [2]. We can see in column 8 that there are significant disparities in the effects of globalization on innovation across income groups. The impact of globalization is largest in the fourth quartile (the point estimate 1.164) and smallest in the third quartile (the point estimate 0.192), while it is at the intermediate levels in the first and second quartiles of the income distribution. From the results, it is noted that globalization has a rather small effect on innovation in the upper-middle range of the income distribution. We return to this issue below.

To connect our results to the large literature that stresses the importance of the differences between coastal provinces and the interior, in Table 4 we report the effect of globalization on innovation for different geographical regions. Columns 1–3 show the results for sub-samples of the eastern, central, and western regions.[10] Across panels we find that the globalization index is significant, which implies a strengthening effect of globalization on innovation in all three geographical areas. Comparing the magnitude of the globalization coefficients, we note that the effect is large in the eastern regions. Importantly, the effects of globalization on innovation are smaller in the relatively developed central regions when compared in the poor western regions. We include in column 4 the interaction terms between globalization and the two location dummies — *East* and *Center* taking the value of one for eastern and central provinces, respectively. The results show that globalization enhances innovation in both the east

---

[8] We estimate the first-differencing model with the current levels as additional explanatory variables and the fixed effects model incorporating the future values of the explanatory variables. Under the null hypothesis of strict exogeneity, the level variables should be insignificant in the first-differenced equation and the leading variables should be insignificant using the fixed effects estimation (Wooldridge, 2002).

[9] The AR (2) test statistics for autocorrelation and the Hansen test statistics of over-identification show that the GMM estimates are valid.

[10] Eastern regions include Liaoning, Hebei, Beijing, Tianjin, Shandong, Jiangsu, Shanghai, Zhejiang, Fujian, Guangdong, and Hainan; Central regions include Heilongjiang, Jilin, Shanxi, Henan, Hubei, Hunan, Anhui, and Jiangxi; Western regions include Sichuan, Guizhou, Yunnan, Shaanxi, Gansu, Ningxia, Qinghai, Xinjiang, Inner Mongolia, and Guangxi.

Table 4. GMM results of geographic regions.

Independent variable	Dependent variable: *Innovation index*			
	(1) East	(2) Center	(3) West	(4) Whole
Globalization index	0.689***	0.269*	0.339*	0.457***
	(0.166)	(0.151)	(0.191)	(0.074)
Globalization*East				0.203**
				(0.088)
Globalization*Center				−0.048
				(0.065)
GRPPC (ln)	0.002	0.446***	−0.032	−0.008
	(0.120)	(0.105)	(0.072)	(0.076)
Education (ln)	0.681***	0.781***	0.302***	0.443***
	(0.075)	(0.094)	(0.097)	(0.048)
R&D expenditure (ln)	−0.052	0.008	0.154***	0.084**
	(0.081)	(0.051)	(0.053)	(0.042)
AR(2) test	0.635	0.696	0.674	0.203
Over-identification	1.000	1.000	1.000	1.000
Tests of exogeneity	1.000	1.000	1.000	1.000

Note: Year dummies are included in all regressions; AR(2) is a test of second-order serial correlation in the first-differenced residuals, under the null of no serial correlation; Hansen test of over-identification is under the null that all instruments are valid; Diff-in-Hansen tests of exogeneity is under the null that instruments used for the equations in levels are exogenous; *P*-values are presented for all the tests. Standard deviations in parentheses, ***significant at 1%, **significant at 5%, *significant at 10%.

coast regions and interior of China. In this interaction specification, the effect of external opening shows no significant difference between the western and central regions, while it is substantially larger in the coastal areas.

4.2. *Different modes of globalization*

Table 5 shows the GMM results of testing separately the impact of different modes of globalization. First, we can see in columns 1 and 2 that exports are an important channel for regional innovation. The results show that the effect of exporting on innovation is stronger in regions with higher income levels. In column 3, we find that high levels of exports by foreign firms have a significantly larger impact on innovation when compared to exports by domestic firms.

Columns 4 and 5 show the connection between imports and innovation. Importing is often seen as an important channel for technology transfer. Importing in high-income regions (the third and fourth quartiles) is positively correlated with innovation, while it has a negative association in the low-income group. As a potential explanation, on top of insufficient absorptive capacity, lower income regions are more likely to import

Table 5. GMM results for different modes of globalization.

	(1) Export	(2) Export	(3) Export	(4) Import	(5) Import	(6) OFDI	(7) OFDI	(8) FDI	(9) FDI	(10) FDI
					Dependent variable: *Innovation index*					
Mode	0.209***	0.162***		0.177***	0.347***	0.250***	−0.094	0.281***	0.329***	0.520***
	(0.037)	(0.038)		(0.045)	(0.051)	(0.070)	(0.063)	(0.059)	(0.028)	(0.039)
Mode*Q3		0.023			0.409***		0.019		−0.014*	0.115
		(0.031)			(0.061)		(0.023)		(0.007)	(0.100)
Mode*Q4		0.119***			0.617***		0.348***		−0.079***	0.476***
		(0.033)			(0.054)		(0.036)		(0.008)	(0.152)
Foreign export			−0.053							
			(0.051)							
Foreign export*Q3			0.232***							
			(0.046)							
Foreign export*Q4			0.305***							
			(0.057)							
Domestic export			0.121***							
			(0.031)							
Domestic export*Q3			−0.047*							
			(0.026)							
Domestic export*Q4			−0.040							
			(0.059)							
Share*FDI*Q3										−0.197*
										(0.107)
Share*FDI*Q4										−0.696***
										(0.193)
Share										−1.069***
										(0.368)

(*Continued*)

Table 5. (*Continued*)

Dependent variable: *Innovation index*

	(1) Export	(2) Export	(3) Export	(4) Import	(5) Import	(6) OFDI	(7) OFDI	(8) FDI	(9) FDI	(10) FDI
GRPPC (ln)	0.158**			1.265***		0.722***		0.156**		
	(0.067)			(0.172)		(0.132)		(0.078)		
Education (ln)	0.397***	0.437***	0.468***	0.236***	0.539***	0.282***	0.437***	0.489***	0.462***	0.384***
	(0.041)	(0.045)	(0.041)	(0.064)	(0.054)	(0.061)	(0.109)	(0.050)	(0.046)	(0.042)
R&D expenditure (ln)	0.167***	0.125***	0.106**	0.373***	0.130***	0.340***	0.306***	0.142***	0.218***	0.284***
	(0.038)	(0.040)	(0.041)	(0.058)	(0.047)	(0.047)	(0.055)	(0.043)	(0.041)	(0.035)
AR(2) test	0.172	0.186	0.266	0.229	0.343	0.354	0.268	0.427	0.641	0.441
Over-identification	0.982	1.000	1.000	0.987	1.000	0.367	0.911	0.891	1.000	1.000
Exogeneity test	1.000	1.000	1.000	1.000	1.000	0.274	0.826	1.000	1.000	1.000

Note: Q3 and Q4 represent the third and fourth quartile of the initial income distribution, respectively; "Foreign funded (domestic) export" is defined as exports by foreign funded (domestic) firms in percent of gross regional product; Year dummies are included in all regressions; AR(2) is a test of second-order serial correlation in the first-differenced residuals, under the null of no serial correlation; Hansen test of over-identification is under the null that all instruments are valid; Diff-in-Hansen tests of exogeneity is under the null that instruments used for the equations in levels are exogenous; *P*-values are presented for all the tests. Standard deviations in parentheses, ***significant at 1%, **significant at 5%, *significant at 10%.

lower value-added products, which embed less advanced technology. Hence, in these regions the competition effect, which crowds out domestic firms and lowers the aggregate innovation performance, may dominate the knowledge spillover effect.

Further, columns 6 and 7 identify a significant effect of outward FDI on innovation. The coefficients increase with income in terms of both economic and statistical significance. These results may signal that firms in the most developed regions have stronger incentives and higher competence to move towards higher value-added production, which highly relies on foreign knowledge and technology. Establishing foreign subsidiaries offers these firms better geographic proximity to the initial innovators (or even acquire them as subsidiaries), so that they can gain from technology diffusion at home.

Finally, we check how inward FDI affects regional innovation and report the results in the last three columns. Across panels, inward FDI is playing an important role in regional innovation. However, different from what have been found for the other modes of globalization, there is an ordering pattern that inward FDI has a relatively smaller effect in regions with higher income level. According to the estimation results presented in column 9, though the differences between the low-income group and the high-income group (-0.014 for the third quartile and -0.079 for the fourth quartile) are small in size, they can still not be neglected given their statistical significance.

4.3. *The nonlinear effect of globalization on innovation*

Observing Table 5, we can see that in general various modes of globalization have different effects on regional innovation in China. Note that inward FDI has a smaller spillover effect in regions with higher income levels. As argued by Antràs and Helpman (2004), firms that invest abroad are among the most productive in their industry. These highly innovative foreign firms tend to invest in the higher income regions, which have a larger demand for higher value-added products and more productive local partners with higher absorptive capacity. The higher income regions therefore have higher initial FDI levels, which results in lower marginal contribution of FDI to innovation due to decreasing returns to technology transfer. In addition, to protect their intellectual property, highly productive foreign firms are inclined to hold full ownership of local subsidiaries, certainly in regions with high income levels where local imitative capabilities are strong. These low local ownership shares in turn provide weak incentives for local innovation and limit technology transfer.[11]

Further, in column 3 of Table 5, we find that the effect of exports by foreign funded firms on innovation increases with income levels. Foreign firms with lower productivity are more likely to locate in lower income regions and produce lower value-added

---

[11] Column 10 in Table 5 shows the estimates by adding a foreign equity share variable and its corresponding interactions. As a region's foreign equity share is defined as the aggregate foreign ratio in total registered capital of foreign funded enterprises, it can be used to capture the relative intensity of direct entry, as compared with acquisition activities. Therefore, the negative estimated coefficients of the foreign share terms reveal that innovation is more likely to occur in regions with a higher presence of equity joint ventures relative to wholly owned subsidiaries.

products. Exports of these simple goods play a smaller role in improving local innovation performance. By contrast, highly productive firms opt for fully owned foreign subsidiaries in high-income regions. Although this gives limited incentives for local innovation, exports by these firms provide for high spillovers to local suppliers that learn of the most productive foreign firms. Moreover, through the link with these innovative foreign firms, the most productive local firms in the high-income regions also engage in venturing abroad themselves. There is ample empirical evidence that exporting, outward FDI, and indirect international activities through interaction with foreign owned firms increase the incentives for innovation in local firms (De Loecker, 2007; Aw *et al.*, 2008; Bustos, 2011).

As argued in Mathews and Zander (2007) and Mathews (2009), innovation and internationalization of local firms and their engagement in international relationships is highly evolutionary. It often starts with (fully owned) inward FDI in region, which boosts the productivity of local firms through initial spillover links in arms-length relations and labor mobility between foreign and local firms (Fosfuri *et al.*, 2001). Over time, local firms start to leverage their capabilities within these relationships, increasing their share of the surplus by providing a larger share of the inputs. Then, further along the timeline, local firms start to dramatically improve their resource base by learning from the foreign partner and taking over the world class capabilities from the foreign firm.

Our results therefore should show substantial nonlinear relations between entry modes, internationalization, and innovation. We provide evidence that the connection between globalization and innovation is high both in the low and in high-income regions. By contrast, the connection is weaker in the upper-middle income regions. In the low-income regions, both FDI levels and foreign equity shares are low, which results in a large positive effect of inward FDI on regional innovation from a low base. In these regions, exporting is important for the upgrading of skills. Thus, the low-income regions mainly benefit from learning spillovers of exports and inward FDI. By contrast, inward FDI has a smaller impact on innovation in the high-income regions given more FDI and more fully owned foreign firms in these regions. However, higher levels of FDI and higher share of exports by foreign funded firms also imply that local firms in the high-income regions are better connected with highly productive foreign firms. This helps these local firms go through the Mathews (2009) LLL process and finally build their own innovative capabilities. The high-income regions therefore mainly rely on exports, especially FDI related exports, and outward FDI to enhance local innovation.

As for the upper-middle income regions, they are "stuck in the middle". Regarding the spillover effect of FDI, these regions have relatively higher FDI levels and foreign equity shares when compared to the low-income regions. This results in a smaller effect of FDI because of lower returns of technology transfer and weaker incentives for local innovation. Also, local firms in these regions are less productive than those in the high-income regions, so that local firms are not able to enter the evolutionary LLL mechanism engaging with strong foreign partners and over time benefiting from outward FDI.

Further, in column 3 of Table 5, we find that the upper-middle income regions gain less from exports by domestic firms. This provides evidence that the upper-middle income regions attract relatively low productivity foreign firms that are mainly interested in outsourcing part of their production to low cost local firms. These outsourcing partnerships have limited scope for technology transfer and provide limited incentives for local firms to innovate. This is because the foreign firm often provides little value added inside the relationship and the potential hold-up problem following a weak bargaining position reduces the incentives for innovation by the local partner. These reasons are behind the U-shaped relationship between on the one axis the strength of the connection between globalization and innovation, and on the other axis the local income level as a proxy for the productivity of local firms.

4.4. *The changing impact of globalization over time*

A further question is how the effect of globalization on innovation changes over time. To examine this issue, in Table 6 we interact the globalization variables with a time period dummy. Breaking for China's WTO entry in the year 2001, we generate a dummy variable *P02* that takes on the value zero for years 1995–2001 and one for years 2002–2010.[12] Columns 1 and 2 report the GMM estimates of the overall globalization index, while the other columns show the corresponding results for the various modes of globalization.

Overall, external opening has a significant positive impact on innovation in both time periods, consistent with the finding derived in Table 3. We find in column 1 that regional innovation capacity increases faster with globalization in the more recent period than in the early years. The estimated difference in the size of the globalization effect for the two periods (the point estimate 0.401) is noticeable in terms of both economic and statistical significance. Column 2 presents the specific time-changing effect of globalization in different quartiles of the initial income distribution. The coefficients of the time dummy interactions are estimated to be positive, which implies that the effect of globalization on innovation increases over time in each quartile of income. Similar as what is found in Table 3, in both periods the fourth quartile of income benefits the most from globalization (point estimates 0.400 for 1995–2001 and 0.957 for 2002–2010), while the third quartile gains the least (0.201 for 1995–2001 and 0.501 for 2002–2010).

We continue by illustrating the impact of international trade on innovation for different time periods, showing exports in column 3 and imports in column 4. The interaction effects show that both exporting and importing play a greater role in recent years.

---

[12] Due to the data availability, the globalization index for the period 1995–2001 does not incorporate information on the outward FDI activities. For the same reason, no time-changing effect of the outward FDI mode on innovation is illustrated in Table 6.

Table 6. GMM results of time trend.

Independent variable	Dependent variable: *Innovation index*				
	(1) Globalization	(2) Globalization	(3) Export	(4) Import	(5) FDI
Mode	0.246***	0.236***	−0.019	0.023	0.082
	(0.047)	(0.048)	(0.031)	(0.035)	(0.082)
Mode*Q3		−0.035***	0.176***	0.066	0.300***
		(0.015)	(0.027)	(0.053)	(0.068)
Mode*Q4		0.164*	0.228***	0.139***	0.229***
		(0.095)	(0.025)	(0.041)	(0.059)
P02*mode	0.401***	0.243***	0.052*	−0.033	0.418***
	(0.037)	(0.062)	(0.031)	(0.050)	(0.084)
P02*mode*Q3		0.057	0.057	0.129**	−0.387***
		(0.075)	(0.035)	(0.065)	(0.069)
P02*mode*Q4		0.314**	0.203***	0.285***	−0.326***
		(0.128)	(0.035)	(0.051)	(0.061)
P02	0.772***	0.785***	1.292***	0.669***	2.937***
	(0.104)	(0.077)	(0.080)	(0.075)	(0.269)
GRPPC (ln)	0.062				
	(0.048)				
Education (ln)	0.462***	0.499***	0.508***	0.611***	0.330***
	(0.037)	(0.035)	(0.033)	(0.038)	(0.044)
R&D expenditure (ln)	0.092***	0.097***	0.101***	0.085***	0.344***
	(0.033)	(0.031)	(0.028)	(0.032)	(0.038)
AR(2) test	0.887	0.739	0.637	0.895	0.686
Over-identification	0.986	1.000	1.000	1.000	1.000
Tests of exogeneity	1.000	1.000	1.000	1.000	1.000

Note: Q3 and Q4 represent the third and fourth quartile of the initial income distribution, respectively; Year dummies are included in all regressions; AR(2) is a test of second-order serial correlation in the first-differenced residuals, under the null of no serial correlation; Hansen test of over-identification is under the null that all instruments are valid; Diff-in-Hansen tests of exogeneity is under the null that instruments used for the equations in levels are exogenous; *P*-values are presented for all the tests. Standard deviations in parentheses, ***significant at 1%, **significant at 5%, *significant at 10%.

Compared to the increase in regions with low income levels, the change of the trade effect is statistically more predominant in richer regions, especially in the fourth quartile of the income distribution. Hence, the pattern that the effect of trade increases with income holds for both time periods. Even so, it is noteworthy in the first and second income quartiles (the base group) that the estimate of exports turns from insignificance before 2002 to significantly positive thereafter. The results can be explained by the fact that the low-income regions, especially in the early stage of development, often engage in international transactions for simple goods, which contribute little to the local technology base and even divert resources away from R&D activities.

The last column of Table 6 presents the relation between inward FDI and regional innovation. In the time frame 1995–2001, innovation is only weakly associated with inward FDI in low-income regions but can significantly be attributed to the increase in FDI inflows in the high-income group. The reason may be that foreign firms mostly concentrate their investments in developed coastal regions in this period. By contrast, in the more recent period 2002–2010, we find that the positive effect of inward FDI on innovation also becomes significant for low-income regions, whereas it declines over time in significance for high-income regions. Referring to the effects of entry modes on technology transfer, the reverse pattern found in high-income regions is consistent with recent observations that foreign firms are increasingly replacing the joint ventures with their fully owned subsidiaries in China (for instance, see Branstetter and Lardy, 2008).

5. Conclusion

The results in this chapter generate insights into the connection between globalization and innovation across Chinese regions for the period 1995–2010. There already exists a large literature that addresses the relation between internationalization and innovation at the level of Chinese firms. In addition, there have been many studies that explain the pattern of entry of foreign firms in China and its effects on local conditions. At the macro level, the ownership, location, and internalization (OLI) motives of Chinese firms when selecting regions for exports and FDI are also informative for the dynamics of innovation in Chinese firms.

Our study adds to the literature by complementing the picture with an analysis of the regional dynamics of innovation and how these are associated with changes in outward orientation of the local economy. The regional unit of this study makes the result suitable as an input for policy analysis, since differences in regional innovation levels are likely to be the most important determinant of future spatial income disparities and internal migration in China. However, in contrast to most other studies, our analysis presents a muddy picture of various nonlinear connections between globalization and innovation. Hence, it is difficult to present a conclusive qualitative story of the empirical finding. Yet, the following elements stand out from the analysis.

First, there is a close overall connection between globalization and innovation. Unlike most other papers in the literature we use various broad measures for these two concepts, so as not to depend on accidental significance. The long time frame of our data allows us to split the analysis into two main questions. The "between" question is whether regions that are more open to external relations are also more innovative when compared to regions that are less open. For this, we find some evidence, though the result seems to depend on the level of development and the influence of foreign firms. The high-income regions in China, often in the coastal area, have both high levels of globalization and innovation. For poorer regions, there is much less evidence that globalization of a region is associated with higher levels of innovation.

Second, the panel analysis is able to focus on causal relation within regions, so as to answer the question whether regions which open up to external influences *over time* become more innovative. Again, overall we find evidence for that. However, if we then separate the effects across regional income levels, a nonlinear effect appears in the data. For top income regions as well as for lower middle-income regions there is a strong connection between globalization and innovation. However, higher middle-income regions seem not to benefit that much from globalization in terms of innovative capacity. Also, the effect of globalization on innovation is weak in the poorest set of regions.

For this reason, a third set of findings digs deeper in the causes of these nonlinear effects. Our data allow us to examine different sub-indicators for globalization. We find that exporting and outward FDI in high-income regions contribute to innovation, whereas inward FDI contributes to innovation in lower middle-income regions. This makes sense, when one looks outside the window. In the high-income regions, a build-up of local technological ownership advantages (owned by domestic or foreign shareholders) is rooted in their capacity for exports, technology joint ventures, and acquisition of (technological) resources abroad. Technology transfer of foreign firms is high in these regions as this is needed to increase productivity in exports with a higher value-added local content. These effects are less strong in lower-income regions. By contrast, the policy to induce foreign firms to invest in low-income regions seems to bear fruit, for especially in those regions inward FDI is associated with stronger innovative capabilities. The analysis also may explain why there are only limited effects of globalization on innovation in higher middle-income regions. Other studies have already pointed to the fact that the nature of cooperation between domestic and foreign firms is important for technology transfer. Middle-income regions are stuck in the middle with respect to innovation. The production-linkage type of relations means that low levels of inclusive FDI provide limited technology transfer, whereas relative low skills steer domestic firms into low value-added export production. By including ownership shares into the analysis we provide some tentative evidence for this mechanism, which so far has been analyzed only at the firm level.

A final finding relates to the relative importance of globalization in inducing innovation. In the data description part, we show the large differences in absorptive capacity across regions. To analyze the effects of absorptive capacity at the regional level, the difficultly is to separate average from marginal effects. In the data, we find important "outliers" where low globalization goes together with high levels of innovation, especially in lower middle-income regions. These are the regions with high levels of schooling and domestic R&D expenditure. Hence, from our data we find evidence for the broader finding that the national R&D system is important for innovation. However, over time a marginal effect is also important, when high levels of human capital and local public R&D spending increase the effect of globalization on innovation at the margin, even when globalization levels are low within those regions. All in all, we find several non-trivial empirical causal connections between globalization and regional innovation in China.

Acknowledgment

This chapter is supported by the National Social Science Foundation of China (No. 13XJY001) and the Fundamental Research Funds for the Central Universities.

Appendix

Data definitions

Index and variable	Explanation
A. Innovation index	
Patents applied	Number of patents applied with types invention, utility mode, and external design (piece).
Patents granted	Number of patents granted with types invention, utility mode, and external design (piece).
Rate of new products	Rate of new products in total sampling products selected from 73 main industrial cities (%).
Rate of products with excellent quality	Rate of products with excellent quality in total sampling products from 73 industrial cities (%).
B. Globalization index	
Exports (percent of GRP)	Exports of goods and services measured as a share of gross regional product (%).
Imports (percent of GRP)	Imports of goods and services measured as a share of gross regional product (%).
Number of FFE	Number of Foreign Funded Enterprises registered at the year-end by region (unit).
Amount of FFE investment	Total Investment by Foreign Funded Enterprises by region (100 million U.S. dollars).
FDI utilized (percent of GRP)	Inward foreign direct investment actually utilised measured as a share of gross regional product (%).
Outward FDI stock (percent of GRP)	Outward foreign direct investment stock measured as a share of gross regional product (%).
C. Education	
Education funds	Total education funds by region (10,000 Yuan).
Higher education enrolment	Total enrolment of higher education schools (person).
Higher education institutions	Number of higher education school (units).
Senior high enrolment	Total enrolment of senior high (person).
Senior high school	Number of senior high school (unit).
D. Others	
GRP	Gross regional product (10,000 Yuan).
R&D expenditure	Expenditure for R&D activities by region (10,000 Yuan).

Note: Data is mainly taken from various issues of China's Statistical Year books published by Chinese National Bureau of Statistics (1995–2011). The outward FDI data is taken from annual Statistical Bulletin of China's Outward Direct Investment, published jointly by Ministry of Commerce, National Bureau of Statistics and State Administration of Foreign Exchange of China (2003–2011).

Factor loadings of indices

Index and variable	Loading
Innovation index	
Patents applied	0.966
Patents granted	0.964
Rate of new products	0.381
Rate of products with excellent quality	0.491
Globalization index	
Exports (percent of GRP)	0.912
Imports (percent of GRP)	0.775
Number of FFE	0.935
Amount of FFE investment	0.931
FDI utilized (percent of GRP)	0.694
Outward FDI stock (percent of GRP)	0.728
Education index	
Education funds	0.877
Higher education enrolment	0.953
Higher education institutions	0.944
Senior high enrolment	0.959
Senior high school	0.765

Note: The proportion of variation explained is 59% for the innovation index and 70% for the globalization index, respectively. The globalization index is imputed as the outward FDI variable has a shorter time span than other variables. For robustness, an alternative globalization index is generated without the outward FDI variable. The correlation between these two globalization indices is 0.961, so we include the outward FDI data for efficiency.

References

Aitken, BJ and AE Harrison (1999). Do domestic firms benefit from direct foreign investment? Evidence from Venezuela. *American Economic Review*, 89, 605–618.

Antràs, P (2003). Firms, contracts, and trade structure. *Quarterly Journal of Economics*, 118, 1375–1418.

Antràs, P and E Helpman (2004). Global sourcing. *Journal of Political Economy*, 112, 552–580.

Aw, BY, MJ Roberts and DY Xu (2008). R&D Investments, exporting, and the evolution of firm productivity. *American Economic Review*, 98, 451–456.

Bernard, AB and JB Jensen (1999). Exceptional exporter performance: Cause, effect, or both? *Journal of International Economics*, 47, 1–25.

Blomstrom, M, A Kokko, M Zejan and K Wakelin (2001). Foreign direct investment: Firm and host country strategies. *Economic Journal*, 111, F524–F525.

Branstetter, L and N Lardy (2008). China's embrace of globalisation. In L Brandt and T Rawski (Eds.), *China's Great Economic Transformation*, New York: Cambridge University Press, pp. 633–728.

Buckley, PJ, J Clegg and C Wang (2002). The impact of inward FDI on the performance of Chinese manufacturing firms. *Journal of International Business Studies*, 33, 637–655.

Bustos, P (2011). Trade liberalisation, exports, and technology upgrading: Evidence on the impact of MERCOSUR on Argentinian firms. *American Economic Review*, 101, 304–340.

Chan, KW, JV Henderson and KY Tsui (2008). Spatial dimensions of Chinese economic development. In L Brandt and T Rawski (Eds.), *China's Great Economic Transformation*, New York: Cambridge University Press, pp. 776–828.

Cheung, KY (2010). Spillover effects of FDI via exports on innovation performance of China's high-technology industries. *Journal of Contemporary China*, 19, 541–557.

Cheung, KY and P Lin (2004). Spillover effects of FDI on innovation in China: Evidence from the provincial data. *China Economic Review*, 15, 25–44.

De Loecker, J (2007). Do exports generate higher productivity? Evidence from Slovenia. *Journal of International Economics*, 73, 69–98.

Dreher, A (2006). Does globalisation affect growth? Evidence from a new index of globalisation. *Applied Economics*, 38, 1091–1110.

Fan, P (2011). Innovation, globalisation, and catch-up of latecomers: Cases of Chinese telecom firms. *Environment and Planning A*, 43, 830–849.

Fosfuri, A, M Motta and T Rønde (2001). Foreign direct investment and spillovers through workers' mobility. *Journal of International Economics*, 53, 205–222.

Grossman, GM and E Helpman (1990). Trade, innovation, and growth. *American Economic Review*, 80, 86–91.

Grossman, GM and E Helpman (1991). Trade, knowledge spillovers and growth. *European Economic Review*, 35, 517–526.

Grossman, GM and E Helpman (2005). Outsourcing in a global economy. *Review of Economic Studies*, 72, 135–159.

Grossman, GM, E Helpman and PM Romer (1993). Innovation and growth in the global economy. *Journal of Economic Literature*, 31, 276–278.

Grossman, GM, E Helpman and A Szeidl (2005). Complementarities between outsourcing and foreign sourcing. *American Economic Review*, 95, 19–24.

Guan, J and N Ma (2003). Innovative capability and export performance of Chinese firms. *Technovation*, 23, 737–747.

Hennart, J and K Brouthers (2007). Boundaries of the firm: Insights from international entry mode research. *Journal of Management*, 33, 395–425.

Hu, AGZ and GH Jefferson (2002). FDI impact and spillover: Evidence from China's electronic and textile industries. *World Economy*, 25, 1063–1076.

Hu, AGZ and GH Jefferson (2008). Science and technology in China. In L Brandt and T Rawski (Eds.), *China's Great Economic Transformation*, New York: Cambridge University Press, pp. 250–285.

Johnson, WHA and Q Liu (2011). Patenting and the role of technology markets in regional innovation in China: An empirical analysis. *Journal of High Technology Management Research*, 22, 14–25.

Li, X (2009). China's regional innovation capacity in transition: An empirical approach. *Research Policy*, 38, 338–357.

Li, Y and YHD Wei (2010). The spatial-temporal hierarchy of regional inequality of China. *Applied Geography*, 30, 303–316.

Liefner, I and S Hennemann (2011). Structural holes and new dimensions of distance: The spatial configuration of the scientific knowledge network of China's optical technology sector. *Environment and Planning A*, 43, 810–829.

Mathews, JA (2009). China, India and Brazil: Tiger technologies, dragon multinationals and the building of national systems of economic learning. *Asian Business & Management*, 8, 5–32.

Mathews, JA and I Zander (2007). The international entrepreneurial dynamics of accelerated internationalisation. *Journal of International Business Studies*, 38, 387–403.

Melitz, MJ (2003). The impact of trade on intra-industry reallocations and aggregate industry productivity. *Econometrica*, 71, 1695–1725.

Sajeva, M, D Gatelli, S Tarantola and H Hollanders (2005). Methodology report on European innovation scoreboard 2005. *European Trend Chart on Innovation*. European Commission, Brussels.

Su, J and GH Jefferson (2012). Differences in returns to FDI between China's coast and interior: One country, two economies? *Journal of Asian Economics*, 23, 259–269.

Sun, J (2012). Study on the interaction of enterprise technological innovation and regional economic development in China. *Studies in Sociology of Science*, 3, 39–43.

Sun, Y and F Liu (2010). A regional perspective on the structural transformation of China's national innovation system since 1999. *Technological Forecasting and Social Change*, 77, 1311–1321.

Sun, Y and D Du (2011). Domestic firm innovation and networking with foreign firms in China's ICT industry. *Environment and Planning A*, 43, 786–809.

Tang, M and C Hussler (2011). Betting on indigenous innovation or relying on FDI: The Chinese strategy for catching-up. *Technology in Society*, 33, 23–35.

Wei, YHD and I Liefner (2012). Globalisation, industrial restructuring, and regional development in China. *Applied Geography*, 32, 102–105.

Wei, YHD, Y Zhou, Y Sun and G Lin (2012). Production and R&D networks of foreign ventures in China: Implications for technological dynamism and regional development. *Applied Geography*, 32, 106–118.

Wooldridge, JM (2002). *Econometric Analysis of Cross Section and Panel Data*. Massachusetts: MIT Press.

Yu, K, M Tan and X Xin (2008). Have China's FDI policy changes been successful in reducing its FDI regional disparity? *Journal of World Trade*, 42, 641–652.

Zhou, Y and YHD Wei (2011). Globalisation, innovation, and regional development in China. *Environment and Planning A*, 43, 781–785.

Chapter 2

Trade and Investment Liberalization in India: Implications for Productivity Gains

Ram Upendra Das

Research and Information System for Developing Countries (RIS),
New Delhi

Abstract

Since 1991, India has witnessed wide-ranging economic reforms in its policies governing international trade and foreign direct investment (FDI) flows which has consequently led to a dramatic rise in both trade and FDI flows since then. Using firm-level panel data, this chapter investigates whether these trends have contributed to significant productivity improvements since 2000, as measured by total factor productivity (TFP). In addition, the chapter also examines the determinants of TFP across a range of different industry categories. The results suggest the existence of significant productivity improvements since 2000 and also identify variables such as imports of raw materials and capital goods, size of operation, quality of employment captured by wage rates, and technology imports as crucial determinants of productivity.

Keywords: Trade; investment; liberalization; India; total factor productivity (TFP).

1. Introduction

The economic growth dynamism of India since the 1990s until the global financial crisis (GFC) of 2008–2009 placed the country amongst the set of "emerging economies" in the global economic arena. One of the primary reasons often attributed for India's dynamism was the whole host of economic reforms undertaken since the 1990s in the domains of domestic industrial policy, trade policy, exchange rate policy and foreign direct investment (FDI) policy.

In the specific area of trade, India embarked upon substantive liberalization of tariffs imposed on imports on a unilateral basis since 1991, which gathered momentum by 2000. The current tariff levels are relatively low in most sectors, except in the agriculture and automobile sectors (Fig. 1). Classifying the sectors into three categories — high, medium and low tariff liberalization, it is worth noting that between 1990 and 2008 most sectors experienced a gradual decline in the tariff levels indicating that liberalization has been wide-ranging over time (Table 1). Almost across-the-board in the industrial sector, trade policy reforms in India — captured by

35

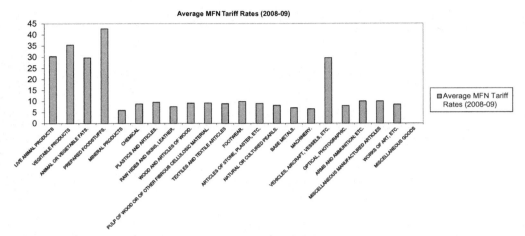

Figure 1. Average MFN tariff rates (2008–2009).
Source: Based on Government of India database.

Table 1. Level and extent of sectoral tariff liberalization in India (1990–2008).

NIC98	Description
	High liberalization
142	Mining and quarrying n.e.c.
369	Manufacturing n.e.c.
173	Knitted and crocheted fabrics and articles
182	Dressing, dyeing of fur and articles of fur
131	Mining of iron ores
323	Sound or video recording, associated goods
132	Non-ferrous metal ores mining, except uranium, tho
243	Man-made fibers
313	Electricity distribution and control apparatus
319	Other electrical equipment n.e.c.
271	Basic iron and steel
292	Special purpose machinery
241	Basic chemicals
353	Aircraft and spacecraft
	Medium liberalization
181	Wearing apparel, except fur apparel
333	Watches and clocks
315	Electric lamps and lighting equipment
332	Optical instruments, photographic equipment
272	Basic precious and non-ferrous metals
192	Footwear
314	Accumulators, primary cells, primary batteries
361	Furniture
251	Rubber products
331	Medical appliances except optical instruments

Table 1. (*Continued*)

NIC98	Description
293	Domestic appliances, n.e.c.
141	Quarrying of stone, sand and clay
261	Glass and glass products
291	General purpose machinery
252	Plastic products
172	Other textiles
242	Other chemical products
342	Coach work for motor vehicles, trailers, semi-trai
101	Mining and agglomeration of hard coal
231	Coke oven products
311	Electric motors, generators and transformers
289	Other fabricated metal products
269	Non-metallic mineral products n.e.c.
222	Printing and printing services
191	Tanning of leather, leather products
201	Saw milling and planing of wood
202	Wood, cork, straw and plaiting materials
312	Electricity distribution and control apparatus
281	Structural metal products, steam generators, etc
359	Transport equipment n.e.c.
210	Paper and paper product
343	Parts, accessories for motor vehicles and their en
351	Building and repair of ships & boats
171	Spinning, weaving and finishing of textiles.
103	Extraction of agglomeration of peat
221	Publishing
352	Railway, tramway locomotives and rolling stock
	Low liberalization
341	Motor vehicles
50	Fishing, operation of fish hatcheries
155	Beverages
154	Other food products
153	Grain products, prepared animal feeds, etc.
152	Dairy product

Note: Indian industry classification NIC-98 is similar to that of ISIC-Rev. 3.
Source: Author's classification based on World Bank, TRAINS-WITS and Government of India, Annual Survey of Industries, various issues.

import tariff liberalization — have been associated with increased import flows, with a greater rise in imports than exports (Fig. 2). There has been a steadily rising trend in imports between 2000 and 2008 except for a marginal decline in 2009 possibly due to the GFC.

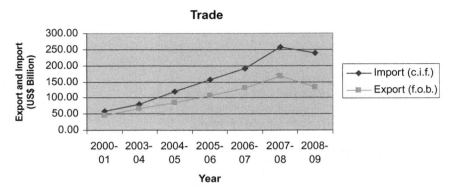

Figure 2. Trade.
Source: Based on Government of India, Ministry of Commerce and Industry database.

As evident from Fig. 3, FDI inflows have also increased during 2000 and 2008, to which liberalization of the FDI policy regime has been one of the major contributors (see Annex 1). The rise in FDI inflows has been especially steep since 2005.

Given the above broad macro trends relating to trade and FDI policy liberalization and their possible impact on increased trade and FDI flows, it is important to examine their implications for productivity gains, if any, especially at the micro level — a dimension often omitted from the macro analysis, sometimes due to data limitations. The firm-level determinants of productivity, especially in terms of the role of trade and investment liberalization, have remained largely unexplored, a gap this chapter aims to fill. The time period used in the chapter is 1990–2008 because Indian economic dynamism is best evident in that period.

The remainder of the chapter is organized as follows. Section 2 presents a brief review of the literature on the subject, including those relating to the Indian context. The analytical framework is discussed in Sec. 3. Section 4 details the methodology,

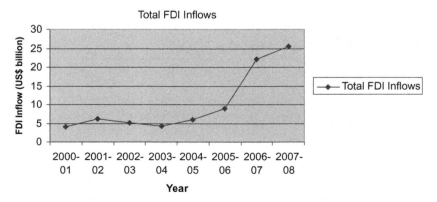

Figure 3. Total FDI inflows.
Source: Based on RBI database.

definitions and data. Section 5 presents an interpretation of results. Section 6 concludes the chapter.

2. Selected Literature Review

There have been several studies trying to explain the inter-linkages of productivity and total factor productivity (TFP) with other variables, including policy-variables. The methods of productivity estimation have also varied from study-to-study depending on the context. In a recent survey of literature on productivity estimates through various methodologies, Kathuria *et al.* (2013) arrive at the conclusion that estimates of productivity are sensitive to the empirical technique used. Hence, there is no unambiguous picture on productivity changes in India post-1991.

While the above is true, it is almost like discovering a *truism*. A conclusion as above would possibly be true of any estimation exercise and analysis of a particular estimate. This does not prevent analysts from adopting a particular methodology to estimate a particular economic phenomenon. This is so, because methodologies and estimation techniques are bound to differ depending on the issues at hand, the hypotheses and adequate data availability.

This section is divided in three sets of studies. It firsts considers selected theoretical studies linking productivity and trade. It is followed by a discussion of selected non-India focused empirical studies, after which India-specific empirical studies are discussed.

2.1. *Theoretical studies*

One of the channels through which trade is linked to productivity improvements is when a market finds a conglomeration of both efficient and inefficient firms, but only the efficient ones empowered by higher TFP gains venture into export markets. The findings on the nexus between exports and TFP as well as the direction of their causality are rather mixed. For instance, Melitz (2003) argues that while the reallocation of productive factors may generate aggregate productive gains, this may not ensure improvement in production efficiency at the individual firm level. In fact, exposure to trade will induce only the more productive firms to enter the export market, while some less productive firms continue to produce only for the domestic market, and will simultaneously force the least productive firms to exit.

To examine how trade liberalization affects firm and industry-level productivity, as well as social welfare, Long and Stähler (2007) develop an oligopolistic model of international trade with heterogeneous firms and endogenous research and development (R&D). Four effects of trade liberalization on productivity are categorized: (i) a direct effect through changes in R&D investment; (ii) a scale effect due to changes in firm size; (iii) a selection effect due to inefficient firms leaving the market; and (iv) a market-share reallocation effect as efficient firms expand and inefficient firms reduce their output. From this what follows for any market structure is that trade liberalization (i) increases (decreases) aggregate R&D for low (high) trade costs; (ii) increases expected firm size if trade costs are high; and (iii) raises expected social welfare if trade costs are low.

The literature has also examined whether trade liberalization increases aggregate productivity through reallocation towards more productive firms or through productivity increases of individual firms. Gibson (2006) addresses this question using a trade model with heterogeneous firms and argues that aggregate productivity gains come from firm-level productivity increases. The chapter considers how trade liberalization affects technology adoption by individual firms. If technological improvements are not costly — for example, if they occur through dynamic spillover effects — then trade liberalization has the potential to generate large increases in productivity.

Topalova and Khandelwal (2011) establish a causal link between changes in tariffs and firm productivity. Reductions in trade protection leading to higher levels of productivity, is a phenomenon observed by them on account of two forces: (i) increases in competition resulting from lower output tariffs causes firms to increase their efficiency and (ii) trade reforms manifested in lowering the tariffs on inputs, led to an increase in the number and volume of imported inputs from abroad (Goldberg *et al.*, 2009). Firms could access more and cheaper imported inputs that resulted in firm-level productivity. According to their estimates, the "input channel was a larger force in driving the productivity gains compared to the pro-competitive channel" (p. 3).

In sum, the theoretical literature provides important insights into trade-productivity linkages. First, exposure to trade, through trade liberalization, will induce only those firms that are empowered by TFP to enter the export market, in other words only the efficient ones venture into export markets. Second, trade liberalization helps increase R&D; firm size; and social welfare under certain enabling conditions. Third, productivity gains come from firm-level productivity increases, especially through technological improvements, rather than through reallocation towards more productive firms. Finally, trade liberalization leads to higher levels of productivity via competition resulting from lower output tariffs and input tariffs, with the latter having greater effects.

2.2. *General empirical studies*

Pavcnik (2000) empirically investigates the effects of trade liberalization on plant productivity in Chile and finds evidence of within-plant-productivity improvements that can be attributed to a liberalized trade policy, especially for the plants in the import-competing sector. In many cases, aggregate productivity improvements stem from the reshuffling of resources and output from less to more efficient producers.

Amiti and Konings (2005) estimate the effects of trade liberalization on plant productivity for Indonesia. They distinguish between productivity gains arising from lower tariffs on final goods relative to those on intermediate inputs. Lower output tariffs can produce productivity gains by inducing tougher import competition whereas cheaper imported inputs can raise productivity via learning, variety or quality effects. Using Indonesian manufacturing census data from 1991 to 2001, which includes plant-level information on imported inputs, their results show that the largest gains arise from reducing input tariffs.

In the case of Brazil, Liu and Nishijima (2012) find that openness and trade liberalization are crucial for productivity gains and openness of firms is a significant determinant of productivity. Similarly in the case of France, Garicano *et al.* (2012) find that regulation impacts distribution of firm-size and productivity levels.

While the foregoing literature is by no means meant to be comprehensive, it does suggest that increased openness should lead to increases in productivity. These increases occur on both the export and import sides and are driven by technology transfers and increases in competition, resulting in the exit of inefficient firms and sectors, the growth of firm-level productivity, and an increasing share of more productive firms in the market.

In contrast, the evidence in the case of Morocco by Augier *et al.* (2009) indicates that productivity growth over 1990–2002 for key manufacturing sectors has been minimal despite liberalization. They conclude that while the mechanisms driving trade and productivity linkages and "creative destruction" are well documented, results reinforce the need to understand more fully the circumstances under which they may or may not arise.

2.3. *India-specific literature*

Turning towards the Indian experience of productivity gains, the results are rather mixed and somewhat incomplete. Different macro-level studies primarily using aggregate data have found a positive relationship between trade liberalization and TFP during the 1980s and 1990s (Goldar, 1986; Ahluwalia, 1991; Chand and Sen, 2002).

Fujita (1994) argues in the case of India that the early liberalization policies during the period 1981–1982 and 1987–1988 improved the productivity of the manufacturing industries and also adds that the improvement in productivity led to the expansion of manufactured product exports. Further, he showed that the improvement in productivity involved mainly labor-intensive industries.

Goldar *et al.* (2004) explore the effect of ownership on technical efficiency — estimated with help of a stochastic frontier production function — at the firm level in the engineering sector for the periods 1990–1991 to 1999–2000. They show that domestically-owned firms display a tendency to catch up with foreign-owned firms in terms of technical efficiency, especially after the reforms were put in place.

In one of the more incisive studies, Topalova (2004), using a panel of firm-level data, examines the effects of India's trade reforms in the early 1990s on firm productivity in the manufacturing sector. The chapter focuses on the interactions between policy shocks and firm characteristics using the methodological advancements of

Levinsohn and Petrin (2003) for estimating TFP. In particular, the chapter tries to establish a causal link between variations in inter-industry and inter-temporal tariffs and the estimates of firm productivity. It finds that reductions in trade protectionism lead to both higher levels and growth of firm productivity.

Turning to somewhat more recent studies on India, Thomas and Narayanan (2012) explore productivity heterogeneity and firm-level export market participation in Indian manufacturing for the period 1990–2009and conclude that "learning by exports" results in productivity gains. On the other hand, using data on Indian manufacturing firms for the period 1991–2004, Haidar (2012) found a "self-selection" hypothesis at work by showing that more productive firms become exporters and that entry into export markets did not enhance productivity in India implying that the causality was not through the "learning by exports" channel.

In contrast, there are some, albeit a few, studies that have found that trade liberalization in India has not resulted in productivity gains (for instance, see Srivastava, 2001; Balakrishnan *et al.*, 2000; Driffield and Kambhampati, 2003).

Overall, the literature on trade-productivity linkages gives a mixed picture. In addition, there have been little attempts to combine both trade and FDI liberalization and assess their incumbent effects on productivity. Thus, there is significant scope to further explore the issues of trade and investment liberalization in India and fill some of the important gaps in the existing literature, especially at the firm-level.[1] Further, evidence is sparse in terms of the Indian experience at the firm-level relating to the determinants of TFP gains. This chapter attempts to contribute to the literature by combining trade and investment liberalization in examining their impact on productivity. The period of analysis covered in the chapter is also different from previous studies and it covers a much more recent period of trade and investment liberalization i.e., 2000–2008. It also explores the issue of determinants of TFP gains at firm level in the context of a liberalized trade and FDI regime, together.

3. Conceptual Contours

At a conceptual level, this chapter attempts to extend the analytical framework to include both trade and investment liberalization and their implications for productivity outcomes. The analysis of the impact of trade and FDI liberalization on productivity

---

[1] While the literature in this section has focussed on trade and productivity, we also consider the impact of investment liberalization in India on productivity. To be sure, there have been relatively few studies focussing on linking TFP and other forms of productivity gains with FDI inflows. Among the group of advanced Organization for Economic Cooperation and Development (OECD) members, FDI is found to be strongly associated with higher growth (in terms of output and productivity) in various sectors. However, among the group of developing economies, low-skilled and resource-intensive industries are the ones in which a positive link between FDI and growth has been observed (Castejón and Woerz, 2005). In a comprehensive survey of the existing literature on the productivity spillovers of FDI presence in China, Hale and Long (2011) suggested that many of the empirical estimates of productivity spillovers from FDI to domestic firms in China contain an upward bias. Bijsterbosch and Kolasa (2009) conclude that foreign capital, in the form of FDI inflows, plays an important role in accounting for productivity growth in the Central and Eastern European (CEE) regions.

can be grouped under different analytical categories such as (a) trade and investment liberalization: aggregate; (b) foreign-owned versus domestic firms; (c) export-oriented versus domestic-market-oriented firms; and (d) import-dependent versus import-independent firms.

Trade and FDI openness have the potential to infuse foreign competition into the domestic economy, especially in a country such as India which followed a protectionist policy in general and an import substitution policy in particular. The competitive pressures through trade and FDI openness thus exerted, force domestic producers to become more efficient and productive, manifested in increased availability of lower-priced and higher-quality products. These in turn help the economy become more export-oriented as well. As mentioned earlier, inefficient firms are forced to exit, whereas newer firms enter the production arena in a liberalized trade and FDI policy environment. Trade liberalization enables firms to use high-quality parts, components, and machinery at lower prices resulting in improved productivity, as noted in the literature surveyed earlier, whereby tariff reduction on inputs have a greater impact on productivity (Topalova and Khandelwal, 2011).

Liberalization of FDI contributes positively to the recipient countries as multinational enterprises (MNEs) bring in not only technologies and management know-how, but also financial resources to be used for fixed investment. All of these resources, which are in short supply in the recipient countries, contribute to improvements in productivity which leads to an increase in production and exports as it tends to enhance competitiveness. In the second round, increased production enables firms to reap benefits from economies of scale. On the other hand, with increased foreign exchange earnings from increased exports, firms' capability to import high-quality components and equipment also rises, resulting in turn in higher productivity Urata (1994). Thus, firm-level productivity is jointly determined by the trade, FDI and technology regimes, among other factors.

The size of the firm could be another important determinant of firm-productivity. Larger firms usually have more options than smaller ones with regard to choices of technology, products and markets. Larger firms may also be better positioned to enter into joint ventures with MNEs (Siddharthan and Lal, 2003). Ownership by a foreign firm is another factor that could help firms to push the productivity frontier favorably due to their well-known inherent advantages. Firms also import technology against royalty and lump sum payments to improve productivity and this could be another determinant of productivity. Import of capital goods is yet another dimension that is crucial for a firms' productivity. With import liberalization, including those of capital goods in the Indian case, this factor assumes greater importance for raising firms' productivity. One of the important constraints on growth and hence productivity is the demand constraint. Firms that are export-oriented are able to overcome this constraint.

Given the above, we examine four scenarios for analysis of firm-productivity (captured by TFP) comprising trade and investment liberalization at the aggregate level including all firms; comparing foreign and domestic-owned firms; export-oriented and domestic-market-oriented firms; import-dependent and domestic-market-dependent firms, in order to bring out similarities and differences among various analytical categories. This is considered crucial since a comparison of this kind would also have important policy implications.

4. Empirical Design

4.1. *Analytical categories for estimation*

4.1.1. *Trade and investment liberalization: Aggregate*

The firm-level panel data estimation for the determinants of TFP was carried out by capturing trade and FDI liberalization simultaneously with the help of the following specification:

$$\text{TFP} = \alpha + \beta_1 \text{IMP} + \beta_2 L + \beta_3 \text{R\&D} + \beta_4 \text{Size} + \beta_5 \text{XI} + \beta_6 \text{Cap} + \beta_7 R$$
$$+ \beta_8 \text{Exp} + \beta_9 \text{COR} + \beta_{10} \text{MNE} + \beta_{11} \text{I} - \text{CG} + \beta_{12} \text{I} - \text{FG} + \mu,$$

where TFP is total factor productivity, IMP is import penetration ratio, L is labor, R&D is research and development, Size is the size of the firm, XI is export incentives, Cap is capacity building, R is royalty and technical fee payments made abroad, Exp is exports, COR is capital-output ratio, MNE is foreign ownership, I-CG is imports of capital goods and I-FG is imports of final goods.

4.1.2. *Foreign-owned versus domestic firms*

The above will also be tested in terms of foreign and domestic ownership of firms, in an attempt to observe their behavioral differences. The hypothesis is that foreign-owned firms are more productive due to their inherently stronger capacities on various fronts such as technological-edge, managerial expertise, skills, etc. This categorization also helps to isolate the effects of FDI policy liberalization. For our purposes, a firm having equity stake greater than 51% has been categorized as a foreign firm.

4.1.3. *Export-oriented versus domestic-market-oriented firms*

The scenarios will be tested separately for export-oriented and domestic market-oriented firms with the hypothesis that export-oriented firms may be more productive due to the pressures of global competition. For the domestic-oriented firms, exports-sales ratio will be taken as zero.

4.1.4. *Import-dependent versus import-independent firms*

The effects of import tariff liberalization would be best captured by conducting analysis separately for import-dependent firms compared to import-independent firms. The import dependent firms will be those with an import penetration ratio greater than 0.50

considering that more than 50% import dependence would be a good criterion for classifying the firms as import-dependent firms as opposed to import-independent firms.

4.2. *Measurement of variables*

Consistent estimates of the parameters of the industry-level production functions in constructing firm-level productivity measures was done using the methodology of Levinsohn and Petrin (2003) similar to Topalova (2004). The details are presented below.

4.2.1. *Estimating TFP*

The dependent variable used was the estimated TFP. The estimation of TFP at for manufacturing firms needs elaboration before the measurement of independent variables is explained.

There have been several approaches towards estimating TFP (see Fig. 4) as summarized by Kathuria *et al.* (2013). Much of this literature has been devoted to the

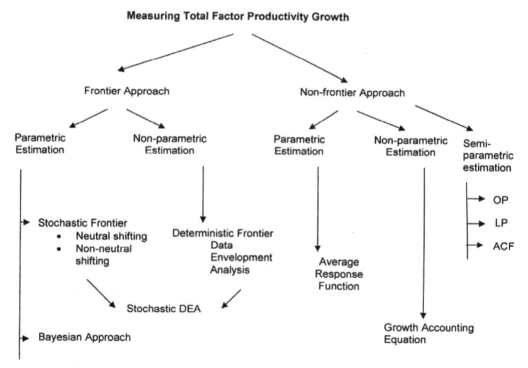

Figure 4. Different approaches to measurement of TFP.
Notes: OP — Olley and Pakes approach; LP — Levinsohn and Petrin approach; ACF — Ackerberg, Caves and Frazer model.
Source: Kathuria *et al.* (2013) as adapted from Mahadevan (2003, p. 372).

estimation of firm productivity levels, obtained as residuals from an estimated production function based on using deflated sales as a proxy. Different researchers have calculated the productivity index using different production functions, for example, Cobb Douglas, translog production function, etc. A great deal of the literature is also devoted to using labor productivity (LP) as a measure of productivity. However, a drawback of LP is that it does not fully consider firms' productivity and is not an accurate measure of productivity when many firms in the dataset are capital intensive.

Usually a functional form for the production function is preferred and in the vast majority of cases, the Cobb–Douglas production function is used. An alternative to the Cobb–Douglas function would be a more flexible translog function, which, in theory, is more attractive because it is less restrictive. In practice, the restriction of the functional form (as in Cobb–Douglas) does not tend to make a significant numerical difference. On the other hand, the advantage of employing the Cobb–Douglas function is that it is relatively easy to assess whether the estimated coefficients and the resulting returns to scale are broadly in line with common sense.

A Cobb–Douglas production function with labour, capital and material taken to be inputs can be captured as follows:

$$Y_t = b_0 + b_l l_t + b_k k_t + b_m m_t + w_t + u_t,$$

where y_t is the logarithm of firm's output, l_t and m_t are the logarithm of the freely variable inputs labour and the intermediate input, and k_t is the logarithm of state variable capital. The error has two components, the transmitted productivity component given by w_t and u_t an error term that is uncorrelated with input choices.

The following problem which can be described as one of simultaneity is usually encountered: At least a part of the TFP will be observed by the firm at a point in time early enough so as to allow it to change the factor input decision. If that is the case then the firm's profit maximization implies that the realization of the error term of the production function is expected to influence the choice of factor inputs. This means that the regressors and the error term are correlated, which makes OLS estimates biased.[2]

A relatively simple solution to this problem can be found if one has sufficient reason to believe that the part of TFP that influences firms' behavior w_t is a plant-specific attribute and invariant over time. In that case, including plant dummies in the regression, i.e., a fixed-effect panel regression, will solve the problem caused by w_t and deliver consistent estimates of the parameters. There are two drawbacks to this method. First, a substantial part of the information in the data is left unused. A fixed-effect estimator uses only the across-time variation, which tends to be much lower than the cross-sectional one. This means that the coefficients will be weakly identified. Second, the assumption that w_t is fixed over time may not always be correct, thus invalidating the entire procedure. As an alternative to fixed-effect regressions, a consistent

---

[2]Awareness of this phenomenon is far from new: It was first pointed out by Marschak and Andrews (1944).

semi-parametric estimator was developed by Olley and Pakes (1996). This estimator solves the simultaneity problem by using the firm's investment decision to proxy unobserved productivity shocks.

A key issue in estimation of production function is the correlation between unobservable productivity shocks and input levels. Profit-maximizing firms respond to positive productivity shocks by expanding output, which requires additional inputs. In such cases, OLS estimates lead to a productivity bias. Olley and Pakes uses investment as a proxy for these unobservable shocks. The method suggested by Olley and Pakes (1996) is able to generate consistent estimates for the production function, provided a number of conditions are met. One of these conditions is that there must be a strictly monotonous relationship between the proxy (investment) and output. This means that any observation with zero investment must be dropped from the data in order for the correction to be valid. Depending on the data, this may imply a considerable drop in the number of observations because it will often be the case that not all firms will make a strictly positive annual investment. Levinsohn and Petrin (2003) offer an estimation technique that is very close in spirit to the Olley and Pakes approach. Instead of investment, however, they suggest the use of intermediate inputs as a proxy. Typically, many datasets will contain significantly less zero-observations in materials than in firm-level investment. Thus the Levinsohn–Petrin procedure uses intermediate input as a proxy for these unobservable shocks.

We have used the Levinsohn and Petrin (2003) procedure in our model in preference to other methods available for various reasons. The most commonly used methods in firm level panel data as mentioned above have drawbacks. The Levinsohn–Petrin procedure overcomes these problems. It takes into account the time variation as well as cross-sectional variation. It also deals with the problem encountered in the Olley and Pakes methodology in which TFP cannot be calculated over time for firms for whom investment is zero. Rather, we use intermediate input as the proxy variable. The estimation takes place in two stages using OLS. First the following equation is estimated:

$$Y_t = b_l l_t + f(k_t, m_t) + u_t, \tag{1}$$

where

$$f(k_t, m_t) = b_0 + b_k k_t + b_m m_t + w_t. \tag{2}$$

This completes the first stage of estimation from which an estimate of b_l and an estimate of f_t (pu to the intercept) are estimated. The second stage identifies the coefficient of b_k. Here function f_t is estimated using OLS. Now w_t is estimated by:

$$w_t = f_t - b_k k_t. \tag{3}$$

Using these values, TFP is estimated from the following regression:

$$w_t = a_0 + a_1 w_{t-1} + a_3 w_{t-1}^2 + a_3 w_{t-1}^3 + e_t. \tag{4}$$

Generally, energy is taken as the proxy variable and in our model, we have also used the variable "power and fuel" as the proxy variable.

In sum, we have adopted the semi-parametric estimation with the help of Levinsohn–Petrin procedure under the overall non-frontier approach.

4.2.2. *Measuring independent variables*

The independent variables included in the study are: Size — measured as the number of employees of a company; labor — measured as wage rates capturing quality of employment; import penetration ratio (IMP) — measured as import of raw material/ (output + total imports); imports of capital goods (I-CG) expressed as a ratio of sales; imports of final goods (I-FG) expressed as a ratio of sales; export incentives (XI); R&D — R&D as a ratio of sales, royalty and technical fee (R) payments made abroad expressed as a ratio of sales; capacity building (CAP) — expenses towards capacity building or training and welfare expenses expressed as a ratio of sales; capital-output ratio (COR); exports to sales ratio (EXP); and MNE — defined as the percentage share of the foreign collaborator's equity of the total equity. In a wholly owned subsidiary it will be 100%.

4.3. *Estimation techniques*

We have used both the generalized least squares (GLS) and the Newey–West estimation procedures. From the basic model of panel data estimation, where the intercept changes for individuals but is constant over time and the slope is constant for both the individuals and over time:

$$Y_{it} = \beta_{1i} + \sum_{k=2}^{K} \beta_k X_{kit} + e_{it}.$$

To estimate the model we can make assumptions about the intercept: $\beta_{1i} = \beta_1 + \alpha_i$. This means that there is a constant portion in the intercept for all individuals (beta) and a portion that changes for each group (alpha). In a fixed effects model, α_i is a fixed parameter $\rightarrow X_{kit}$ and α_i are correlated. In a random effects model, α_i is a random variable $\rightarrow X_{kit}$ and α_i are uncorrelated.

We use fixed and random-effects models when N is large and T is small. A fixed-effects model is preferred if we have data on all members of the population. If the population is too large and we have a sample, then a random-effects model is better and it saves us degrees of freedom because some of the parameters are random variables. This is precisely the case with our estimation since the sample is very large. We also estimate GLS specifications that account for various patterns of correlation between the residuals due to the need for varying weights across firms and over time. We also take into account the problem of non-stationarity in a panel with the help of the Hadri test.[3]

---

[3] It is a residual-based lagrange multiplier (LM) test for a null that the individual observed series are stationary around a deterministic level or around a deterministic trend against the alternative of a unit root in panel data (Hadri, 2000).

In the context of linear regression, well-known large sample tests, such as the Wald and LM tests, usually require estimating the asymptotic covariance matrix of the normalised OLS estimator. This estimation may be cumbersome when data have complex dynamic properties. Newey and West (1987) and Gallant (1987) suggested non-parametric kernel estimators that are consistent even when there are serial correlations and conditional heteroskedasticity of unknown forms.

The *firm_identifier* is the variable which denotes each firm and *time_identifier* is the variable that identifies the time dimension, such as year. This specification allows for observations on the same firm in different years to be correlated (i.e., a firm effect). If we want to allow for observations on different firms but in the same year to be correlated we need to reverse the firm and time identifiers. We can specify any lag length up to $t - 1$, where t is the number of years per firm. It was found that the Newey–West estimations were more robust than the GLS estimates as they tackled the problems of multicollinearity and heteroskedasticity.

4.4. *Data*

Data used for estimation is taken from the Prowess data base by CMIE which covers approximately 11,230 firms in the organized sector, including both public and private firms (covering around 70% of the economic activity in the organized industrial sector of India). A good summary of the dataset is provided by Topalova (2004).

The time period taken was 2000–2008 for the reasons explained in the beginning of the chapter and the focus was limited to firms engaged in the manufacturing sector. The measurement of TFP was undertaken with the help of Levinsohn–Petrin method as discussed earlier. Data are drawn on the following variables: Sales, inventory, number of employees, capital employed, raw material used and power and fuel used. Real values of all of these variables have been obtained by deflating the nominal figures by the wholesale price index (WPI) (base 1993–1994 = 100). Gross output is calculated adding sales and inventory data. Number of employees is taken as a measure of labor input. Capital employed is taken as a measure of capital input. Raw material is taken as a measure of raw material input. Power and fuels is taken as a proxy for energy input. Since complete data for all the firms for all variables were not available, many companies had to be dropped from the dataset. The total number of observations is 3138.

5. Results

The Newey–West results based on panel data estimation (as opposed to random effects chosen on the basis of Hausman test under GLS[4]) are summarized in Table 2 for the aggregate as well as different categories.

---

[4] The Hausman test tests the null hypothesis that the coefficients estimated by the efficient random effects estimator are the same as the ones estimated by the consistent fixed effects estimator. If they are insignificant, then it is safe to use random effects. If a significant *P*-value is obtained, however, it is advisable to use fixed effects.

Table 2. Determinants of TFP.

Dependent variables	Aggregate	X-oriented	Import-dependent	Foreign-owned
Size	0.00165*	0.00003	0.000476**	0.000172*
	−0.00037	−0.00002	−0.00023	−0.000054
R&D	−0.000319**	−0.022312*	0.01334	−0.2022*
	−0.00015	−0.00813	0.0071	−0.0506
XI	0.01016	−0.00502	0.3331	0.02912**
	0.01406	−0.0116	0.40798	0.01328
R	0.08593*	0.04736*	−0.00499	−0.00817
	0.0203	0.01023	−0.02056	−0.0396
L	8.332*	65.997*	616.99*	66.97*
	2.2707	16.514	179.52	15.631
COR	0.00001	−0.04309	−0.00365	−0.6915**
	0.00002	−0.0398	−0.00328	−0.322
Cap building	0.0004	−0.0008	−152.64**	−147.09*
	0.0003	−0.001	−62.24	−30.755
X-sales	0.0002	−1.2475*	4.603**	−2.078*
	0.0004	−0.3289	2.2796	−0.685
MNE	0.00204	0.00414	3.0364	
	0.00583	0.0058	3.5638	
IMP	0.6974**	0.6904*	7.058 (4.5298)	1.1718*
	0.3166	0.1938		0.448
N	3138	2322	616	778
F Stat	22.15*	18.70*	894.18*	27.50*

Note: Newey West Std error in parenthesis.
*Significant at 99%; **significant at 95%.

For the *aggregate*, in the first scenario where *trade and investment liberalization* have been taken together with the former captured by the imports and the latter in terms of foreign equity participation, it is found that royalties, import penetration ratio, and employment are significantly positive, whereas R&D and size are significantly negative. While the significantly positive variables can be expected to determine TFP, according to the literature, a negative sign for R&D is puzzling. One explanation for this could be the fact that in India R&D was mostly undertaken by the public sector and private sector R&D is only catching up now.

On the other hand, our results are in agreement with Amiti and Konings (2005) whereby imported inputs can raise productivity via learning, variety or quality effects. Size being negative has important implications too, indicating that there is ample scope for economic activity levels to be stepped up in India through scale expansion.

Our results also conform to Topalova and Khandelwal (2011), according to which externally-imposed trade reform, i.e., increased import competition infused into the Indian economy, establishes a causal link between changes in tariffs and firm productivity. This is effected through tariff liberalization in all variety of products but it is most pronounced in lower tariffs on final goods, as well as access to better inputs, due to lower input tariffs.

In the second scenario of *export-oriented firms*, import penetration ratio, royalties, and employment are positive and significant. Additionally, imports of capital goods are also significantly positive. This is important to note as it shows the positive productivity gains appear to be accruing due to import liberalization of both raw materials and capital goods, the latter possibly embodying technology and hence the effect. R&D remains significantly negative even in this scenario, conforming to explanation given above.

The third scenario of *import-dependent firms* has size, employment and import of capital goods emerge significant. This is interesting as these suggest that import-dependent firms generally do reap productivity gains with greater number of workers employed at higher wage rates. This might possibly be due to the technological improvements in their operations assisted by capital goods import regulations which have been extensively liberalized in India. This is evident from the fact that capital goods imports turn out to be positive and significant. An important insight one gets from this result is the significant and negative exports to sales ratio, which indicates that import-dependent firms have been oriented towards the Indian domestic market and a possible import-export link is yet to be established. In other words, it may be argued that import liberalization especially of capital goods has largely helped consumers in the domestic market via productivity effects.

The fourth scenario of *foreign ownership* has size, employment, export incentives, and import penetration ratio turn positive and significant. These indicators suggest that foreign firms in India contribute to employment with higher wage rates; as foreign firms are responsive to the availability of export incentives and derive benefits from liberalised imports of raw materials as denoted by the import penetration ratio. On the other hand, foreign firms' productivity is negatively related to R&D, capital goods imports, and exports. The significant and negative exports to sales ratio perhaps indicates that until now MNEs in India have largely catered to the Indian domestic market and have yet to turn India into a major export platform.

In a nutshell, the results at the aggregate level suggest that variables capturing import and FDI liberalization effects have contributed to TFP gains. The merit of the scenarios is that it is possible to isolate the effects of trade and investment liberalization on productivity gains in terms of export-orientation, import-dependence and foreign ownership, providing interesting insights.

6. Conclusion

Post-1991, India has witnessed wide-ranging economic reforms in its policies governing international trade and FDI flows. Consequently, both trade and FDI flows have risen dramatically since 1991. In the era of reforms, productivity improvements have taken place and the findings of this chapter support several other studies on the subject.

The chapter further explores the important determinants of productivity improvements across different categories. Based on the findings of the chapter, some of the important determinants of productivity measured by TFP include imports of raw materials and capital goods, size of operation, quality of employment captured by wage rates and technology imports measured by royalty payments. It also appears that R&D in the organised manufacturing is still at a nascent stage possibly because of the inadequate emphasis this sphere has been given by the private sector. However, further exploration of this issue is required in order to draw any firm conclusions. Broadly, foreign firms have catered to the domestic market and as a result, India is yet to develop as an export platform. Finally, the import-export linkage is not shown to be significant in the sample of import-dependent firms.

While the issue of productivity gains needs to be viewed from a holistic perspective,[5] some of the broad conclusions of the chapter are that the aggregate-level variables capturing import and FDI liberalization effects have contributed to TFP gains. Taken together, these conclusions have important policy implications for tariff liberalization, especially for imports of raw materials and capital goods, FDI liberalization, and technology imports along with the case for a sound wage rate regime, primarily determined by market forces. Size being negative at the aggregate level has important implications too, indicating that the there is ample scope for the level of economic activity to be stepped up in India at the firm-level by scale expansion with increased employment of skilled human resources. However, in the context of a global slowdown, this may mean focussing on domestic sources of scale expansion alongside tapping regional sources of demand impulses via enhanced and more structured co-operation agreements.

Acknowledgments

The author would like to thank Ramkishen Rajan and anonymous referees for their valuable comments. However, usual disclaimers apply.

Annex 1: FDI Policy Framework in India

The FDI policy regime in India has been liberalized considerably since 1991. Industrial policy reforms gradually removed restrictions on investment projects and business expansion on the one hand and allowed increased access to foreign technology and funding on the other.

---

[5] In particular, it is important to place productivity gains in a proper perspective. This can be done at two levels: First, assessing the employment effects of LP and secondly, by studying productivity gains in conjunction with work-hours. With regard to the former, in the absence of scale expansion, LP gains could result in a lower demand for labor per unit of output production, precisely because labor has become more productive (Das, 2007). With regard to the latter, it has been found that in different sectors where LP has increased at a very high rate, the length of shifts has reportedly increased too (Ghosh, 2009). Both these dimensions should be kept in mind while envisaging any policy conclusions for productivity gains with the help of trade and investment liberalization policies.

A series of measures that were directed towards liberalizing foreign investment included:

(i) Introduction of dual route of approval of FDI — Reserve Bank of India (RBI)'s automatic route and Government's approval (SIA/FIPB) route.

(ii) Automatic permission for technology agreements in high priority industries and removal of restriction of FDI in low technology areas as well as liberalization of technology imports.

(iii) Permission to non-resident Indians (NRIs) and overseas corporate bodies (OCBs) to invest up to 100% in high priorities sectors.

(iv) Hike in the foreign equity participation limits to 51% for existing companies and liberalisation of the use of foreign "brands name".

(v) Signing the convention of multilateral investment guarantee agency (MIGA) for protection of foreign investments.

These efforts were boosted by the enactment of less stringent regime under Foreign Exchange Management Act (FEMA), 1999, replacing the Foreign Exchange Regulation Act (FERA), 1973. This along with the sequential financial sector reforms paved way for greater capital account liberalization in India.

FDI under the automatic route does not require any prior approval either by the Government or the RBI. The investors are only required to notify the concerned regional office of the RBI within 30 days of receipt of inward remittances and file the required documents with that office within 30 days of issuance of shares to foreign investors. Under the approval route, the proposals are considered in a time-bound and transparent manner by the FIPB. Approvals of composite proposals involving foreign investment/foreign technical collaboration are also granted on the recommendations of the FIPB.

Overall, the movement has been towards more and more sectors brought under the automatic route and increased equity participation even up to 100% in large number of sectors.

Source: Excerpted from RBI (2014).

References

Ahluwalia, IJ (1991). *Productivity and Growth in Indian Manufacturing*. New Delhi: Oxford University Press.

Amiti, M and J Konings (2005). Trade liberalisation, intermediate inputs and productivity: Evidence from Indonesia. Working Paper No. 05/146, International Monetary Fund, Washington DC.

Augier, P, M Gasiorek and G Varela (2009). Paradoxes of productivity: Trade liberalisation and Morocco. Draft, DEFI, France, Université de la Méditerranée.

Balakrishnan, P, K Pushpangadan and M Suresh Babu (2000). Trade liberalisation and productivity growth in manufacturing: Evidence from firm level panel data. *Economic and Political Weekly*, 7, 3679–3682.

Bijsterbosch M and M Kolasa (2009). FDI and productivity convergence in central and eastern europe: An industry-level investigation. Working Paper Series No. 992, European Central Bank, Germany.

Castejón, CF and JM Woerz (2005). Good or bad? — The influence of FDI on output growth — An industry-level analysis. Working Paper No. 38, The Vienna Institute for International Economic Studies, Vienna.

Chand, S and K Sen (2002). Trade liberalisation and productivity growth: Evidence from Indian manufacturing. *Review of Development Economics*, 6, 120–132.

Das, RU (2007). Technological advances and industrial characteristics: Some evidence from developed and developing countries. *Economics Bulletin*, 15, 1–13.

Driffield, N and US Kambhampati (2003). Trade liberalisation and the efficiency of firms in Indian manufacturing. *Review of Development Economics*, 7, 419–430.

Ferreira, PC and JL Rossi (2003). New evidence from Brazil on trade liberalisation and productivity growth. *International Economic Review*, 44, 1383–1405.

Fujita, N (1994). Liberalisation policies and productivity in India. *The Developing Economics*, XXXXII, 509–524.

Gallant, AR (1987). *Nonlinear Statistical Models*. New York: Wiley.

Garicano, L, C Lelarge and JV Reenen (2012). Firm size distortions and the productivity distribution: Evidence from France. Mimeo, March.

Ghosh, S (2009). *Sub-Contracting in Organised Manufacturing Sector in India*, M.Phil dissertation, Jawaharlal Nehru University, New Delhi.

Gibson, MJ (2006). Trade liberalisation, reallocation and productivity, Job Market Paper, University of Minnesota and Federal Reserve Bank of Minneapolis.

Goldar, B (1986). *Productivity Growth in Indian Industry*. New Delhi: Allied Publishers Private Limited.

Goldar, B, VS Ranganathan and R Banga (2004). Ownership and efficiency in engineering firms in India. *Economic and Political Weekly*, 39, 441–447.

Goldberg, P, A Khandelwal, N Pavcnik and P Topalova (2009). Trade liberalisation and new imported inputs. *American Economic Review*, 99, 494–500.

Hadri, K (2000). Testing for stationarity in heterogeneous panel data. *The Econometrics Journal*, 3, 148–161.

Haidar, JI (2012). Trade and productivity: Self-selection or learning-by-exporting in India. *Economic Modelling*, 29, 1766–1773.

Hale, G and C Long (2011). Are there productivity spillovers from foreign direct investment in China? *Pacific Economic Review*, 16, 135–153.

Kathuria, V, SNR Rajesh and K Sen (2013). Productivity measurement in Indian manufacturing: A comparison of alternative methods. *Journal of Quantitative Economics*, 11, 148–179.

Levinsohn, J and A Petrin (2003). Estimating Production Functions Using Inputs to Control for Unobservables. *Review of Economic Studies*, 70(243) (April).

Liu, W and S Nishijima (2012). Productivity and openness: Firm level evidence in Brazilian manufacturing industries. Discussion Paper No. 2012–01, Kobe University.

Long, R and F Stähler (2007). The effects of trade liberalisation on productivity and welfare: The role of firm heterogeneity, R&D and Market Structure. Economics Discussion Paper No. 0710, Dunedin, University of Otago.

Marschak, J and W Andrews (1944). Random simultaneous equations and the theory of production. *Econometrica*, 12, 143–153.

Melitz, MJ (2003). The impact of trade on intra-industry reallocations and aggregate industry productivity. *Econometrica*, 71, 1695–1725.

Newey, WK and K West (1987). A simple, positive semi-definite, heteroskedasticity and autocorrelation consistent covariance matrix. *Econometrica*, 55, 703–708.

Olley, S and A Pakes (1996). The dynamics of productivity in the telecommunications equipment industry. *Econometrica*, 64, 1263–1297.

Pavcnik, N (2000). Trade liberalisation, exit, and productivity improvements: Evidence from Chilean plants, Working Paper No. 7852, National Bureau of Economic Research, Cambridge.

Reserve Bank of India (2014). Foreign direct investment flows to India. Department of Economic and Policy Research.

Siddharthan, NS and K Lal (2003). Liberalisation and growth of firms in India. *Economic and Political Weekly*, 38, 1983–1988.

Srivastava, V (2001). The impact of India's economic reforms on industrial productivity, efficiency and competitiveness: A panel study of Indian companies, 1980–1997. Report by National Council of Applied Economic Research, New Delhi.

Thomas, R and K Narayanan (2012). Productivity heterogeneity and firm level exports: Case of Indian manufacturing industry. Presented at *The 11th Annual GEP Postgraduate Conference 2012 Leverhulme Centre for Research on Globalisation and Economic Policy (GEP)*, University of Nottingham, United Kingdom.

Topalova, P and A Khandelwal (2011). Trade liberalisation and firm productivity: The case of India. *Review of Economics and Statistics*, August, 93, 995–1009.

Topalova, P (2004). Trade liberalisation and firm productivity: The case for India. Working Paper No. WP/04/28, International Monetary Fund, Washington DC.

Urata, S (1994). Trade liberalisation and productivity growth in Asia: Introduction and major findings. *The Developing Economies*, XXXXII, 363–372.

Chapter 3

Foreign Direct Investment, Intellectual Property Rights, and Productivity Growth

Sasatra Sudsawasd and Santi Chaisrisawatsuk

School of Development Economics,
National Institute of Development Administration (NIDA)
Thailand

Abstract

Using panel data for 57 countries over the period of 1995–2012, this chapter investigates the impact of intellectual property rights (IPR) processes on productivity growth. The IPR processes are decomposed into three stages — innovation process, commercialization process, and protection process. The chapter finds that better IPR protection is directly associated with productivity improvements only in developed economies. In addition, the contribution of IPR processes on growth through foreign direct investment (FDI) appears to be quite limited. Only inward FDI in developed countries which creates better innovative capability leads to higher growth. In connection with outward FDI, only the increase in IPR protection and commercialization are proven to improve productivity in the case of developing countries, particularly when the country acts as the investing country.

Keywords: Foreign direct investment; intellectual property rights; productivity growth.

JEL Classifications: F23, O34.

1. Introduction

Foreign direct investment (FDI) has been a critical component of the economic development process in most economies. Fundamentally, it points to the fact that FDI not only develops and utilizes idle resources, but also uses all the available resources more efficiently. Contributions by FDI to the growth of national output and economic efficiency improvements have been the focal points of most previous studies (see Hansen and Rand, 2006; Basu *et al.*, 2003). It has been widely argued that FDI is complementary to growth in the host countries. Influx of FDI is empirically found to be a major factor supporting job creation and efficiency improvements in the host economies (see Chowdhury and Mavrotas, 2005; De Mello, 1999; Alguacil *et al.*, 2011). Providing the capital needed for economic development is another primary role of FDI. Many countries also look for greater economic benefits in terms of technology transfers to domestically owned firms — i.e., the so called "spillover effects" — so as to help them move up the value chain.

In this connection, intellectual property rights (IPR) protection has received a great deal of attention (Furukawa, 2010; Acemoglu and Akcigit, 2011). It has been argued that the positive contribution of FDI on growth depends on the stage of IPR development. For instance, Chang (2001) provides a summary of how IPR contributes to economic development via some historical experiences and identifies various circumstances where IPR regimes can supplement economic development. In part, those differences in the IPR environment particularly for the host economy are related to activities involving technological transfers through FDI. A better IPR regime is argued to be more conducive to technology spillovers and hence stimulates productivity enhancements in the host economies.

Generally, there are two channels through which IPR leads to productivity enhancements through FDI. First there is a direct channel wherein a tightening of IPR would create a better investment environment for a technology-intensive or knowledge-intensive sector such that it helps accelerate output growth. In one sense, this implies a greater vertical FDI type where different products in the production chain are manufactured in the home and host economy.[1] Branstetter and Saggi (2009) empirically show that there is a net benefit of FDI to the recipient economy by strengthening IPR protection schemes as the declining rate of imitation will be more than offset by an increasing flow of FDI. The second possibility involves simply changing the IPR regulations to attract greater FDI inflows. An increase in FDI in a host country creates more opportunities for economies of scale and also encourages a more efficient allocation and utilization of resources, thus creating a higher output growth potential (see, for example, Alguacil *et al.*, 2011; Borensztein *et al.*, 1998; Choe, 2003).

In this context, this chapter is interested in identifying some of the crucial IPR aspects together with both inward and outward FDI that help promote productivity growth. In addition, the chapter is also interested in investigating how the interaction between FDI and IPR may impact productivity growth. For instance, is it true that the greater innovative capability of a country will attract more FDI and thus promote growth in output? Or, considering the case of outward FDI, does investing in a country with better innovative capability lead to productivity improvements in the home economy from where FDI originates? If that is the case, the destination of outward FDI ought to be concentrated more toward highly technologically advanced economies.

While most of the previous studies focussed mainly on IPR protection (Chin and Grossman, 1988; Deardorff, 1992; Helpman, 1993), this chapter considers the differences in the stages of the IPR process consisting of the innovation process, commercialization process, and protection process. In each of these processes, it is hypothesized that there will be a differential impact on productivity enhancement through FDI inflows

---

[1] A "forward vertical FDI" refers to the type of FDI that bring in intermediate goods from the home country to produce finished goods in the host country. A "backward vertical FDI" refers to the type of FDI that produces intermediate goods in the host country to be used in the host country for the production of finish goods. Horizontal FDI, on the other hand, refers to the type of FDI that invests and produces similar products as those manufactured at home and thus, it benefits from better knowledge and technology of production the firms have experienced.

and outflows. Ambiguous effects have been discovered in earlier studies. For instance, Kashcheeva (2013) reported that while positive impacts of IPR on productivity improvement in the host economy are confirmed, providing a stricter IPR environment in the host country does not necessarily guarantee productivity enhancement via FDI and that it is contingent on the level of FDI in the host economy. Another set of studies using a general equilibrium analysis has also indicated that a stricter IPR environment might have an adverse effect on output growth.[2] Rising rates of unemployment and the cost of IPR usage are cited as the major factors driving the possibility of such a negative effect.

In this chapter, three IPR related indicators are introduced to illustrate the impact of each stage of the IPR processes on the host and home country's productivity growth. First, the number of patents per resident is used to represent the degree of innovative capability of the host country as the first stage of the IPR process. If a country has a greater IPR innovative capability — "IPR producer" measured as an increase in the number of innovations, then it is expected to have a positive impact on output growth. Thus, an increase in the number of innovations should have a positive effect (or at least will not produce a harmful effect) on economic growth. However, there is also the possibility of a diminishing factor setting in as more innovations are introduced. This could imply that the marginal benefit obtained from innovation activities in terms of output growth may decrease as the earlier innovations appear to achieve a greater leap in value creation.

Second, the degree to which innovations translate into greater production in the economy (and also economic value added) as well as the IPR commercialization process are represented by the ease of knowledge transfer (or the amount of activities) between universities and the private sector. Better links between the two entities indicate successful communication and a healthy IPR development that is expected to promote productivity growth.

Finally, the IPR protection is the stage of IPR development widely considered in literature as the key element that is essential to improve a nation's competitiveness in the long-run. Basically, it is argued that a stricter protection scheme supports the growth in output. However, the empirical evidence has not shown solid support for this argument.[3] For example, it is argued that for a user of new technology, a tighter IPR protection means that it is more costly to obtain access to advanced and up to date production technology and this makes it more difficult to use existing innovations as a basis for further creative activities.

The remainder of the chapter is organized as follows. Section 2 outlines the methodology used in the chapter. Section 3 discusses the data and empirical issues and empirical findings are presented in Sec. 4. The final section concludes the chapter.

---

[2] For a more detailed discussion, see Helpman (1993) and Fisch and Speyer (1995).

[3] For instance, see Ferrantino (1993), Braga and Fink (1997), and Charlton and Davis (2007).

2. Methodology

This chapter employs a variation of the Alfaro *et al.* (2009) model that was originally used to examine the role of FDI on growth in financial markets. The model is modified in a way that can capture the effects of the IPR process on total factor productivity (TFP) growth via two main channels. First, the IPR may have a direct relationship with TFP growth, as IPR development on its own is a productivity enhancement activity. Greater innovation achievements, smoother transfer of knowledge (or better links between IPR producers and IPR users), and a tighter IPR protection scheme are expected to improve national output growth. Under various circumstances, IPR development is expected to act as a mechanism for developing economies to pull themselves out of the so-called "middle income trap" by building up more economic value added activities and moving up the global value chain.

For the second channel, the IPR may have an indirect effect on growth through interactions with FDI. This perhaps rests on the fact that a more suitable IPR environment might be able to attract more inward FDI, which may lead to a higher growth rate of output by realizing the benefits of economies of scale and more efficient utilization of production resources. In addition, with a better IPR environment, the types of FDI that is attracted possibly generate higher economic value added and greater positive FDI spillovers, which will help improving the country's competitiveness and stimulating economic growth.

The growth impact of IPR via outward FDI rests more heavily on resource-seeking and efficiency-seeking FDI. For a home country to benefit, potential gains from specific type of resources such as knowledge, innovation technology and special skills are expected. This opens a door for developing economies to place more emphasis on the role of outward FDI on growth. An outward FDI that focusses on improving efficiency is another channel for growth stimulating activities in the home country. Sound IPR schemes tend to encourage such types of FDI movement. For instance, a better IPR protection environment supports FDI abroad to capture a more advanced production technology. Likewise, it also gives greater confidence for research and development (R&D) cooperation in the private sector so that more efficient production technology can be realised.

In terms of the relationship between inward FDI and growth, it is widely believed that multinational enterprises (MNEs) not only bring new investment to the economy but also generate "positive spillovers" to domestic firms, resulting in productivity growth (see Görg and Greenaway, 2004). In the view of Moran (2007), the positive spillovers may come in various forms. For instance, workers employed by MNEs after having acquired skills and knowledge may leave foreign firms and become available to domestic firms which will raise the productivity level of the domestic firms. Likewise, domestic firms may observe and learn from MNEs about their production techniques, management practices, or quality-control practices. In addition, MNEs may provide advice and direct production assistance to domestic suppliers which may raise quality as well as productivity of domestically owned firms. Moreover, entry of MNEs may bring in more competition, putting pressure on domestic firms to be more efficient and more productive (Görg and Greenaway, 2004).

The relationship between outward FDI and economic growth is less clear. On the one hand, the decision to invest abroad reduces the likelihood of investment at home due to the scarcity of available resources. Hence, outward FDI may substitute domestic investment, which inevitably reduces employment, productivity, and thereby economic growth of the home country (Herzer, 2010; Stevens and Lipsey, 1992). On the other hand, outward FDI may allow firms to enter new markets, to produce intermediate goods in the host countries at lower costs and to acquire new technology, which may encourage technology transfer back to the home country. In turn, these promote economic growth in the home country (Herzer, 2010; Desai *et al.*, 2005).

The model presented in this chapter has TFP growth as a dependent variable, and the variables of interest are the IPR related indicators (Policy) and their corresponding interaction with FDI (FDI * Policy) as regressors. In particular, it is presented in the form:

$$\text{TFPgrowth}_{it} = \beta_0 + \beta_1 X_{it} + \beta_2 \text{FDI}_{it} + \beta_3 \text{Policy}_{it} + \beta_4 \text{FDI}_{it} * \text{Policy}_{it} + \varepsilon_{it},$$

where i represents a country and t is a time period. β s are the estimated coefficients and ε_{it} is the error term.

The TFP growth variable corresponds to the growth rate of TFP. X is the set of control variables including the share of the nonagricultural sector as a percentage of GDP (NonAgri), level of development measured by real GDP per capita (GDPPC), size of population (in millions) (POP), domestic credit in the private sector as a percentage of GDP (Credit), inflation rate (Inflation), share of government consumption as a percentage of GDP (GOV), trade openness measured by the sum of export and import as a percentage of GDP (Openness), and local institutional quality in which the rule of law index (RuleofLaw) is used as a proxy.

FDI is the FDI stock as a percentage of GDP. Both FDI inflows (FDIin) and FDI outflows (FDIout) are investigated since they may have different effects on productivity growth. Although economic theory can offer reasons for several possible channels for positive spillovers from inward FDI as described above, existing empirical studies generally found mixed evidence on the role of FDI in generating productivity growth (through technology spillovers to domestic firms). Further, the positive effects of FDI on productivity growth are found to be conditional on local conditions and policies (such as, the policy environment, human capital, local financial markets, market strictness, etc.).

Görg and Greenaway (2004) concluded that the empirical evidence on spillover effects from inward FDI is mixed at best. Lipsey (2002) came to the conclusion that there is no confirmed correlation between FDI and output growth. Besides, several studies even found negative effects of MNEs on domestic firms. For instance, Konings (2001) found negative FDI spillovers to domestic firms in Bulgaria and Romania. Aitken and Harrison (1999) used panel data on Venezuela firms to measure the effects of foreign ownership to domestically owned firms and found that productivity of domestic firms declined when FDI increased, suggesting a negative spillover effect. Konings (2001) and Aitken and Harrison (1999) argued that there can be a negative effect of inward FDI on the productivity of domestically owned firms, particularly in the short run because the competition as a result of the entry of MNEs could force the domestic firms to reduce production and move back up their average cost curves. If this demand effect is large enough, net domestic productivity can decline even if there are some positive spillover effects from MNEs to domestic firms.

Likewise, findings from previous empirical studies on how outward FDI affects domestic economy are also not unambiguous. Using data for the U.S. MNEs, Stevens and Lipsey (1992) suggested that outward FDI and domestic investment are substitutes. In contrast, a chapter by Desai *et al.* (2005) found that greater FDI is associated with higher levels of domestic investment. Moreover, Herzer (2010), using cross country regressions for a sample of 50 countries, found that outward FDI is positively associated with growth; whereas, Braconier *et al.* (2001) found no evidence that outward FDI transmitted international technological spillovers and productivity improvements in Sweden.

To investigate the impact of IPR process on productivity enhancement, a set of IPR related indicators (Policy) is introduced, such that the role of each IPR process in stimulating production growth in an economy can be monitored. The three IPR related indicators are: (1) IPR (IPRprotect) as a proxy of the IPR protection process, (2) the number of patents granted to residents (PATENT) as a proxy of the IPR innovation process, and (3) knowledge transfer (KTRANSER) as a proxy of the IPR commercialization process. All are drawn from the IMD's World Competitiveness Yearbook 2013. The IPRprotect and KTRANSER indicators are based on the executive opinion survey response to the questions, "Are IPRs adequately enforced?" and "Is knowledge transfer highly developed between companies and universities?". As stated, the existing empirical findings on the relationship between IPR process and productivity growth are not entirely unambiguous. Hence, one of the objectives of the chapter is to explore this relationship for both the direct and indirect channels (through the interaction with inward and outward FDI).

3. Data and Empirical Issues

Since unbalanced panel data from 57 countries during the period of 1995–2012 is used, this chapter performed the Im *et al.* (2003) panel unit roots test. The test results rejected the null hypothesis that all series contain a unit root. In addition, the Hausman (1978) specification test was employed to test whether a fixed effect or random effect model specification is more appropriate. The result from the Hausman test rejected the null hypothesis, in which the estimated coefficients between the two estimators were statistically indifferent, which suggested the use of a fixed effect model estimator. In order to control for potential serial correlation and heteroskedasticity problems, a fixed effect model with a robust covariance matrix is selected as the main estimator. Since estimation results for developed and developing countries could vary substantially, the TFP growth model is estimated for both developed- and developing-country datasets separately for the purpose of comparative analysis.

In summary, this chapter estimates the TFP growth model by using a fixed effects regression with a robust covariance matrix estimator employing three datasets: The "all-country", "developing-country", and "developed-country" datasets.[4] The estimation results are reported in Tables 1–6. Tables 1–3 focus on the effects of FDI inflows; whereas, the effects of FDI outflows are shown in Tables 4–6. The estimation results are discussed and presented in Sec. 4.

4. Empirical Findings

For the set of control variables, the baseline estimation results (column 1 in Tables 1–6) show that the share of the nonagricultural sector, level of development, domestic credit, inflation, government consumption, and trade openness have some impact on TFP growth. While trade openness appears to have a robust positive impact, the coefficient of inflation is negative and significant, suggesting that a higher inflation rate would result in a lower TFP growth rate. It is useful to note that the coefficients of the share of the non-agricultural sector, level of development, domestic credit, and government consumption emerge significant in some regressions, while they are insignificant in others. The coefficient varies on the basis of the dataset used and/or the choice of explanatory variables (FDI inflows or outflows) included in the model. Finally, the coefficients of population size and local institutional quality are found to be insignificant.

4.1. *Effects of FDI inflows*

Based on the estimation results in Tables 1–3, inward FDI turns out to have a negative effect on TFP growth. The finding once again suggests that the benefits obtained by the host country in terms of productivity growth depend on the level of FDI inflows. However, this negative relationship is not robust and significant in any of the regressions. This nonrobust relationship between inward FDI and growth concurs with the findings from Alfaro *et al.* (2009) and Lipsey (2002), in which the relationship is ambiguous depending on the influence of other factors, such as the level of human capital (Borensztein *et al.*, 1998) and the development of the domestic financial markets (Alfaro *et al.*, 2009).

When the IPR related indicators are added without the interaction term (columns 2, 4, and 6), the IPR protection and commercialization indicators appear to have a positive and significant effect on TFP growth according to the all-country dataset, but only

---

[4] The list of 57 countries and data sources for all variables is reported in Appendix A.

Table 1. Regression results, FDI inflows, all countries, dependent variable: TFP growth.

	(1) Baseline	(2) Policy = IPRprotect	(3) Policy = IPRprotect	(4) Policy = Patent	(5) Policy = Patent	(6) Policy = KTransfer	(7) Policy = KTransfer
NonAgri	−0.1992	−0.1518	−0.1496	−0.2753	−0.2662	−0.1748	−0.1702
	(0.1089)*	(0.1167)	(0.1157)	(0.1987)	(0.1958)	(0.1156)	(0.1164)
lnGDPPC	−1.7667	−0.2526	−0.0220	−3.5427	−3.5704	−0.2476	−0.1855
	(1.7127)	(1.5300)	(1.5916)	(2.1836)	(2.1722)	(1.4862)	(1.5594)
lnPOP	2.5680	3.1066	2.4593	−1.1413	−1.2542	1.6999	1.5405
	(2.3568)	(3.1241)	(3.0766)	(2.3198)	(2.2824)	(3.0943)	(3.1391)
Credit	−0.0266	−0.0238	−0.0233	−0.0256	−0.0263	−0.0256	−0.0255
	(0.0099)***	(0.0084)***	(0.0084)***	(0.0159)	(0.0160)	(0.0083)***	(0.0083)***
Inflation	−0.1180	−0.1013	−0.1069	−0.2239	−0.2229	−0.0998	−0.1017
	(0.0343)***	(0.0633)	(0.0648)	(0.0684)***	(0.0683)***	(0.0639)	(0.0660)
GOV	−0.1687	−0.2635	−0.2705	−0.3521	−0.3577	−0.2463	−0.2479
	(0.0573)***	(0.0851)***	(0.0831)***	(0.0963)***	(0.0959)***	(0.0795)***	(0.0788)***
Openness	0.0647	0.0545	0.0524	0.0724	0.0729	0.0545	0.0537
	(0.0118)***	(0.0112)***	(0.0115)***	(0.0223)***	(0.0222)***	(0.0114)***	(0.0122)***
RuleofLaw	−0.9144	0.0889	−0.0379	−0.2485	−0.2511	0.3349	0.2418
	(1.0978)	(1.0009)	(0.9826)	(1.6248)	(1.6158)	(1.0133)	(1.0790)
FDIin	−0.0163	−0.0158	−0.0550	−0.0236	−0.0265	−0.0160	−0.0250
	(0.0065)*	(0.0058)***	(0.0576)	(0.0081)***	(0.0091)***	(0.0060)*	(0.0500)
Policy		0.4812	0.3202	0.0000	−0.0000	0.3604	0.3097
		(0.2185)*	(0.3108)	(0.0000)	(0.0000)*	(0.1884)*	(0.2675)
FDIin*Policy			0.0055		0.0000		0.0015
			(0.0074)		(0.0000)*		(0.0076)
Constant	29.7331	7.5129	8.6251	67.5114	67.3059	14.9034	14.8422
	(13.3336)*	(10.1405)	(9.3756)	(21.9102)***	(21.8595)***	(9.9966)	(9.9287)
R²	0.20	0.17	0.18	0.19	0.20	0.17	0.17
Observation	671	608	608	481	481	608	608
No. of countries	57	57	57	57	57	57	57

Note: Figures in parentheses are robust standard errors. ***, **, * indicate significance levels at 1%, 5%, 10%, respectively.

Table 2. Regression results, FDI inflows, developed countries, dependent variable: TFP growth.

	(1) Baseline	(2) Policy = IPRprotect	(3) Policy = IPRprotect	(4) Policy = Patent	(5) Policy = Patent	(6) Policy = KTransfer	(7) Policy = KTransfer
NonAgri	−0.0759	0.0405	0.0415	−0.6868	−0.6749	−0.0211	−0.0397
	(0.1868)	(0.1827)	(0.1817)	(0.6958)	(0.6912)	(0.1903)	(0.1903)
lnGDPPC	−4.6870	−3.4059	−3.4727	−6.1888	−6.6289	−3.1968	−3.7037
	(2.4071)*	(2.5872)	(2.7118)	(4.6818)	(4.6208)	(2.5209)	(2.7959)
lnPOP	0.1755	−0.0405	0.2545	−4.0377	−4.1562	−1.1333	−0.1594
	(1.2686)	(2.8120)	(3.1733)	(1.9045)*	(1.9285)*	(2.9705)	(3.3040)
Credit	−0.0166	−0.0154	−0.0155	−0.0110	−0.0114	−0.0174	−0.0176
	(0.0091)*	(0.0082)*	(0.0082)*	(0.0101)	(0.0102)	(0.0084)*	(0.0086)*
Inflation	−0.1985	−0.1485	−0.1416	−0.3110	−0.3060	−0.1574	−0.1328
	(0.0592)***	(0.0764)*	(0.0709)*	(0.0565)***	(0.0580)***	(0.0797)*	(0.0772)*
GOV	−0.1396	−0.2798	−0.2788	−0.5123	−0.5248	−0.2423	−0.2490
	(0.1253)	(0.1320)*	(0.1312)*	(0.1623)***	(0.1616)***	(0.1289)*	(0.1327)*
Openness	0.0697	0.0655	0.0661	0.0642	0.0653	0.0650	0.0689
	(0.0145)***	(0.0148)***	(0.0155)***	(0.0290)*	(0.0289)*	(0.0150)***	(0.0171)***
RuleofLaw	−0.3556	−0.1960	−0.1861	0.0015	0.0782	0.2226	0.6834
	(1.7157)	(1.6733)	(1.6670)	(2.4964)	(2.4900)	(1.6811)	(1.6507)
FDIin	−0.0115	−0.0125	−0.0022	−0.0159	−0.0185	−0.0122	0.0236
	(0.0048)*	(0.0045)***	(0.0443)	(0.0056)***	(0.0068)*	(0.0047)*	(0.0357)
Policy		0.6559	0.7094	0.0000	−0.0000	0.2881	0.5031
		(0.2336)***	(0.3264)*	(0.0000)	(0.0000)	(0.1858)	(0.2776)*
FDIin*Policy			−0.0014	0.0000	0.0000		−0.0059
			(0.0061)	(0.0000)	(0.0000)*		(0.0060)
Constant	53.5260	27.8707	27.2430	145.2400	148.7843	36.5843	38.8450
	(26.7213)*	(26.9476)	(26.2563)	(66.5196)*	(65.7850)*	(27.1287)	(28.9745)
R^2	0.17	0.18	0.18	0.19	0.19	0.17	0.17
Observation	437	410	410	312	312	410	410
No. of countries	−0.0759	0.0405	0.0415	−0.6868	−0.6749	−0.0211	−0.0397

Note: Figures in parentheses are robust standard errors. ***, **, * indicate significance levels at 1%, 5%, 10%, respectively.

Table 3. Regression results, FDI inflows, developing countries, dependent variable: TFP growth.

	(1) Baseline	(2) Policy = IPRprotect	(3) Policy = IPRprotect	(4) Policy = Patent	(5) Policy = Patent	(6) Policy = KTransfer	(7) Policy = KTransfer
NonAgri	-0.0760	-0.1688	-0.1700	-0.0244	-0.0146	-0.1644	-0.1069
	(0.0930)	(0.1052)	(0.1073)	(0.1412)	(0.1392)	(0.1018)	(0.1100)
lnGDPPC	-0.0039	2.2555	2.0875	-1.4239	-2.2419	2.2002	1.4959
	(2.1196)	(2.7594)	(2.9326)	(4.4319)	(3.7980)	(3.0844)	(3.1685)
lnPOP	3.2605	3.7750	5.6523	7.9370	9.4222	4.3526	6.6509
	(5.4442)	(6.4311)	(6.2753)	(8.1581)	(7.9548)	(7.4388)	(6.7837)
Credit	-0.1051	-0.0853	-0.0861	-0.1024	-0.0992	-0.0896	-0.0856
	(0.0274)***	(0.0255)***	(0.0235)***	(0.0339)***	(0.0319)***	(0.0244)***	(0.0242)***
Inflation	-0.1052	-0.1067	-0.1055	-0.1968	-0.2001	-0.1075	-0.1149
	(0.0358)***	(0.0638)	(0.0593)*	(0.0929)*	(0.0986)*	(0.0654)	(0.0630)*
GOV	-0.2847	-0.3327	-0.3105	-0.4260	-0.4257	-0.3211	-0.3428
	(0.0595)***	(0.1041)***	(0.0906)***	(0.0779)***	(0.0803)***	(0.0949)***	(0.0942)***
Openness	0.0749	0.0595	0.0558	0.1095	0.1074	0.0635	0.0677
	(0.0255)***	(0.0257)*	(0.0261)*	(0.0306)***	(0.0283)***	(0.0249)*	(0.0244)*
RuleofLaw	1.2843	1.9703	1.8139	0.9589	0.9838	2.4540	2.2783
	(1.4146)	(1.2517)	(1.1491)	(2.0970)	(2.0199)	(1.0145)*	(0.9332)*
FDIin	-0.0515	-0.0962	-0.2462	-0.0648	-0.0574	-0.0883	-0.2149
	(0.0225)*	(0.0354)*	(0.1110)*	(0.0264)*	(0.0217)*	(0.0323)*	(0.1097)*
Policy		0.4110	-0.3354	-0.0000	0.0001	-0.0703	-0.9968
		(0.4324)	(0.6475)	(0.0000)	(0.0002)	(0.4820)	(0.8291)
FDIin*Policy			0.0290		-0.0000		0.0304
			(0.0197)		(0.0000)		(0.0254)
Constant	2.3878	-10.1737	-12.9808	-9.2555	-9.5344	-10.7721	-16.3875
	(14.9290)	(13.0249)	(13.3738)	(25.1099)	(24.8619)	(18.4963)	(15.1561)
R^2	0.36	0.31	0.33	0.32	0.32	0.30	0.32
Observation	234	198	198	169	169	198	198
No. of countries	20	20	20	20	20	20	20

Note: Figures in parentheses are robust standard errors. ***, **, *, indicate significance levels at 1%, 5%, 10%, respectively.

Table 4. Regression results, FDI outflows, all countries, dependent variable: TFP growth.

	(1) Baseline	(2) Policy = IPRprotect	(3) Policy = IPRprotect	(4) Policy = Patent	(5) Policy = Patent	(6) Policy = KTransfer	(7) Policy = KTransfer
NonAgri	−0.2143	−0.1598	−0.1583	−0.2899	−0.2899	−0.1830	−0.1813
	(0.1178)*	(0.1213)	(0.1217)	(0.2122)	(0.2126)	(0.1206)	(0.1215)
lnGDPPC	−1.8953	−0.2797	−0.2406	−4.1593	−4.0771	−0.3132	−0.2954
	(1.7923)	(1.6418)	(1.6729)	(2.3112)*	(2.3226)*	(1.5891)	(1.6132)
lnPOP	2.4255	2.8743	2.7272	−1.1605	−1.1958	1.5428	1.5248
	(2.3127)	(3.1819)	(3.2626)	(2.4725)	(2.4712)	(3.1660)	(3.1807)
Credit	−0.0255	−0.0219	−0.0219	−0.0213	−0.0214	−0.0236	−0.0236
	(0.0101)*	(0.0084)*	(0.0084)*	(0.0166)	(0.0166)	(0.0084)***	(0.0083)***
Inflation	−0.1129	−0.0969	−0.0977	−0.2188	−0.2188	−0.0957	−0.0963
	(0.0332)***	(0.0613)	(0.0621)	(0.0680)***	(0.0684)***	(0.0625)	(0.0631)
GOV	−0.1529	−0.2625	−0.2639	−0.3542	−0.3578	−0.2450	−0.2454
	(0.0553)***	(0.0859)***	(0.0852)***	(0.1038)***	(0.1046)***	(0.0803)***	(0.0802)***
Openness	0.0566	0.0488	0.0482	0.0710	0.0707	0.0495	0.0493
	(0.0118)***	(0.0122)***	(0.0125)***	(0.0215)***	(0.0216)***	(0.0122)***	(0.0125)***
RuleofLaw	−0.9717	0.2060	0.1962	0.0218	0.0158	0.4617	0.4354
	(1.1201)	(0.9762)	(0.9730)	(1.6774)	(1.6768)	(0.9973)	(1.0092)
FDIout	−0.0089	−0.0109	−0.0219	−0.0194	−0.0201	−0.0118	−0.0158
	(0.0051)*	(0.0051)*	(0.0422)	(0.0060)***	(0.0060)***	(0.0051)*	(0.0386)
Policy		0.4977	0.4672	0.0000	−0.0000	0.3666	0.3481
		(0.2277)*	(0.2609)*	(0.0000)	(0.0000)	(0.1886)*	(0.2339)
FDIout*Policy			0.0015		0.0000		0.0007
			(0.0057)		(0.0000)		(0.0060)
Constant	32.8276	9.0454	9.2594	73.8657	73.2997	16.5756	16.4564
	(14.1110)*	(10.4467)	(10.2513)	(23.3737)***	(23.4387)***	(10.1536)	(10.2563)
R^2	0.19	0.17	0.17	0.18	0.18	0.16	0.16
Observation	663	604	604	474	474	604	604
No. of countries	57	57	57	57	57	57	57

Note: Figures in parentheses are robust standard errors. ***, **, * indicate significance levels at 1%, 5%, 10%, respectively.

Table 5. Regression results, FDI outflows, developed countries, dependent variable: TFP growth.

	(1) Baseline	(2) Policy = IPRprotect	(3) Policy = IPRprotect	(4) Policy = Patent	(5) Policy = Patent	(6) Policy = KTransfer	(7) Policy = KTransfer
NonAgri	−0.0866	0.0335	0.0310	−0.7065	−0.6847	−0.0278	−0.0324
	(0.1894)	(0.1839)	(0.1855)	(0.7064)	(0.7108)	(0.1919)	(0.1943)
lnGDPPC	−5.4560	−4.2113	−4.2368	−7.3172	−7.5928	−4.0118	−4.0680
	(2.4767)*	(2.6208)	(2.6867)	(4.7055)	(4.7519)	(2.5567)	(2.6555)
lnPOP	0.3383	0.5803	0.7395	−3.8566	−3.8922	−0.4515	−0.3877
	(1.3444)	(2.9371)	(3.1570)	(1.9164)*	(1.9162)*	(3.0147)	(3.0923)
Credit	−0.0129	−0.0114	−0.0114	−0.0052	−0.0051	−0.0134	−0.0135
	(0.0091)	(0.0082)	(0.0083)	(0.0096)	(0.0096)	(0.0083)	(0.0084)
Inflation	−0.2019	−0.1571	−0.1536	−0.3131	−0.3102	−0.1663	−0.1627
	(0.0619)***	(0.0815)*	(0.0762)*	(0.0530)***	(0.0543)***	(0.0848)*	(0.0806)*
GOV	−0.1448	−0.2909	−0.2903	−0.5261	−0.5378	−0.2553	−0.2565
	(0.1255)	(0.1330)*	(0.1327)*	(0.1611)***	(0.1627)***	(0.1301)*	(0.1314)*
Openness	0.0737	0.0708	0.0713	0.0714	0.0717	0.0708	0.0715
	(0.0141)***	(0.0148)***	(0.0152)***	(0.0308)*	(0.0309)*	(0.0151)***	(0.0157)***
RuleofLaw	−0.2415	0.1210	0.1063	0.1987	0.2710	0.5384	0.5992
	(1.7267)	(1.6429)	(1.6638)	(2.5061)	(2.5093)	(1.6470)	(1.6262)
FDIout	−0.0132	−0.0152	−0.0071	−0.0190	−0.0202	−0.0155	−0.0079
	(0.0054)*	(0.0055)***	(0.0450)	(0.0068)***	(0.0072)***	(0.0056)***	(0.0409)
Policy		0.6313	0.6678	0.0000	−0.0000	0.2945	0.3447
		(0.2315)***	(0.3054)*	(0.0000)	(0.0000)	(0.1854)	(0.2821)
FDIout*Policy			−0.0011		0.0000		−0.0013
			(0.0061)		(0.0000)		(0.0064)
Constant	61.1085	34.2222	34.0227	156.7924	157.6776	42.6449	43.1050
	(26.8414)*	(26.1870)	(26.0139)	(65.8823)*	(65.5544)*	(26.3013)	(27.1765)
R^2	0.17	0.18	0.18	0.19	0.20	0.17	0.17
Observation	437	410	410	312	312	410	410
No. of countries	37	37	37	37	37	37	37

Note: Figures in parentheses are robust standard errors. ***, **, * indicate significance levels at 1%, 5%, 10%, respectively.

Table 6. Regression results, FDI outflows, developing countries, dependent variable: TFP growth.

	(1) Baseline	(2) Policy = IPRprotect	(3) Policy = IPRprotect	(4) Policy = Patent	(5) Policy = Patent	(6) Policy = KTransfer	(7) Policy = KTransfer
NonAgri	-0.1322	-0.1936	-0.1829	-0.0522	-0.0511	-0.1865	-0.1062
	(0.1000)	(0.1210)	(0.1240)	(0.1425)	(0.1415)	(0.1153)	(0.1189)
LnGDPPC	1.5370	4.3506	4.1249	-1.2116	-1.4902	4.0458	3.0751
	(2.2061)	(2.8308)	(2.6190)	(4.7124)	(4.7913)	(3.1647)	(3.1495)
LnPOP	3.9947	1.8358	2.9967	8.8732	8.7661	2.1751	3.3603
	(5.0110)	(6.5344)	(6.2726)	(9.9467)	(10.2555)	(7.6117)	(7.3593)
Credit	-0.1178	-0.1098	-0.1049	-0.1223	-0.1166	-0.1119	-0.0965
	(0.0271)***	(0.0291)***	(0.0261)***	(0.0400)***	(0.0391)***	(0.0295)***	(0.0286)***
Inflation	-0.0838	-0.0855	-0.0854	-0.1671	-0.1578	-0.0881	-0.0945
	(0.0282)***	(0.0569)	(0.0545)	(0.0814)*	(0.0781)*	(0.0589)	(0.0593)
GOV	-0.2034	-0.2749	-0.2779	-0.3696	-0.3858	-0.2656	-0.2898
	(0.0488)***	(0.0949)***	(0.0835)***	(0.0966)***	(0.0874)***	(0.0900)***	(0.0868)***
Openness	0.0582	0.0386	0.0458	0.0969	0.0933	0.0447	0.0635
	(0.0244)*	(0.0254)	(0.0239)*	(0.0278)***	(0.0263)***	(0.0249)*	(0.0268)*
RuleofLaw	1.4915	2.2191	1.9802	1.2262	1.1207	2.6797	2.2305
	(1.2594)	(1.0315)*	(1.1700)	(1.8000)	(1.7049)	(1.0000)*	(1.1366)*
FDIout	-0.1351	-0.1434	-0.7360	-0.0711	-0.0587	-0.1268	-0.6131
	(0.0525)*	(0.0326)***	(0.2804)*	(0.0612)	(0.0662)	(0.0386)***	(0.2449)*
Policy		0.4970	0.0900	-0.0000	0.0001	-0.0089	-0.5649
		(0.4671)	(0.5070)	(0.0000)	(0.0002)	(0.5196)	(0.5928)
FDIout*Policy			0.0943		-0.0000		0.0862
			(0.0413)*		(0.0000)		(0.0408)*
Constant	-8.1150	-17.0188	-19.3378	-12.8559	-10.2673	-14.7729	-18.2611
	(17.2276)	(14.8282)	(15.6639)	(31.7052)	(31.4872)	(20.0683)	(19.1155)
R^2	0.36	0.30	0.31	0.29	0.29	0.29	0.31
Observation	226	194	194	162	162	194	194
No. of countries	20	20	20	20	20	20	20

Note: Figures in parentheses are robust standard errors. ***, **, * indicate significance levels at 1%, 5%, 10%, respectively.

the effects of the IPR protection indicator remain significant when using the developed-country dataset. This finding indicates that providing an environment of greater IPR protection for investors can significantly induce growth in developed countries. This is perhaps because better IPR protection creates more suitable conditions for techno-logical transfer and technology development that would enhance growth. Developed economies are considered to have a higher innovative capability in which investment may be used to finance high technology activities. Hence, the relationship between IPR protection and growth appears stronger in developed countries. On the contrary, none of the IPR related indicators seem to have significant impact on TFP growth in de-veloping countries. As IPR users rather than producers, developing countries tend to have less incentive to provide IPR protection. Although improving IPR protection helps increase the value of input used (as it enhances technology transfers), it may also increase the cost of accessing or utilizing such updated innovative knowledge.

Next, after the inclusion of the interaction terms of the FDI and IPR related indi-cators (columns 3, 5, and 7), only the interaction of inward FDI with the number of patent indicators is significant and positive at 10% level of significance in the all-country and developed country datasets. This suggests that a developed country with a higher number of patents granted is in a better position to seize the benefits from FDI promoting positive spillovers which, in turn, stimulates productivity growth. However, none of the interaction terms appear significant in developing countries.

4.2. Effects of FDI outflows

Column 1 in Tables 4–6 illustrates that the estimated coefficient of outward FDI is significant and negative. However, after the IPR related indicators (without interaction term) are added, the negative coefficient of outward FDI appears to be nonrobustly significant, as shown in column 4 in Table 6. For the coefficient on the IPR related indicators, only the IPR protection indicator (column 2) is shown to have a positive and significant effect on TFP growth in the all-country and developed-country datasets. This finding strengthens the important role of IPR protection environment for en-hancing productivity in developed countries.

When considering the interaction of outward FDI with IPR related indicators (columns 3, 5, and 7), these interactions appear to have no significant impact on TFP growth according to the developed-country dataset. Rather, the interaction of outward FDI with the IPR protection and knowledge transfer indicators have a significant positive effect on growth when the dataset of the developing countries is employed. It suggests that better levels of IPR protection and commercialization between companies and universities benefit developing countries through positive FDI spillover enhancing productivity growth.

A summary of the estimated impact of the IPR processes directly on TFP growth is presented in Table 7. Better IPR protection environment contributes positively to productivity improvement in developed economies. While innovative capability and

Table 7. A summary of the direct impact of IPR processes on TFP growth.

Stage of economic development	The impact of IPR processes		
	Innovation	Commercialization	Protection
Developed economy	X	X	(+)
Developing economy	X	X	X

Note: X = It indicates a nonrobust or insignificant impact of IPR process on TFP growth; (+) = It indicates a robust positive impact of IPR process on TFP growth. (−) = It indicates a robust negative impact of IPR process on TFP growth.

knowledge transfers are found to have a modest impact on growth, the relationships do not appear to be robustly significant. The effects of all three IPR related indicators directly affecting growth are rated weak and ambiguous in developing countries. The results suggest that improving the IPR protection environment in a developing country does not guarantee greater productivity growth, as the increasing cost of accessing the available technology and know-how eliminates the positive gains from IPR protection.

The effects of IPR activities through commercialization and innovative capability are also found to be limited in developing economies. These raise the question about the effectiveness of how innovation can be translated into marketable products and how developing economies should conduct their IPR policies. In addition, IPR innovative capability has not been proven to be beneficial for productivity enhancement, which could be linked to the fact that most developing countries have not been able to generate new technology consistent with their comparative advantages. More convincing evidence is seen for developed economies where IPR protection activities are shown to stimulate growth.

Table 8. A summary of the indirect impact of IPR processes on TFP growth (through FDI).

Stage of economic development	The impact of IPR processes through inward FDI		
	Innovation	Commercialization	Protection
Developed economy	(+)	X	X
Developing economy	X	X	X
	The impact of IPR processes through outward FDI		
	Innovation	Commercialization	Protection
Developed economy	X	X	X
Developing economy	X	(+)	(+)

Note: X = It indicates a nonrobust or insignificant impact of IPR process on TFP growth; (+) = It indicates a robust positive impact of IPR process on TFP growth. (−) = It indicates a robust negative impact of IPR process on TFP growth.

The contribution of IPR processes on growth through inward and outward FDI, summarised and presented in Table 8, appears rather ambiguous. The possibility of productivity enhancement in the host country through inward FDI is quite limited, as the results suggest that better innovative capability can help generating positive spillover effects from inward FDI only in developed countries. As far as outward FDI is concerned, IPR protection and commercialization (through outward FDI) are proven to improve productivity in the case of developing countries, particularly when the country acts as the investing country.

5. Concluding Remarks

The chapter has examined the impact of IPR processes on productivity growth. Better IPR protection environment is found to have a direct and positive impact on productivity growth in developed countries. In addition, the contribution of IPR processes on growth through inward and outward FDI appears to be very limited and is shown to be different in developed and developing economies. Innovative capability has important implications for spillover effects from inward FDI only in the case of developed countries; whereas, IPR protection and commercialization are shown to boost productivity spillovers from outward FDI in developing countries.

Based on the findings, IPR protection acts as a policy for stimulating growth in developed countries and innovative capability remains a key driver to productivity enhancement in these economies. This is perhaps because inward FDI in developed economies appears to be more of a vertical FDI type.

In contrast, IPR policy implications related to inward FDI for developing countries are less obvious. Inward FDI in developing economies tends to be of the horizontal type where the flows of such FDI rely more on the benefits of economies of scale and getting access to cheap resources. Moreover, there is the possibility that inward FDI might bring in production technology that is inconsistent with the host country's comparative advantage, and it may further have a negative spillover effect on the productivity of domestically owned firms. Rather than building innovative capability in the host economies, dependence on greater inflows of FDI could lead the country to inherit a so called "buying technology" habit or mentality which may hinder future productivity improvements.

Interestingly, it appears that developing countries are empirically shown to benefit from IPR conditions through outward FDI. Instead of passively waiting for inward FDI to generate spillover effects that will improve growth, using IPR schemes to facilitate outward FDI seems to be an encouraging and alternative investment policy.

Acknowledgment

This research was conducted as part of a project "Macroeconomy and Economic Policy Research for Thailand," which was funded by the Thailand Research Fund under the contract number RDG5710022. We would like to thank Dr. Somprawin Manprasert for his support, Dr. Kazunobu Hayakawa and other seminar participants at Institute of Developing Economies (IDE), Japan, for their invaluable comments, and Siam Sakaew for his research assistance.

Appendix A. Data Appendix

Country lists

Argentina, Australia, Austria, Belgium, Brazil, Bulgaria, Canada, Chile, China, Colombia, Croatia, Czech Republic, Denmark, Estonia, Finland, France, Germany, Greece, Hong Kong, Hungary, Iceland, India, Indonesia, Ireland, Israel, Italy, Japan, Jordan, Kazakhstan, Korea, Lithuania, Luxembourg, Malaysia, Mexico, Netherlands, New Zealand, Norway, Peru, Philippines, Poland, Portugal, Qatar, Romania, Russia, Singapore, Slovak Republic, Slovenia, South Africa, Spain, Sweden, Switzerland, Thailand, Turkey, Ukraine, United Kingdom, USA, Venezuela.

Variable and source

Variable	Definition and source
TFPgrowth	Growth rate of TFP at constant national prices (2005 = 1). (*Source*: Penn World Table (PWT) 8.)
NonAgri	Share of nonagriculture sector as a percentage of GDP (*Source*: IMD's *World Competitiveness Yearbook*, 2013.)
GDPPC	Real GDP per capita (constant 2005 US$). (*Source*: World Bank's World Development Indicators (WDI).)
POP	Population (in millions). (*Source*: Penn World Table (PWT) 8.)
Credit	Domestic credit to private sector as a percentage of GDP. (*Source*: World Bank's World Development Indicators (WDI).)
Inflation	Inflation rate, consumer prices (annual percent). (*Source*: World Bank's World Development Indicators (WDI).)
GOV	Share of government consumption as a percentage of GDP. (*Source*: Penn World Table (PWT) 8.)
Openness	Trade openness, measured by the sum of export and import as a percentage of GDP. (*Source*: World Bank's World Development Indicators (WDI).)
RuleofLaw	Rule of law indicator. (*Source*: Worldwide Governance Indicators (WGI).)
FDIin	FDI stock (inflow) as a percentage of GDP. (*Source*: UNCTAD.)
FDIout	FDI stock (outflow) as a percentage of GDP. (*Source*: UNCTAD.)
IPRprotect	Intellectual property rights indicator. (*Source*: IMD's *World Competitiveness Yearbook*, 2013.)
PATENT	Number of patents granted to residents indicators. (*Source*: IMD's *World Competitiveness Yearbook*, 2013.)
KTRANSER	Knowledge transfer indicator. (*Source*: IMD's *World Competitiveness Yearbook*, 2013.)

References

Acemoglu, D and U Akcigit (2011). Intellectual property right policy, competition and innovation. *Journal of the European Economic Association*, 10, 1–42.

Aitken, BJ and AE Harrison (1999). Do domestic firms benefit from direct foreign investment? Evidence from Venezuela. *American Economic Review*, 89, 605–618.

Alfaro, L, A Kalemli-Ozcan and S Sayek (2009). FDI, productivity and financial development. *World Economy*, 32, 111–135.

Alguacil, M, A Cuadros and V Orts (2011). Inward FDI and growth: The role of macroeconomic and institutional environment. *Journal of Policy Modeling*, 33, 481–496.

Basu, P, C Chakraborty and D Reagle (2003). Liberalization, FDI, and growth in developing countries: A panel cointegration approach. *Economic Inquiry*, 41, 510–516.

Borensztein, E, J De Gregorio and K-W Lee (1998). How does foreign direct investment affect economic growth? *Journal of International Economics*, 45, 115–135.

Braconier, H, K Ekholm and KHM Knarvik (2001). In search of FDI-transmitted R&D spillovers: A study based on Swedish data. *Review of World Economics*, 137(4), 644–665.

Braga, CAP and C Fink (1997). The economic justification for the grant of intellectual property rights: Patterns of convergence and conflict. In *Public Policy and Global Technological Integration*, FM Abbott and DJ Gerber (Eds.), The Netherlands: Kluwer Academic Publishers.

Branstetter, L and K Saggi (2009). Intellectual property rights, foreign direct investment, and industrial development. *Economic Journal*, 121, 1161–1191.

Chang, HJ (2001). Intellectual property rights and economic development — Historical lessons and emerging issues, Third World Network, Jutaprint, Pinang, Malaysia.

Charlton, A and N Davis (2007). Does investment promotion work? *The B.E. Journal of Economic Analysis & Policy*, 7, 1–19.

Chin, JC and GM Grossman (1988). Intellectual property rights and north–south trade. NBER Working Paper No. 2769, MA: National Bureau of Economic Research.

Choe, JI (2003). Do foreign direct investment and gross domestic investment promote economic growth? *Review of Development Economics*, 7(1), 44–57.

Chowdhury, A and G Mavrotas (2005). FDI and growth: A causal relationship. UNU-WIDER research paper, United Nations University.

De Mello, L (1999). Foreign direct investment, international knowledge transfers, and endogenous growth: Time series evidence. *Oxford Economic Papers*, 51, 133–151.

Deardorff, AV (1992). Welfare effects of global patent protection. *Economica*, 59, 35–51.

Desai, MA, F Foley and JR Hines Jr. (2005). Foreign direct investment and domestic capital stock. *American Economic Review*, 95, 33–38.

Ferrantino, MJ (1993). The effect of intellectual property rights on international trade and investment. *Weltwirtschaftliches Archiv*, 129, 300–331.

Fisch, G and B Speyer (1995). TRIPs as an adjustment mechanism in north–south trade. *Intereconomics*, 30, 65–69.

Furukawa, Y (2010). Intellectual property protection and innovation: An inverted-U relationship. *Economics Letters*, 109, 99–101.

Görg, H and D Greenaway (2004). Much ado about nothing? Do domestic firms really benefit from foreign direct investment? *World Bank Research Observer*, 19, 171–197.

Hansen, H and J Rand (2006). On the causal links between FDI and growth in developing countries. *The World Economy*, 29, 21–41.

Hausman, JA (1978). Specification tests in econometrics. *Econometrica*, 46, 1251–1271.

Helpman, E (1993). Innovation, imitation, and intellectual property rights. *Econometrica*, 61, 1247–1280.

Herzer, D (2010). Outward FDI and economic growth. *Journal of Economic Studies*, 37, 476–494.

Im, KS, MH Pesaran and Y Shin (2003). Testing for unit roots in heterogeneous panels. *Journal of Econometrics*, 115, 53–74.

Kashcheeva, M (2013). The role of the intellectual property rights in the relation between foreign direct investment and growth. *Oxford Economic Papers*, 65, 699–720.

Konings, J (2001). The effects of foreign direct investment on domestic firms: Evidence from firm-level panel data in emerging economies. *Economics of Transition*, 9, 619–633.

Lipsey, RE (2002). Home- and host-country effects of foreign direct investment. In *Challenges to Globalisation: Analysing the Economics*, RE Baldwin and LA Winters (Eds.), Ch. 9. University of Chicago Press.

Moran, TH (2007). How to investigate the impact of foreign direct investment on development and use the results to guide policy. Brookings Trade Forum 2007, MD: Project MUSE.

Stevens, GVG and RE Lipsey (1992). Interactions between domestic and foreign investment. *Journal of International Money and Finance*, 11, 40–62.

Chapter 4

A New Regime of SME Finance in Emerging Asia: Enhancing Access to Growth Capital and Policy Implications

Shigehiro Shinozaki

Financial Sector Specialist (SME Finance),
Office of Regional Economic Integration Asian Development Bank,
Philippines

Abstract

While finance is critical for small and medium-sized enterprises (SMEs) to survive and grow, most SMEs suffer from poor access to finance. Given the pronounced global financial uncertainty, stable access to appropriate funding sources has become even more difficult for SMEs to attain. Lessons from the global financial crisis have motivated many countries to consider SME access to finance beyond conventional bank credit and to diversify their domestic financial systems. This chapter uses empirical analysis to point out the limitations of traditional bank lending to SMEs and suggests possible policy approaches facilitating them to access growth capital.

Keywords: Access to finance; bankability; diversified financing; financial inclusion; growth capital; SME finance.

1. Introduction

Asia's rapid growth is increasingly influencing the global economy and positioning the region as a global growth driver. Continuing global imbalances require Asian countries to rebalance their economies by promoting intra-regional trade and mobilizing domestic demand, areas in which small and medium-sized enterprises (SMEs) can play a pivotal role. SMEs stimulate domestic demand through job creation, innovation, and competition. In addition, SMEs involved in global supply chains have the potential to encourage international trade. Prioritizing SME development is, therefore, critical for promoting inclusive economic growth in most economies in Asia and the Pacific.

Adequate access to finance is crucial for SMEs to survive and eventually grow beyond the SME status. In Asia, the reality is that SMEs have poor access to finance, which is one of the core factors impeding their development. As the global financial system has become increasingly advanced, the root causes of financial crises become more complex. Amid continuing global financial uncertainty, stable access to appropriate funding sources has become even more difficult for SMEs to attain. These conditions are restricting the region's development of resilient national economies.

Among the Asia and Pacific countries, fostering supporting industries (e.g., parts suppliers) and promoting the internationalization of SMEs are crucial to stimulating inclusive economic growth and escaping the middle income trap.

Given the diversified nature of SMEs, there is no "one-size-fits-all" financing solution. Continuing supply–demand gaps in SME finance suggest the limitations of relying on bank lending to safely and sustainably raise funds for businesses. The global regulatory response to the recent global financial crisis (GFC) — the Basel Capital Accord (Basel III) — may further constrain bank lending to SMEs as it requires banks to have tighter risk management as well as greater capital and liquidity. The resulting asset preferences and deleveraging of banks, particularly European banks with a significant presence in Asia, could further limit the availability of funding for SMEs in the region. Since the GFC, many countries have begun to consider SME access to finance beyond conventional bank credit and to diversify their domestic financial systems. Both the improvement of lending efficiency and the diversification of financing models can help increase SME financial access, given the largely bank-centered financial systems in Asia and the Pacific. Accordingly, national policy makers and regulators need to develop a comprehensive policy and regulatory framework that supports innovative instruments and services to promote SME access to finance, well serving their various financing needs.

This chapter focusses on two policy priorities to promote financial accessibility for SMEs — enhancing bankability and diversified financing models — and identifies missing areas that policies and regulations should cover to reduce barriers for SMEs to enter formal financial markets and access innovative products, as well as to smooth the cash flow cycle among growth-oriented SMEs.

2. SME Growth and External Funding

Not all kinds of SMEs are eligible to be economic growth drivers. SME is a generic term for entities that operate on different scales in a range of sectors and with varying management styles, which makes a discussion of SMEs as a homogenized grouping impossible. However, SMEs can be roughly classified into one of two types to facilitate discussion of their role in the national economy: (i) stability-oriented and (ii) growth-oriented. The former is typically a self-employed enterprise or family business that operates with the intent of providing for minimum or moderate needs, and with no interest in further growth. The latter is a high-end SME or a small but growing venture firm that explores new business opportunities with innovative technology and ideas.

National policies on SME finance basically comprise two layers of financial inclusion strategies to account for these different types of SMEs. One includes policies for developing the microfinance industry, which aims at social stability and poverty alleviation through enhancing access to finance for low income households and stability-oriented SMEs. The other includes policies for scaling up funding opportunities for SMEs, which aims at macroeconomic stability and sustainable economic growth through enhancing access to finance for growth-oriented SMEs. Although both sets of policies are critically important for the development and welfare of a country, the latter policy approach is rather crucial to create and stimulate the growth cycle of SMEs toward a resilient national economy. The policies for expanding SME finance should be addressed in a holistic manner that goes beyond conventional discussions of SMEs' bankability.

This section reviews the literature related to SME growth factors and discusses the underlying conditions of what makes SMEs survive and grow during a financial crisis.

2.1. SME growth factors

There have been many studies on the growth structure of SMEs where the discussions focus mainly on (i) the factors that enable SMEs' survival, (ii) stages of firm growth, and (iii) SME growth strategies.[1] Tambunan (2006) discussed two factors that contribute to SMEs' survival: (i) subcontracting with large firms and (ii) establishing a niche market that is not in direct competition with large firms. He concluded that the latter is the most suitable for SMEs — for instance, handicraft manufacturers that rely on a simple production process since the former strategy requires just-in-time delivery and a high level of quality control. Subcontracting may be effective for highly organized SMEs but would not be appropriate for average SMEs lacking developed technology and the benefit of scale economies.

Attempting a theoretical analysis on SME growth, Anderson (1982), among others, classified the growth stage of enterprises by the maturity level of the economy. In doing so, they revealed that (i) household industries such as garments, metal manufacturing, shoe making, and handicraft are dominant in the early stages of economic development; (ii) SME manufacturers arise as incomes increase with the development of commodity markets; and (iii) large-scale manufacturers dominate the economy in the later stages of economic development.

Tambunan (1994) and Snodgrass and Biggs (1996) concluded from their surveys that the number of employees in small firms decreases as average income levels increase. The impact may be most significant in higher income countries. Biggs and Oppenheim (1986) pointed out that the type of products made by small firms shifts from simple manufacturing products to sophisticated modern ones as income levels increase, which encourages the growth of enterprises. However, less sophisticated SMEs will not entirely fade away over time, but rather industries with special skills and production specialization can survive in limited market areas.

The accumulated studies also touched upon differences in growth patterns between rural and urban SMEs even within the same industry and among firms of similar sizes, with urban SMEs recording higher growth rates than rural ones. Anderson (1982)

---

[1]See Byerlee (1973); Anderson (1982); Piore and Sabel (1984); Biggs and Oppenheim (1986); Steel (1993); Tambunan (1994, 2005, 2006) and Snodgrass and Biggs (1996).

analyzed several unique factors in urban areas — including market potential, larger populations, relatively higher incomes per head, and the presence of a middle- and high-income customer base — that offer advantages to urban SMEs. Byerlee (1973) also concluded that different supply–demand patterns exist in rural and urban markets even for SMEs of the same size and in the same industry.

As for the growth strategies of SMEs, the role of specialized SMEs (flexible specialization) has been discussed, especially with regard to Europe, since the 1980s when globalization deepened. Piore and Sabel (1984) pointed out that globalization has generated new consumer demand for non-mass-produced products that cater to special needs and interests, and has led to the formation of areas where specialized handicraft SMEs gather. Specialized SMEs are characterized as entities with a high level of human resource skills focused on a single method of production within a closed market. They pursue innovation under a limited competitive environment and often cooperate closely with other enterprises. Specialized SMEs have the ability to grow faster than large firms, although the timely renewal of technologies is a precondition for them to survive. SME clusters can also be discussed in this context, with the banking sector now seeing clusters as a source of potential clients. Clustering is expected to more effectively protect SMEs from unexpected external shocks such as a financial crisis (Sandee, 1999).

SME growth patterns have been often discussed in terms of (i) real income, (ii) population density, (iii) market demand, and (iv) labor supply. Combining these factors as variables, Tambunan (2006) classified the growth patterns into four types. First is the relation between income and market demand, which suggests that market demand shifts to modern products as per capita income increases and the demand for inferior products from manual industries decreases. Even in this case, however, specialized SMEs promptly responding to market demand will be able to grow further, cultivating a new market opportunity or niche market. In rural areas, income increases can stimulate demand for sophisticated urban products and imported goods, while reducing demand for handmade products. Still, market infrastructure in rural areas can be improved as urban enterprises enter into rural markets. Whether rural SMEs can compete with urban enterprises or not determines their survivability. Second is the relation between income and the labor supply. The labor force is expected to shift to more sophisticated enterprises in the event that rising labor productivity triggers higher incomes, while it will remain with microenterprises if better work opportunities bring higher incomes. Third is the relation between population density and market demand, which indicates that rural areas with higher population densities have increased demand for SME products. Fourth is the relation between population density and the labor supply, which explains that rural areas with higher population densities generate an excess supply of labor for SMEs, gradually reducing incomes and lowering labor productivity in these areas.

Moving beyond theoretical discussions, Steel (1993) found that many large firms in Indonesia had grown from SMEs, indicating that the ratio of enterprises with more than 500 employees to the total number of medium and large firms increased from 28.8% in 1975 to 63.7% in 1990. However, whether or not this demonstrates SME growth was not clearly determined.

Based on the discussion in the above mentioned literature, the growth structure of SMEs can be summarized below. It should be noted, however, that these findings were derived from the analyses of manufacturing SMEs and did not analyze other sectors or the correlation between SME growth and external funding.

(i) SMEs can increase their chance of survival by either subcontracting with large firms or establishing a niche market. The average SME that does not enjoy economies of scale can benefit from establishing a niche market rather than subcontracting. Flexible specialization or clustering can be the key for an SME's survival and growth.

(ii) The dominant growth stage of SMEs differs across economies depending on their level of maturity, with household industries in the early stages of economic development and manufacturers in the later stages. Urban SMEs grow faster than rural ones due to advantageous business conditions in urban areas.

(iii) Rising incomes can generate new market demand through customer preferences shifting to sophisticated modern products, and will encourage the growth of enterprises, which also brings a more competitive environment and more open markets to rural economies. Micro businesses will decrease in number as incomes rise but they can still maintain demand in niche markets. The transfer of labor caused by rising incomes encourages the development of sophisticated micro businesses.

(iv) Areas with higher population densities have increased demand for SME products, which encourages the growth of enterprises unless the labor supply is excessive.

2.2. *Financial crisis, SMEs, and financial access*

The 1997/1998 Asian financial crisis led to many studies on SMEs' performance during and after the crisis, with most focusing on SME manufacturers, especially exporters. Berry *et al.* (2001) pointed out that SMEs were less impacted by the financial crisis than large firms due to SMEs' flexible production processes. This contention is supported by data from the Ministry of Cooperatives and SMEs in Indonesia, which indicate that the annual increase in sales value per worker in the manufacturing industry was negative in 1998 in medium firms and large firms at -27.2% and -5.4%, respectively. Meanwhile, sales value per worker increased 34.9% in small firms in 1998, mainly due to their low dependency on formal commodity markets for material procurement and on financial institutions for funding, which enabled small firms to promptly and flexibly respond to the crisis situation.[2]

---

[2] However, the severity of the impact of the financial crisis on SMEs in Indonesia differed by sector and region.

Magiera (1999) surveyed Indonesian export-oriented SME manufacturers and found that they performed better than large firms after the crisis. Small exporters (e.g., garments and leather products) increased their trade volume 3.6% in 1998, while large firms only saw a 0.8% increase.

Thee (2000) comparatively analyzed the impact of the financial crisis in Indonesia by scale of enterprise and developed a different opinion. The manufacturing industry was one of the sectors most seriously impacted by the financial crisis, with growth slipping by −12.9% in 1998. Although other studies evaluated the post-crisis performance of SME manufacturers (especially exporters) positively when compared with large firms, Thee (2000) stressed that the financial crisis led to a sharp decrease in the number of SMEs and their employees by −23.4% and −19.8%, respectively, between 1996 and 1998, thus signaling reduced domestic demand for SME products. The banking crisis further restricted SME access to finance. Despite these conditions, however, SMEs that shifted production to cheaper goods for export were able to profit in light of the rupiah's depreciation.

Wengel and Rodriguez (2006) analyzed the performance of export-oriented SME manufacturers in Indonesia in the aftermath of the financial crisis and again found differences in the impact between SMEs and large firms. During the crisis, large firms reduced their trade volumes while SMEs expanded theirs. As large firms relied heavily on imported materials, high procurement costs caused by the rupiah's depreciation and increasing amounts of bad debt resulting from the banking crisis seriously hampered the recovery of large firms. Meanwhile, the slowdown in domestic markets and increasing production costs drove some SMEs toward international markets. Due to their low dependency on imported materials, SMEs' competitiveness tended to remain high and they achieved moderate growth after the crisis.

As for the funding environment of export-oriented SME manufacturers, Wengel and Rodriguez (2006) conducted an empirical analysis which showed that SMEs would experience an increase in their estimated trade volume by 1.8% if they were able to borrow from financial institutions compared to a scenario in which SMEs had no access to finance. The increase was smaller in the case of large firms (1.0%), which implies that external funding can improve the business performance of SMEs to a greater degree than for large firms.

Musa and Priatna (1998) also surveyed the funding environment for SMEs after the financial crisis. Analyzing 300 samples from eight provinces in Indonesia, the findings showed that 75% of SMEs relied on their own capital for financing while less than 13% had access to formal finance. Access to formal finance was found to have decreased after the Asian financial crisis. Musa and Priatna explained that the relatively quick recovery of SMEs after the crisis could be attributed to their limited access to finance prior to the crisis, with SMEs overcoming the crisis period by making use of cheap materials. However, 80% of the SMEs surveyed reported reducing business activities after the crisis, while the 8% that reported increased profits were exporters who were not dependent on imported materials. Several studies highlighted that SMEs suffered less impact from the crisis compared to large firms, but a significant portion of SMEs (mainly non-exporters) experienced serious losses. Against this backdrop, it is natural to consider that limited access to finance may have adversely affected the survival and growth rate of SMEs.

Based on the discussion above, the factors that contributed to an SME's survival during the 1997/1998 Asian financial crisis included the following.

(i) *Financial accessibility*: SMEs relying on their own capital and with limited access to finance were better positioned to avoid the serious shocks from the financial and banking crisis than large firms. However, low access to finance negatively affected SME survival and growth rates in general.

(ii) *Localization and niche marketing*: Creating a niche market separate from open markets enabled SMEs to survive the crisis. Locally based business operations, in which SMEs were not involved in subcontracts with large firms, also enabled SMEs to survive.

(iii) *Internationalization and export-orientation*: SMEs that shifted from domestic to international markets with no reliance on imported materials were able to weather the crisis.

(iv) *Specialization and clustering*: SMEs that successfully cooperated with other enterprises — to reduce their production costs, share and renew technologies, and form wide-ranging sales networks — were able to survive the crisis.

Findings from the studies referenced above imply that stability-oriented SMEs could survive a financial crisis by not relying on open markets and formal funding sources. Growth-oriented SMEs could do so by pursuing management efficiency and technological innovation, and flexibly shifting market strategies to overcome their financial difficulties. Taking account of the long-term growth trend of Asian economies, the number of growth-oriented SMEs is expected to increase and they will seek increased access to the formal financial system. Thus, enhancing financial accessibility through broadening financing instruments and infrastructure is critical to support growth-oriented SMEs.

3. Supply-Demand Gap in SME Finance

While there are plenty of factors that can slow the pace of SME growth, such as weak internal control systems and governance, restricted access to finance is one of the most critical factors inhibiting their growth. How large is SMEs' unmet financing demand or the supply–demand gap? Stein *et al.* (2010) estimated the value of the gap in formal SME credit in 2010 at US$700 billion–US$850 billion, which is equivalent to 21–26% of the total formal SME credit outstanding in the developing world (Table 1). The financing gap varies by region. For instance, the gap in East Asia accounted for US$250 billion–US$310 billion of the total, while in South Asia it accounted for US$30

Table 1. SME access to finance.

		Value of credit gap ($ billion)	Number of firms (million)	With deposit accounts	With loans or overdraft
East Asia	MSMEs	900–1,100	170–205	115–140	17–19
	Formal SMEs	250–310 [11–14%]	11.2–13.6	7.6–9.1	2.0–2.5
South Asia	MSMEs	310–370	75–91	47–57	15–17
	Formal SMEs	30–40 [29–35%]	2.0–2.8	1.0–1.2	0.5–0.7
Central Asia &	MSMEs	215–260	18–22	13–17	8–10
Eastern Europe	Formal SMEs	105–130 [16–20%]	2.7–3.3	2.5–3.0	1.5–1.9
High-income	MSMEs	1,000–1,300	56–68	51–63	24–30
OECD	Formal SMEs	600–700 [5–6%]	11–14	11–14	5–6
Total	MSMEs	2,100–2,500	365–445	240–290	75–90
excluding high-	Formal SMEs	700–850	25–30	18–22	8–10
income OECD		[21–26%]			

Note: Based on World Bank analytical classifications.
[ ] = gap as percentage of current outstanding SME credit; MSMEs = micro, small, and medium-sized enterprises; OECD = Organisation for Economic Co-operation and Development; SMEs = small and medium-sized enterprises.
Source: IFC and McKinsey & Company. 2010. *Two trillion and counting*. Washington, DC: IFC.

billion–US\$40 billion. If informal SMEs and microenterprises are included, the total gap in developing countries in terms of unmet financing demand exceeds US\$2 trillion.

Based on the disequilibrium models of the credit market developed by academics such as Fair and Jaffee (1972); Rimbara and Santomero (1976); Laffont and Garcia (1977); Pazarbasioglu (1997); Ghosh and Ghosh (1999) and Agung *et al.* (2001), this section investigates the financing gap in Indonesia between lenders and SME borrowers by establishing regression models that measure both supply-side and demand-side factors to determine the provision of bank credit. The data used were extracted from various issues of Bank Indonesia's[3] *Banking Statistics* and *Financial Statistics* and reports from the Central Bureau of Statistics (BPS),[4] covering the period between January 2007 and December 2011.

A credit supply curve is formulated with the assumption that banks' loan supply is determined by their lending capacity (defined as total liabilities minus equity capital and required reserves), lending rate, production outputs, and non-performing loan (NPL) values. The equation is described by:

$$L_t^s = a + b_1 \text{cap}_t + b_2 r_t + b_3 y_t + b_3 \text{npl}_t + u_t, \qquad (1)$$

[3] Bank Indonesia. *Data Perbankan Indonesia/Indonesian Banking Statistics*. Various Issues. Jakarta. *Statistik Ekonomi dan Keuangan Indonesia/Indonesian Financial Statistics*. Various Issues. Jakarta.
[4] Badan Pusat Statistik. http://www.bps.go.id/.

where L^s is a credit supply function; a and b are coefficients to be estimated; cap is lending capacity in local currency (LCY) values calculated based on commercial bank balance sheets; r is the average lending rate for working capital; y is the value of real gross domestic product (GDP); NPL is the value of non-performing SME loans; t is an observed point in time; and u is a residual.

A credit demand curve is formulated with the assumption that the demand for bank loans is determined by bank lending rates and production outputs. GDP is considered as an indicator to represent the potential demands on firms' business operations, although some arguments exist for selecting independent variables in the demand function (Ghosh and Ghosh, 1999). The equation is described by:

$$L_t^d = a + b_1 r_t + b_2 y_t + u_t, \tag{2}$$

where L^d is a credit demand function; a and b are coefficients to be estimated; r is the average lending rate for working capital; y is the value of real GDP as a determinant of credit demand; t is an observed point in time; and u is a residual.

The outstanding values of SME bank loans are used as dependent variables in the credit supply and demand curves. To measure the change of the credit supply and demand in pre- and post-GFC period, a dummy for the GFC is included in both curves, where 0 denotes the period from January 2007 to December 2008 while 1 represents the period from January 2009 to December 2011. Due to the truncated nature of data, maximum likelihood (ML) estimation is adopted as analysis of limited dependent variable in both models.

Given that the price of credit (lending rate) is not sufficiently adjusted and credit rationing arises, the disequilibrium of the credit market is denoted by:

$$L_t = \min (L_t^s, L_t^d), \tag{3}$$

where L_t is the actual lending value observed at period t. L corresponds to the credit supply curve (L^s) if the credit demand exceeds the credit supply ($L^d > L^s$), while it follows the credit demand curve (L^d) if the credit supply exceeds the credit demand ($L^s > L^d$).

The result of the estimates (Table 2) indicates that the credit supply for SMEs increases if banks' lending capacity and production outputs increase. It also increases if lending rates decline. However, SME credit supply increases even if NPLs rise in pre-crisis periods, though such a trend is reversed in the post-crisis period. Meanwhile, SME credit demand increases if production outputs rise. It remains high even if lending rates go up prior to a crisis, but this trend is reversed in the post-crisis period. These estimates imply that the banking sector actively provides SME credit with concessional lending rates in line with government policies to improve SME access to finance, but banks' credit risk sensitivity in the post-crisis period tends to exceed that prior to a crisis. As for credit demand, SMEs maintain their appetite for finance during the pre-crisis period regardless of lending rates, but their credit price sensitivity tends to go up in the post-crisis period.

Table 2. Supply–demand gap in SME finance — Indonesia ML estimation.

	Total		Before GFC		After GFC	
	Credit supply	Credit demand	Credit supply	Credit demand	Credit supply	Credit demand
Lcap	0.4273		0.4928		0.2652	
	[16.91]***		[14.51]***		[3.95]***	
wcr	−0.014	0.0141	−0.0175	0.0043	−0.0203	−0.0297
	[−5.39]***	[2.87]***	[−5.56]***	[0.51]	[−3.33]***	[−4.62]***
y	2.4389	3.6983	2.1641	3.4470	2.6804	2.8202
	[29.31]***	[70.24]***	[20.94]***	[19.87]***	[24.94]***	[26.25]***
sme_npl	0.0150		0.1206		−0.0391	
	[0.60]		[2.02]**		[−1.28]	
Constant	−24.8248	−35.6477	−23.1225	−32.2203	−25.0756	−23.4047
	[−33.40]***	[−48.36]***	[−24.16]***	[−13.94]***	[−19.54]***	[−15.54]***
sigma	0.0111	0.0271	0.0095	0.0305	0.0099	0.0123
N	60	60	24	24	36	36

$*p < 0.1$, $**p < 0.05$, $***p < 0.01$.
Notes: (1) Dependent variables are total outstanding value of SME lending. (2) The upper section is the estimate, while the lower section is the z-value.
Lcap = banks' lending capacity, wcr = working capital lending rate, y = real gross domestic product, sme_npl = non-performing SME loans, SME = small and medium-sized enterprise, GFC = global financial crisis.
Source: Author's calculations based on various issues of Bank Indonesia's *Banking Statistics* and *Financial Statistics* and BPS statistics.

The supply–demand gap in SME finance is simply measured by credit demand minus credit supply as defined by:

$$S-D\,gap_t = L_t^d - L_t^s, \tag{4}$$

where S–D gap_t is the lending quantity denoting the difference between credit demand and supply at period t. If a positive gap is identified, there might have been a credit contraction by banks during the time observed.

Figure 1 shows the estimated supply–demand gap in total and SME bank lending in Indonesia. The result of these estimates identified large SME financing gaps at some points in time. In particular, the gap is large in late 2008. External factors such as the GFC, rather than internal factors such as seasonal and country-specific events, may largely affect bank lending attitudes toward SMEs. Triggered by the Lehman shock in late 2008, the GFC led to credit contractions all over the world including Indonesia relatively soon after the crisis began, with SMEs being the most impacted among Indonesian firms. The estimated large financing gap indicated in Fig. 1 is somewhat synchronized with the GFC. Due to several policy prescriptions for SME lending in Indonesia, the insufficiency of financing SMEs was relatively quickly diminished.

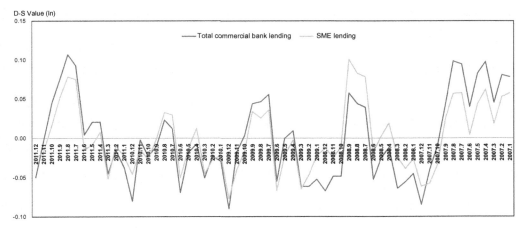

Figure 1. Supply–demand gap in SME finance — Indonesia.
Note: The supply–demand gap is calculated by estimates on the credit demand curve (D) minus those on the credit supply curve (S).
Source: Author's calculations based on various issues of Bank Indonesia's *Banking Statistics* and *Financial Statistics* and BPS statistics.

However, large gaps in terms of unmet financing demand for SMEs still appeared from time to time even after expanding policy support measures for SME bank lending.

The result of supply–demand gap analysis suggests the limitations of relying on bank lending to raise sustainable and safe funds for business, especially for SMEs. Once unexpected events such as a financial crisis occur, the banking sector will naturally respond to such events and take actions to mitigate associated risks, which will cause a credit crunch in the banking sector and seriously affect SME access to finance. Moreover, Basel III might have a risk accelerating this trend in banks by further restricted financing for SMEs. The root causes of financial crises change as global financial systems become more advanced. Well-established SME finance policies will alleviate credit contraction, but cannot remove it entirely. To supplement the limitations of bank lending for SMEs amid the complex global financial environment, the diversification of financing models, with flexibility and innovation, is indispensable.

4. Enhancing Bankability for SMEs

Given the preponderance of bank-centered financial systems in Asia, the issue of how to enhance bankability for SMEs is a core policy subject in the context of financial inclusion. The major obstacles to bank lending to SMEs are attributed to banks' funding conditions, insufficient capital, and more importantly weak risk perception among clients. Against this backdrop, information asymmetry between lenders and borrowers underlies bank lending attitudes, which deepens the supply–demand gap in SME finance. Due to high costs for transactions and information collection, as well as immeasurable risks, financial institutions generally hesitate to finance SMEs. To mitigate such risks and reduce the cost burden, financial institutions tend to apply high interest rates and require SMEs to fulfil steep collateral and guarantee requirements. Not surprisingly, SMEs tend to regard these measures as serious supply-side barriers.

It is useful to elaborate on the strategic framework needed to reduce the supply-demand gap of SME finance through public-private initiatives. The policy framework to improve SMEs' bankability should address the following key areas:

  (i) proper legal and financial infrastructure for SMEs,
 (ii) innovative financing instruments that facilitate SME access to banks, and
(iii) sustainable guarantee schemes for mitigating SME credit risks.

4.1. *Legal and financial infrastructure for SMEs*

There is a perceived negative correlation between credit constraints and sound legislation as indicated in Fig. 2. Referring to the study conducted by Kuntchev *et al.* (2012), the credit-constrained firms are extracted from the World Bank's *Enterprise Surveys* (including 11 countries from Asia) as a percentage of total surveyed firms in the observed countries. The extent of legislative deepening is measured by the strength of a country's legal rights index in the World Bank's *Doing Business 2013*, on a scale of 0–10, which illustrates the level of protecting borrower and lender rights through collateral laws and secured creditor rights through bankruptcy laws;

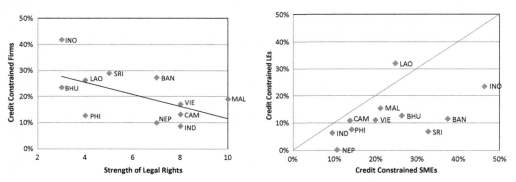

Figure 2. Credit constrained firms and legal rights.
Notes: (1) Credit-constrained firms as a percentage of total surveyed firms. (2) Strength of legal rights is measured on a scale of 0 to 10, where higher scores mean better-designed collateral and bankruptcy laws for protecting borrowers, lenders, and secured creditors. (3) Valid samples: Bangladesh 409, Bhutan 52, Cambodia 55, India 40, Indonesia 603, Lao People's Democratic Republic (Lao PDR) 94, Malaysia 205, Nepal 36, the Philippines 166, Sri Lanka 176, and Viet Nam 178. LEs = large enterprises, SMEs = small and medium-sized enterprises. *Source*: Author's calculations based on the World Bank's *Enterprise Surveys* and *Doing Business 2013*.

higher scores indicate better-designed collateral and bankruptcy laws for expanding access to finance. The credit-constrained firms are those that had no external finance and were rejected for loan applications or hesitated to apply for a loan due to strict bank policies (e.g., interest rates, collateral requirements, and loan size) and complex procedures. The estimates explain that strengthened legal rights for collateralized assets and bankruptcy remote reduce the level of firms' credit constraints. Taking into account that SMEs are more constrained than large firms in bank lending (right chart of Fig. 2), the findings imply that well-designed collateral and bankruptcy laws are beneficial, especially for SMEs in accessing finance, and suggest the importance of laws and regulations that support financial infrastructure development such as collateral registries. The legal framework for creating and operating collateral registries is expected to encourage secured lending and asset-based financing for SMEs.

A credit bureau is another example of core infrastructure that mitigates asymmetric information conditions. According to the International Finance Corporation (IFC) Stocktaking Report to the G20 (2010), credit bureau coverage in developing economies is much lower than the Organisation for Economic Co-operation and Development (OECD) country average.[5] Credit bureaus are expected to reduce obstacles to small firms' access to finance and increase their use of external financing. An enabling regulatory environment that facilitates credit information sharing among financial institutions is needed at the national level.

Multi-country data sharing on SME access to finance is also necessary to promote evidence-based policymaking and regulations. There are several regional and global efforts on creating a consolidated SME data platform under the context of financial inclusion. For instance, the Association of Southeast Asian Nations (ASEAN) plans to create a regional development fund for SME-friendly infrastructure that will include a regional SME web portal by 2015. The G20 endorsed a basic set of financial inclusion indicators at the Los Cabos Summit in 2012. The World Bank's Global Financial Inclusion Database (Global Findex) and the International Monetary Fund's (IMF) Financial Access Survey (FAS) provide comprehensive supply- and demand-side data on financial inclusion. The FAS has expanded data on SME access to finance since 2012. The OECD also issues annual country profiles on SME finance called an SME Scoreboard. The structured needs survey on SME information sharing in Asia conducted by the Asian Development Bank (ADB) in 2012 and 2013 indicated the tangible demand facing policy makers and regulators for multi-country SME data sharing (Fig. 3). The survey respondents understood the value added potential of data sharing, addressing that the evidence-based SME policymaking and regulations are promoted (score 4.41 out of 5.0).

---

[5] Private bureaus cover only 14.4% of adults in East Asia and the Pacific, while covering 59.6% in OECD countries. Public registries cover 7.2% of adults in East Asia and the Pacific, while covering 8.8% in OECD countries.

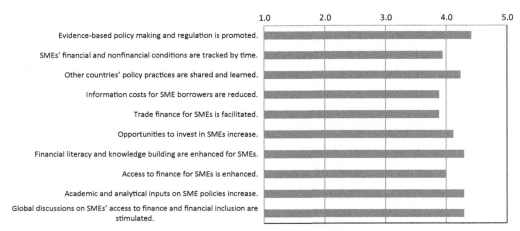

Figure 3. Value added of the regional SME information sharing platform.
Notes: Average score of 17 institutions in ten countries. (1) Brunei Darussalam: Ministry of Industry and Primary Resources*; (2) Cambodia: (i) Ministry of Industry, Mines and Energy and (ii) National Bank of Cambodia; (3) Indonesia: Ministry of Cooperatives and SMEs*; (4) Lao PDR: SME Promotion and Development Office, Ministry of Industry and Commerce*; (5) Myanmar: Ministry of Industry*; (6) Philippines: (i) Bureau of MSME Development, Department of Trade and Industry, (ii) Bangko Sentral ng Pilipinas, and (iii) Small Business Corporation; (7) Thailand: (i) Office of SME Promotion*, (ii) Bank of Thailand, and (iii) Board of Investment of Thailand; (8) Viet Nam: (i) State Bank of Vietnam, (ii) Ministry of Industry and Trade, and (iii) State Agency for Technology Innovation; (9) Singapore: SPRING Singapore*; and (10) Papua New Guinea: Bank of Papua New Guinea. The survey was conducted during August – September 2013. *The survey in June 2012. 5 = agree; 4 = relatively agree; 3 = neutral; 2 = relatively disagree; 1 = disagree.
Source: ADB Survey on SME Information Sharing Platform in Asia, 2012 and 2013.

4.2. *Innovative product design*

As financial technology advances, various innovative products and services to improve SME access to finance are being developed and delivered by diverse players, which creates a competitive environment for SME credit markets. Accordingly, financial regulations are required to be updated on a timely basis and regulators need to appropriately regulate financing activities, not focus on financial institutions, to secure a level playing field and minimize the risk of regulatory arbitrage. Regulations should facilitate new approaches and innovation, not stifle them, and stimulate competitive SME credit markets. This can bring about a change of regulatory policies in the banking sector. The following instruments are of particular importance to banking regulators:

- *Asset-based finance* (ABF) is often discussed as a tool to mitigate over-dependence on real estate security for bank lending. ABF is a generic term for financing instruments that make use of a firm's valued assets such as movables (e.g., inventory, machinery, and equipment) and accounts receivable as collateral, or through sale or lease, while not depending on real estate securities and third party guarantees. There are roughly four types of instruments: (i) asset-based lending (ABL), (ii) factoring, (iii) financial lease, and (iv) asset-backed securities (ABS). ABL is a lending scheme collateralized by movables and accounts receivable. Factoring is a short-term financing for suppliers, selling accounts receivable. Financial lease is a mid-term financial instrument, giving the right to use an owner's assets for specific period. ABS is a securitized product in which the underlying assets are SME loans in this context. Collecting reliable information on SMEs for financing is costly due to their small size, which results in their limited access to financial markets. Securitization will mitigate uncertainty for investing in SMEs and vitalize both SME credit and capital markets. ABF is a promising alternative to mortgage-based lending and is expected to expand banks' client base, especially among SME borrowers.

- *Credit-score-based lending* is a promising instrument for banks to reduce transaction costs by making use of technology and credit risk database. One thing to be concerned with, however, is that credit-score-based lending can be inflexible due to the rote assessment of borrowers, in which banks may fail to consider special conditions of SME borrowers.

- *SME cluster financing* is another innovative approach to enhance the efficiency of SME finance. Clustering is beneficial for SMEs, especially smaller manufacturers, because it facilitates connections with the external economy including suppliers, workers, trade parties, and financial institutions. Banks may be unwilling to finance small borrowers on an individual basis due to high transaction costs, but they may be willing to provide loans for a cluster that assembles small borrowers at a reduced cost.

- *Crowdfunding* is a new approach where individuals lend to each other or small businesses through specialized lending websites. This technique has been growing in popularity in the United States (US), the United Kingdom (UK), Germany, and the People's Republic of China (PRC). It has a simple and low cost structure as compared with traditional bank lending, provides relatively higher returns to investors, and is released from regulatory burdens (Wehinger, 2013). In 2012, US$2.7 billion was raised through crowdfunding, driven by an annual growth rate of 81% (Kleverlaan, 2013). OECD has pointed out some concerns with crowdfunding, addressing a no "money back guarantee," which means that investors are attracted by higher rates with no risk perception efforts. A proper policy and regulatory framework for crowdfunding is needed, especially for consumer protection. The US JOBS Act provides legal support for crowdfunding so that start-ups can raise a maximum of US$1 million per annum through online and social media. In Asia, the Philippines has been discussing a proposed Crowdsourcing Act since 2012.

- *Exit financing*, or debtor-in-possession financing, may be of interest when it is necessary to rescue innovative SMEs from bankruptcy.

4.3. *Credit guarantee systems*

Credit guarantees are a popular tool to improve SME access to finance in line with national SME development policies and poverty reduction strategies. In Asia, credit guarantees are provided by specialized institutions — either partially sponsored or fully owned by the government — and target micro, small, and medium-sized enterprises (MSMEs) as main clients, including female entrepreneurs and agro-businesses.

Various guarantee products have been developed in Asia in response to specific country needs, with risk-sharing arrangements between guarantee institutions and financial institutions being relatively well established. Credit guarantee systems have been centralized in most Asian economies, while some countries such as Indonesia are seeking to develop regional guarantee systems through newly established local guarantee institutions, given that guarantee benefits are effectively reaching rural SMEs. At present, re-guarantee (credit insurance) systems are yet to be established in emerging Asia.

Credit guarantees are expected to (i) fill the supply–demand gap in SME finance, (ii) lower funding costs for SMEs, (iii) alleviate financing constraints for SMEs by partially or fully releasing them from collateral requirements, and (iv) respond in a timely fashion to external shocks such as a financial crisis. In addition, credit guarantees can reduce social opportunity costs — by increasing outreach to the underserved — and contribute to (i) mobilizing SME savings for investment, (ii) increasing the survival rate of SMEs, (iii) providing growth opportunities, and (iv) promoting a resilient national economic foundation.

However, there are potential negative effects of credit guarantee systems: (i) Basel Capital Accord's risk weighting system may drive banks to increase guaranteed SME lending but reduce unsecured SME lending to strengthen their capital adequacy ratios; (ii) the increased risk of adverse selection and moral hazard since credit guarantees may tempt malicious SME borrowers and discourage financial institutions from closely monitoring borrowers, resulting in the use of funds inconsistent with loan objectives; (iii) the life of poorly performing SMEs might be prolonged; (iv) less incentive to improve SME management if guarantees do not include any collateral requirements because owner assets are not at risk in the case of default; and (v) the increased risk of bloated national budgets and the crowding out of private businesses since credit guarantee institutions are mostly public entities in Asia.

To diminish the negative aspects of credit guarantee schemes, four key issues should be addressed: (i) business sustainability, shifting from a public-dependent to private-led business model to effectively deliver guarantee benefits to SMEs; (ii) risk-conscious arrangements, developing re-guarantees, partial guarantees, and second credit screenings to hedge against risks associated with the guarantee business; (iii) decentralization, promoting regional guarantee schemes with a proper regulatory and supervisory framework to expand guarantee availability for SMEs; and (iv) credit infrastructure (credit risk database).

Although there is no universal prescription for increasing SME access to finance, credit guarantees are playing an important role in filling the SME financing gap in Asia. At the same time, credit guarantees open the door for a debate on potentially negative effects. Due to their strong public nature, business sustainability is a critical concern in credit guarantees. Balancing government intervention with a private-led guarantee industry is needed. Innovation and technology are key to developing demand-driven and risk-based credit guarantee products. SME data infrastructure is also crucial to establish a sustainable credit guarantee system at the national level. Such data infrastructure will support credit guarantee institutions in proper pricing and risk-based management. Promoting credit guarantee literacy for all stakeholders is a necessary component of the development of a national credit guarantee industry. A comprehensive policy and regulatory framework on credit guarantees should be well designed to avoid market distortions and to facilitate innovative products, given the industry's public nature in Asia.

4.4. *Roles of public financial institutions*

Besides credit guarantees, there are other modalities of public intervention such as direct lending and interest subsidies. The expected role of public finance is two-fold. One is to increase outreach to growth-potential SMEs deemed underserved by commercial banks, which will result in reducing opportunity costs in economic growth. The other is to respond in a timely fashion to external shocks such as a financial crisis and a natural disaster, in which the banking sector may be damaged as well. This means that the roles of public financial institutions will not disappear even if a private-sector-led economy is established. The challenge is how to attain and maintain balance between the fiscal costs and macroeconomic benefits to sustain public financial institutions. In this context, *ex post facto* evaluations of public intervention should be done by the government periodically to assess their efficiency.

4.5. *Basel III*

The Basel Capital Accords (Basel I, II, and III) have been developed as a framework for reducing global systemic risks that may be triggered by the collapse of the banking system. As capital markets are yet to become a popular source of funding for enterprises in Asia, the banking sector plays a pivotal role in supporting firms' growth through external funding. In the era of global financial uncertainty, risk-based regulations and supervision aligning with global standards such as the Basel Core Principles are critically important to establish a healthy banking system and a resilient national economy against financial crises.

Basel III requires tighter risk management of banks, which has generated debate on the potential negative impacts on SME lending. As a risk mitigation technique, Basel Accords' risk weighting system may encourage banks to concentrate their portfolios on lower weighted assets such as government bonds and mortgage loans. Guaranteed SME loans may increase because the risk weight can either be reduced or zero, but banks may be still willing to finance large firms with AAA ratings rather than unrated SMEs to reduce their total high-risk weighted assets. The experience of the GFC led to the introduction of new rules for liquidity management in Basel III, such as the liquidity coverage ratio, which encourages banks to hold "easy-to-sell assets" or higher liquid assets, meaning that the increase of payment services and/or relatively low-risk short-term finance such as trade finance may be promoted rather than SME loans.

From a long-term perspective, the procyclical effects of the regulations should be taken into account, which means that micro- and macroprudential regulations and supervision need to be sophisticated enough to account for SME lending. For microprudential measures, minimum capital and loan size requirements for defining risk weighting are critical for SME lending. The European Central Bank pointed out that small loans enjoy preferential treatment for SMEs but larger loans are not applicable in Europe, which will create an environment in which high-growth SMEs encounter difficulty in raising needed growth capital from the banking sector.

Macroprudential measures are tools with a long-term perspective to address systemic risks and secure countercyclical capital buffers. While poor access to finance has become a new normal for SMEs, another concern has arisen in the aftermath of the financial crisis: excessive credit growth. Facilitated by deregulation at the national level as a response to the GFC, the sharp growth of credit has occurred in several countries. This raises questions on the roles and scopes of financial regulations in SME lending, including the question of tighter regulation versus credit facilitation since ample credit availability may smooth SME's cash flow cycle but also create difficulties in holding sufficient capital buffers against possible financial crises in the future. A balanced regulatory approach is needed to support SME access to finance while maintaining financial stability and a safety net.

5. Diversified Financing Models

As discussed, there are the limits imposed on SME bank lending in complex global financial systems. Besides improving bankability, the issue of how to respond to SME growth capital needs, arising from a continuously changing business environment, is another core policy subject for scaling up the SME sector. To this end, diversified funding alternatives beyond conventional bank credit are needed for growth-oriented SMEs, which can be promoted by financial institutions that have yet to focus on SME financing. Accordingly, new regulatory approaches should be examined and designed for newly emerging financial institutions in the field of SME finance. In this section, the role of non-bank financial institutions (NBFIs), the potential of short-term risk capital financing (supply chain finance), and long-term financing modalities (SME capital markets) are reviewed.

5.1. *Non-bank financial institutions*

NBFIs are expected to play an important role by supplementing available bank lending for SMEs. Diverse institutions such as specialized financiers (e.g., credit cooperative, credit union, pawnshop, finance company, leasing company, and factor), capital market organizers (e.g., stock exchange, and securities dealer and broker), and risk-taking institutions (e.g., venture capital, private equity fund, pension fund, and mutual fund) are collectively categorized into NBFIs. To encourage the NBFI industry, the establishment of a sound competitive environment between banks and NBFIs is a critical challenge, in which a holistic approach is needed in developing a regulatory framework for NBFIs that provide finance to SMEs.

5.2. *Supply chain finance*

Trade finance and supply chain finance (SCF) for SMEs is of importance as their internationalization is helping to promote inclusive economic growth in Asia. As a supporting industry, SMEs contribute to intra-regional trade through subcontracts with large firms. In the globalized economy, large firms seek the division of labor to enhance business efficiency to win over their competitors, which accelerates their dependency on overseas markets for efficient production. This trend can lead subcontracted SMEs into foreign markets to establish or maintain business relations with large firms, where trade finance and SCF can help SMEs survive.

SCF is a relatively new concept. Although there is not yet a standardized definition, it can be expressed as a combination of trade finance and a technological platform that connects trading partners and financial institutions, and provides various services related to supply chain events, as defined by the International Factors Group (IFG).[6] Various combinations of financing instruments and services can be arranged under SCF.

Data extracted from the ADB Trade Finance Survey (2013) indicated that 42% of banks surveyed recognized SCF as a tool for filling trade finance gaps and that 50% of banks felt existing SCF modalities insufficient. Although valid samples were quite limited (24 banks), this implies that SCF has yet to penetrate banks deeply. Before designing the regulatory framework, SCF products should be properly targeted to respond to small suppliers' financing needs, and product literacy should be promoted for potential users including SMEs.

5.3. *Factoring*

Factoring is generally interpreted as a short-term supplier financing scheme where companies sell their accounts receivable to the factor with or without recourse and in return receive cash-in-advance at a discount from the factor. It is referred to as domestic factoring when the seller and the buyer domicile in the same country and as

---

[6] International Factors Group. http://www.ifgroup.com/.

international factoring when the seller (exporter) and the buyer (importer) are located in different countries.

The factoring industry has grown rapidly around the world. Annual global turnover increased 22.3% in 2011 and reached EUR2 trillion according to the Factors Chain International (FCI).[7] The factoring business is quite active in Europe (60.4% of global volume in 2011) and relatively less active in Asia (25.2%). The leading factoring companies are mostly bank subsidiaries or bank divisions that dominate the global factoring market.

In general, factoring enables companies to improve their business efficiency and risk management by (i) improving cash flow or providing needed working capital in a flexible and timely way; (ii) not counting as a liability on the balance sheet, but rather as an off-balance-sheet transaction; and (iii) transferring risk to the factor, resulting in a hedge against settlement risks. Basically, factoring companies do not see SMEs as an underwriting risk due to factoring's nature of individual-transaction-based financing. Therefore, factoring is beneficial for start-ups, rapidly growing SMEs with weak credit history and no collateral, and SMEs in emerging economies with less developed commercial laws and regulations. Particularly, reverse factoring enables factoring companies to reduce information costs and finance even risky SMEs.[8]

International factoring complements trade finance for SMEs by guaranteeing (i) cross-border payment and settlement (credit protection), (ii) individual transactions (SMEs have no disadvantage), and (iii) non-letter-of-credit-based trade. This scheme enables SME exporters to increase business opportunities, rationalizing the process of supplier financing in terms of time and cost. International factoring also facilitates SME and new entrant participation in trade in goods and services, and as a result promotes intra-regional trade in Asia.

Factoring is a growing business in the world. Asia is following the same path, though factoring is still small in scale in the region. Ideally, factoring takes on a catalytic role in connecting SMEs to the growth-and-graduation cycle of enterprises. To this end, the factoring industry may target growing SMEs to develop its niche market. In this regard, the factoring industry in Asia has dual potential. At the national level, domestic factoring as part of diversified financing mechanisms will support growth-oriented SMEs in expanding given additional funding flexibility. At the global level, international factoring as a complement to trade finance will support SME exporters and promote intra-regional trade that serves global rebalancing.

Increased trade in Asia is creating more business opportunities for the factoring industry. The majority of enterprises are SMEs in any country and their contribution to

---

[7] Factors Chain International. http://www.fci.nl/. *Annual Review 2011, Annual Review 2012.*

[8] In the reverse factoring scheme, the factor purchases all accounts receivable from the suppliers of a single high-quality buyer, such as a creditworthy large company, and in return respective suppliers receive cash-in-advance at a discount from the factor. Before concluding factoring contracts, the factor collects credit information and calculates the credit risk only for high-quality buyers, which is less costly than traditional factoring. Because the credit risk is basically equal to the default risk of a high-quality buyer, reverse factoring is a promising financing tool for risky SMEs.

total exports is not insignificant. The more SMEs are internationalized, the more intra-regional trade is encouraged. The factoring industry is in part expected to promote SMEs' internationalization in support of intra-regional trade. The more SMEs' savings are mobilized through intra-regional trade, the more that global rebalancing is promoted. At the same time, the factoring industry can support financial inclusion in Asia.

5.4. *Capital market financing for SMEs*

Capital market financing is one of the hot issues in long-term financing for high-growth SMEs. Long-term financing for investment, including SMEs, is key for sustainable growth and job creation in all countries as stated at the G20 Finance Ministers and Central Bank Governor Meeting in Moscow in July 2013. On the occasion of the Saint Petersburg Summit in September 2013, the G20 Leaders also addressed the importance of promoting long-term financing for SMEs in the context of investment.

SMEs have long-term funding needs but banks' hesitation to provide long-term financing owing to uncertain economic circumstances is seriously affecting them. Bank-centered financial systems in Asia require robust capital markets as an alternative channel for providing growth capital. The development of long-term financing instruments for SMEs and proper regulatory frameworks for new instruments will be a key growth agenda among policy makers and regulators.

Capital markets are typically susceptible to changing external economic conditions, especially during a financial crisis. In OECD countries, most economies were severely impacted by the GFC, with the level of equity investments in 2011 still below pre-crisis levels in several countries (Fig. 4). This suggests that SME capital markets need more innovative institutional arrangements with sophisticated risk management mechanisms so as to effectively attract investors as risk capital providers for SMEs.

SME capital markets are still in the early stages of development in Asia. Some countries have pursued a trial-and-error approach for creating a well-functioning equity financing venue for growth-oriented SMEs. This can be roughly classified into two types, an (i) exchange market and (ii) organized over-the-counter (OTC) market. For the exchange market, besides a typical SME Board under the stock exchange, a sponsor-driven alternative investment market (AIM) modeled on the UK-AIM has been established in some emerging Asian countries such as Malaysia, Singapore, and Thailand. As for the organized OTC market, self-regulatory organizations (SROs), such as the Korea Financial Investment Association (KOFIA) and the Japan Securities Dealers Association (JSDA), have operated a trading venue for unlisted SME stocks that is separate from the exchange market. There is a new movement for creating an SME bond market in countries such as the PRC and the Republic of Korea. In the latter, a qualified institutional buyer (QIB) system was established for SME bond trading in May 2012.[9]

---

[9] SME bond transactions under the QIB system, however, are quite limited and not attractive to individual and institutional investors due to the existence of low investment grade bonds (BB or below).

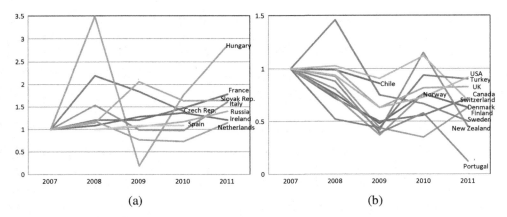

Figure 4. Growth capital investment in OECD areas. (a) Countries where growth capital investment increases. (b) Countries where growth capital investment declines.
Note: 2008 (base year) = 1 for Russia, Spain, and the United Kingdom; 2007 = 1 for other countries.
Source: OECD (2013). *Financing SMEs and Entrepreneurs 2013 – An OECD Scoreboard.* p. 34.

In emerging Asia, equity financing venues for SMEs have been mostly created under stock exchange operations. In the PRC, the Shenzhen Stock Exchange[10] has developed a three-tier market venue comprising the Main Board, SME Board, and ChiNext (high-tech venture board), in line with national economic development strategies. Hong Kong, China's Growth Enterprise Market (GEM)[11] is an alternative stock market for high-growth enterprises, operated by the Stock Exchange of Hong Kong Ltd. India has recently developed dedicated stock exchanges for SMEs, following the recommendation of the Prime Minister's Task Force in June 2010. The Bombay Stock Exchange launched the SME Exchange[12] in March 2012 and has 41 listed SMEs as of 19 November 2013. The National Stock Exchange has also launched an SME platform, named Emerge, with three listed SMEs. KOSDAQ is the largest organized market for SMEs and venture businesses in the Republic of Korea and a new market named KONEX was launched under the Korea Exchange[13] in July 2013. MESDAQ under Bursa Malaysia[14] was re-launched as the ACE (Access, Certainty, Efficiency) market in August 2009, a sponsor-driven alternative market. Catalist in Singapore,[15] launched in December 2007, is a Singapore Exchange-regulated but

---

[10] Shenzhen Stock Exchange. http://www.szse.cn/.
[11] Growth Enterprise Market. http://www.hkgem.com/.
[12] BSE SME Platform. http://www.bsesme.com/.
[13] Korea Exchange. http://eng.krx.co.kr/.
[14] Bursa Malaysia. http://www.bursamalaysia.com/.
[15] Singapore Exchange. http://www.sgx.com/.

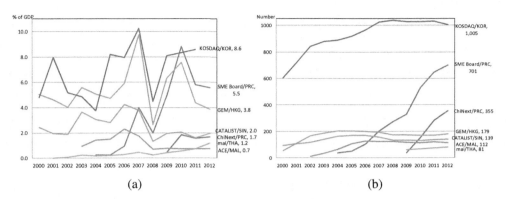

Figure 5. SME capital markets in emerging Asia. (a) Market capitalization (percent of GDP). (b) Number of listed companies.
Note: Emerging Asia comprises the PRC; Hong Kong, China; the Republic of Korea; Malaysia, Singapore, and Thailand. GDP = gross domestic product.
Source: Various statistics from respective stock exchange websites.

sponsor-supervised market for rapidly growing enterprises, modeled on the UK-AIM. The Stock Exchange of Thailand[16] has operated the market for alternative investment (mai) since June 1999, targeting SMEs as potential issuers.

Equity markets for SMEs in emerging Asia are typically small in scale, with market capitalization equal to less than 10% of GDP and market performances that significantly vary by country (Fig. 5). In the PRC, both SME Board and ChiNext have been sharply expanding in terms of size and the number of listed companies, with more than 1,000 listed companies in both markets combined, although their growth rates have slowed recently. KOSDAQ and Hong Kong, China's GEM enjoyed V-shape recoveries from the GFC, but the growth of these markets tends to be slowing with little new listings. Catalist Singapore, ACE Malaysia, and mai Thailand have not performed well on the whole and their listed companies are not increasing at a sufficient pace. This suggests that equity markets in Asia, except for those in the PRC and the Republic of Korea, have not yet become a financing venue for SMEs. Extensive national policies and strategies for improved SME access to capital markets are needed.

Considering the present conditions of capital markets that SMEs can tap in Asia, two types of specialized market infrastructure are worth exploring in greater detail:

• Exercise equity market for SMEs.
• Social capital market.

The creation of an "exercise" equity market for SMEs, separate from the exchange market, can be beneficial, especially in developing Asia. The concept is to create a preparatory market for "smaller but growing" firms that will eventually tap the regular

---

[16] Stock Exchange of Thailand. http://www.set.or.th/en/.

market of stock exchange. This market will provide a chance for SMEs to learn more market rules and obligations such as disclosure before tapping the organized market, and to improve corporate culture through learning the importance of increased corporate value for growth. The exercise market should have a comprehensive mechanism for supporting SMEs in equity finance from various angles, which is combined with (i) fostering the venture capital industry as an initial risk capital provider for SMEs; (ii) developing the base of professionals supporting the SME disclosure process, such as certified public accountants (CPA); and (iii) designing government policy support measures such as tax incentives for SME issuers and investors.

Developing SME capital markets presents a two-fold challenge: (i) demand creation and (ii) market sustainability. To this end, a well-organized investor base and supporting professionals with government preferential measures are prerequisite to stimulating demand for an SME market. Meanwhile, with low cost operations, liquidity enhancement mechanisms — such as market making and obligatory shareholder allotment — are indispensable to market sustainability.

There is also the potential of developing social capital market and impact investment in Asia, given the increased concerns of socially-oriented business and green finance. The social capital market is a place where social enterprises can link up with impact investors. Social enterprises are defined as business-oriented not-for-profits, or mission-oriented for-profits, having a social and/or environmental mission at the core of their work while seeking to operate in a financially sustainable manner (ADB, 2011). This includes microfinance institutions (MFIs) and innovative SMEs in the education, energy, health, and agro-business sectors. Impact investors are defined as investors seeking to make investments that create a positive social and environmental impact beyond financial return (JP Morgan, 2010), including social venture capital funds, microfinance investment vehicles, pension funds, mutual fund managers, institutional fund managers, sovereign wealth funds, endowments, and family foundations. JP Morgan (2010) estimated that the impact investment market has the potential to absorb between US$400 billion–US$1 trillion over the next decade, particularly in the areas of housing, rural water delivery, maternal health, primary education, and financial services. An ADB survey (2011) indicated that 74% of investors in the sample who were not currently impact investing would consider transacting on a social stock exchange.[17] A social stock exchange has similar functions as the regular market of stock exchange, where social enterprises can raise capital through offerings of shares, bonds, or other financial instruments.

---

[17] There are two social stock exchanges operating in the world: (i) Impact Exchange and (ii) the UK Social Stock Exchange. Both platforms were established in June 2013. The Impact Exchange, located in Mauritius, is operated by the Stock Exchange of Mauritius and supervised by the Singapore-based Impact Investment Exchange Asia (IIX), targeting Asian and African social enterprises. The UK Social Stock Exchange, with initially 11 listed social enterprises, was launched by the London Stock Exchange Group as part of the national strategies for fostering social impact businesses in the UK. The recent survey conducted by JP Morgan and the Global Impact Investing Network showed that impact investors planned to commit US$9 billion in 2013, up from US$8 billion in 2012.

6. Conclusion

Asia's largely bank-centred financial systems require enhancing bankability as a core policy pillar to improve SME access to finance. Challenges include (i) financial infrastructure development for SMEs, e.g., the promotion of SME data infrastructure and the legal reform for secured transactions; (ii) innovative financial product design, e.g., asset-based finance, credit-score-based lending, and SME cluster financing; (iii) sustainable credit guarantee systems; and (iv) clarifying the roles of public financial institutions. Meanwhile, the diversification of financing models is another core policy pillar to expand financial accessibility for SMEs, given the limitations of bank lending amid global financial uncertainty. Challenges include (i) increasing the role of NBFIs in SME finance, (ii) promoting supply chain finance for SMEs, and (iii) developing capital market financing for SMEs. A review of these financing models is needed to design a new regime of SME finance in emerging Asia.

To move forward, SME policy makers and financial regulators should develop a comprehensive menu of policy options that supports diversified financing models accessible for SMEs, rather than strictly regulating new financing modality. A holistic and balanced policy approach is needed to design the extensive regulatory and policy measures that improve financial accessibility for SMEs and safeguard financial stability. Well-organized coordination between regulations and policies, with good intragovernmental coordination, is the key for successful implementation of the national SME policy framework beyond already established ways and for the avoidance of financial vulnerabilities.

References

Agung, J, B Kusmiarso, B Pramono, EG Hutapea, A Prasmuko and NJ Prastowo (2001). *Credit Crunch in Indonesia in the Aftermath of the Crisis: Facts, Causes and Policy Implications.* Jakarta.

Anderson, D (1982). Small-scale industry in developing countries: A discussion of the issues. World Development. Vol. 10.

ASEAN Economic Community (2010). *ASEAN Strategic Action Plan for SME Development (2010–2015).*

Asian Credit Supplementation Institution Confederation (2012). *The 25th Anniversary Publication of ACSIC — The 25-Year History of ACSIC.*

Asian Development Bank (2011). *Impact Investors in Asia: Characteristics and Preferences for Investing in Social Enterprises in Asia and the Pacific.* Manila: ADB.

Beck, S, Q Zhang, S Shinozaki, E Mangampat and MI Ferino (2013). ADB trade finance survey: Major findings. *ADB Briefs* No. 11. Manila: ADB.

Berry, A, E Rodriguez and H Sandee (2001). Small and medium enterprises dynamics in Indonesia. *Bulletin of Indonesian Economic Studies*, 37(3), 363–384.

Biggs, T and J Oppenheim (1986). What drives the size distribution of firms in developing countries? EEPA Discussion Paper No. 6, Harvard Institute for International Development.

Boston University Center for Finance Law & Policy and the Consultative Group to Assist the Poor. Financial Inclusion Guide. http://www.bu.edu/bucflp/initiatives/financial-inclusion-guide/.

Byerlee, DR (1973). Indirect employment and income distribution effects of agricultural development strategies: A simulation approach applied to Nigeria. African Rural Economy Paper No. 9, Michigan State University.

Coeure, B (2013). *SME Financing, Market Innovation and Regulation.* Eurofi High Level Seminar, Dubline, April.

Consultative Group to Assist the Poor and International Finance Corporation (2012). *Financial Access 2012: Getting to a More Comprehensive Picture.* Washington, DC.

Fair, RC and DM Jaffee (1972). Methods of estimation for markets in disequilibrium. *Econometrica*, 40, 497–514.

Ghosh, SR and AR Ghosh (1999). East Asia in the aftermath: Was there a crunch? IMF Working Paper No. 99/38.

International Finance Corporation (2006). *Credit Bureau Knowledge Guide.* Washington, DC.

International Finance Corporation (2010). *Scaling-Up SME Access to Financial Services in the Developing World.* Washington, DC.

JP Morgan (2010). *Impact Investments: An Emerging Asset Class.*

JP Morgan (2013). *Perspectives on Progress: The Impact Investor Survey.*

Klapper, L (2006). The role of factoring for financing small and medium enterprises. *Journal of Banking and Finance*, 30, 3111–3130.

Kleverlaan, R (2013). Crowdfunding in Europe — Funding innovation and growth of SMEs. In *9th International Network for SMEs Annual Meeting.* Izmir, 21–23 May.

Kuntchev, V, R Ramalho, J Rodriguez-Meza and J Yang (2012). What have we learned from the enterprise surveys regarding access to finance by SMEs? World Bank Research Paper.

Laffont, JJ and R Garcia (1977). Disequilibrium econometrics for business loans. *Econometrica*, 45, 1187–1204.

Magiera, SL (1999). Indonesia's trade performance during the economic crisis, partnership for economic growth. Department of Industry and Trade, USAID.

Musa, A and P Priatna (1998). The policy reform for capital of SME (small-medium enterprises) in Indonesia: Impact analysis of financial crisis. Jakarta: The Asia Foundation.

Organisation for Economic Co-operation and Development (2012). *Financing SMEs and Entrepreneurs 2012: An OECD Scoreboard.* Paris: OECD.

Organisation for Economic Co-operation and Development (2013). *Financing SMEs and Entrepreneurs 2013: An OECD Scoreboard.* Paris: OECD.

Pazarbasioglu, C (1997). A credit crunch? Finland in the aftermath of the banking crisis. *IMF Staff Papers*, 44, 315–327.

Piore, MJ and CF Sabel (1984). *The Second Industrial Divide: Possibilities for Prosperity.* New York: Basic Books.

Rimbara, Y and AM Santomero (1976). A study of credit rationing in Japan. *International Economic Review*, 17, 567–580.

Shinozaki, S (2012). A new regime of SME finance in emerging Asia: Empowering growth-oriented SMEs to build resilient national economies. ADB Working Paper Series on Regional Economic Integration No. 104, ADB.

Snodgrass, DR and T Biggs (1996). *Industrialisation and the Small Firm: Patterns and Policies.* San Francisco: International Center for Economic Growth and Harvard Institute for International Development.

Steel, WF (1993). Small Enterprises in Indonesia: Role, growth, and strategic issues. Development Studies Project, No. 194. Jakarta.

Stein, P, T Goland and R Schiff (2010). Two trillion and counting: Assessing the credit gap for micro, small, and medium-size enterprises in the developing world, McKinsey & Company and International Finance Corporation.

Tambunan, TTH (1994). The role of small-scale industries in rural economic development: A case study in Ciomas subdistrict, Bogor District, West Java, Indonesia. Amsterdam: Thesis Publishers.

Tambunan, TTH (2005). Promoting small and medium enterprises with a clustering approach: A policy experience from Indonesia. *Journal of Small Business Management*, 43, 138–154.

Tambunan, TTH (2006). Development of small & medium enterprises in Indonesia from the Asia–Pacific perspective. Jakarta: LPFE-Usakti Universitas Trisakti.

Thee, KW (2000). The impact of the economic crisis on Indonesia's manufacturing sector. *The Developing Economies*, 38, 420–453.

Wehinger, G (2013). SME finance: The role of banks, institutional investors and long-term investment. The OECD Working Party on SMEs and Entrepreneurship 43rd Session. Paris, 18–19 April.

Wengel, J and E Rodriguez (2006). SME export performance in Indonesia after the crisis. *Small Business Economics*, 26, 25–37.

World Bank. The World Bank Enterprise Survey Portal. http://www.enterprisesurveys.org/.

World Bank and International Finance Corporation (2013). *Doing Business 2013: Smarter Regulations for Small and Medium-Size Enterprises*. Washington, DC.

Chapter 5

Informal Firms and Financial Inclusion: Status and Determinants

Subika Farazi

Development Economics Research Group and
Financial and Private Sector Development, The World Bank,
The United States

Abstract

Many firms in the developing world — including a majority of micro, small, and medium enterprises (MSMEs) — operate in the informal economy. The informal firms face a variety of constraints, making it harder for them to do business and grow. Lack of access to finance is often cited as the biggest operational constraint these firms face. This chapter documents the use of finance and financing patterns of informal firms, highlights differences between use of finance by formal and informal firms, and identifies the most significant characteristics of informal firms that are associated with higher use of financial services.

Keywords: Informal sector; financial inclusion; firm registration.

1. Introduction

Like its formal counterpart, the informal economy is multi-faceted, comprising different sectors or markets and engaging in diverse activities. It can include — but is not necessarily limited to — informal labor markets, informal financial sectors and informal corporate or business sectors. Because of its heterogeneous nature, researchers have found it difficult to come up with a precise single definition of informality. Researchers and policy makers usually tend to focus on a particular definition of informality based on a specific aspect of informality they are interested in analyzing. For example, if informality is approached from the social protection point of view, then researchers tend to focus on employment and see how some legal requirements (e.g., contributions to pension schemes or social security) are not met. If fiscal considerations of informality are the focus, then a more useful definition will be one that looks at tax revenue losses associated with firms and individuals engaged in untaxed activities. However, if accurate estimation of gross domestic product (GDP) is the objective, then a more comprehensive definition of informality may be needed.

The commonly used definitions of informality (or informal economy) in the literature include Schneider *et al.* (2010) that define informal economy as comprising of market-based legal production of goods and services deliberately concealed from public authorities to avoid paying taxes, social security contributions, and to meet legal obligations/requirements and market standards. Smith (1994) defines it as "market-based production of goods and services, whether legal or illegal, that escapes detection in the official estimates of GDP". Dell'Anno and Schneider (2004); Dell'Anno (2003) define informality as those economic activities and the income derived from them that evade government regulation, taxation or observation. Loayza *et al.* (2009) rely on the definition put forward by de Soto (1989) whereby informal economy is defined as collection of firms, workers, and activities that operate outside legal and regulatory frameworks. One central feature of informal economy observed in these various definitions is that it is unregulated by the institutions of a society. Participants of informal sectors avoid the burden of taxes and regulations but at the same time, do not get a chance to fully utilize the protection and services that the law and the state provide.

Informal activities are a major part of the overall economy in developing countries and deserve attention for a number of reasons. The informal sectors in developing countries are estimated to be around 40–50% of official GDP (Schneider *et al.*, 2010). This shows that economic agents working in the informal sector contribute extensively to the overall economic activity. Informal economies are also significant in terms of the labor force they employ. They provide livelihood to large segments of the population and can absorb around 60% of the labor force engaged in non-agricultural activities in many developing countries (ILO, 2012). Such high levels of informality can have an impact on growth and productivity of a country.[1]

Whether one views the informal sector as a burden or takes it as a sector that contributes positively to the overall economy, there is no doubt that informality is a pervasive and substantive phenomenon in developing countries. It is thus important to explore different aspects of informal economies, especially the working of informal firms. According to the IFC (2012), around 80% of total micro, small and medium sized enterprises (MSMEs) are informal today. Firms in the informal sector face a number of challenges that can negatively impact their operations and growth. These challenges can be related to public infrastructure (power, land and water); they can represent weak institutions (property rights, legal protection, and corruption) or lack of access to benefits associated with participation in the formal sector (access to credit, new technologies, and greater visibility of business through publicity). According to data collected by the World Bank through Informal Enterprise Surveys, firms in the informal sector identify lack of access to finance as the biggest obstacle they face (Fig. 1).

A substantial amount of recent research around informal firms has focussed on understanding different aspects of the business environment that discourages these firms

---

[1] Empirically, it is not very clear whether informality lowers growth and productivity or whether it is a symptom of low growth and productivity.

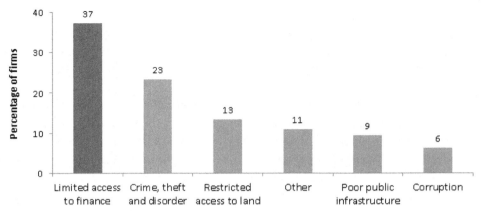

Figure 1. Biggest obstacle affecting operations of informal firms (percent).
Note: The bars represent the percentage of firms identifying a given option as a major obstacle to business. The option "Other" includes problems associated with difficult business registration procedures, workforce, limited demand for product or services, and political instability.
Source: Informal Enterprise Surveys for 13 countries covering micro (0–5 employees) and small (6–20 employees) firms.

from formalizing. These can include rule of law, property rights, corruption and regulatory requirements for formalization. Previous research has shown that countries with more burdensome entry regulations have larger informal sectors (Djankov *et al.*, 2002). However, many recent randomized experiments which made the formalization process easy — by providing firms with information on how to register and the potential benefits of registration and by lowering costs associated with registration — found very few informal firms formalize as a result (de Mel *et al.*, 2012 in Sri Lanka; Jaramillo, 2009 in Peru; de Andrade *et al.*, 2013 in Brazil, De Giorgi and Rahman, 2013 in Bangladesh). These experiments suggest that direct costs of registration might not be the binding constraint firms' face when attempting to formalize. The indirect costs associated with it might be more important, especially in environments where the majority of informal enterprises are small and have low productivity and where benefits of formalization are not very high. The relationship between formalization and firms' productivity is possibly driven by firms' underlying characteristics and not by formality *per se*. It is thus important to look at informal firms more closely and assess which characteristics are positively correlated with their growth.

Most of the recent research on informal firms has been country case studies, focussing frequently on a couple of localities/districts or villages. Not too many cross-country studies on informal firms are available in the literature, especially on the topic of financial access and inclusion of these firms. This could partly be explained by unavailability of data that uniformly describe informality across countries. The present chapter attempts to add to the literature on cross-country analysis and takes a deeper look at issues around financial inclusion of informal firms.[2] In particular, the chapter (i) documents the use of finance by informal firms and their financing patterns, (ii) compares the use of finance by firms both in the formal and informal sector, and (iii) identifies the most significant characteristics of informal firms that are associated with higher use of financial services.

This chapter attempts to identify significant associations between financial inclusion of informal firms and different firm and country characteristics. Its goal is to add to and complement the literature already available on informal firms, and hopes that readers would interpret the results with the caveat in mind that they do not show causal relationships. No claim is made that informality is the only barrier firms' face in their use of finance. Previous literature has identified a number of other factors that affect firms' use of finance. For example, de Soto's (1989) work focusses on lack of property rights as the reason small firms cannot use their assets as collateral to obtain financing, while Field and Torero (2006) look at the impact of land titling on getting credit. However, as shown in Fig. 1, informal firms claim lack of access to finance as the most important barrier they face in their operations and the chapter aims to take a deeper look at the dimension of informality and its link to use of finance by firms. The objective of the chapter is to provide estimates of actual use of finance by informal firms, while identifying key characteristics significantly associated with financial inclusion and to quantify the differences of use of finance between formal and informal firms.

The rest of the chapter is structured as follows. Section 2 explains the methodology used for data collection and describes the dataset used for the analysis. Section 3 provides a snapshot of different characteristics of an average informal firm in the sample to identify any common traits observed among informal firms across different countries. Section 4 provides a comparative analysis of formal and informal firms. This is done in two parts. First, a simple bivariate analysis is undertaken to document the differences in financial inclusion of formal and informal firms. Second, a multivariate regression analysis is done to see the robustness of the results obtained from the bivariate analysis after controlling for a number of firm and country level characteristics. Section 5 provides a regression analysis that explains informal firms' use of finance and their financing pattern while highlighting the significant factors that are important for financial inclusion of informal firms. Section 6 concludes the chapter.

2. The Data Set

The chapter focusses on one sector of the informal economy, viz. the corporate or business sector and defines informal firms as those firms that are not registered with the registration office, municipality or tax authority. This definition is used by the

---

[2] Financial inclusion is defined as the share of firms that use of financial services (World Bank, 2013).

Enterprise Survey unit of the World Bank and the motivation behind its simplicity is to facilitate the standardization of methodology for data collection and its comparability across countries.[3]

The data used in this chapter are from World Bank Informal Enterprise Surveys.[4] These surveys collect data on non-registered business activities and are implemented in parallel to World Bank Enterprise Surveys, which interview formal, private, non-agricultural firms. The Informal Enterprise Surveys are conducted using a uniform sampling methodology in order to minimize measurement error and yield data that are comparable across the world's economies. In each country, the Informal Enterprise Surveys are conducted in two selected urban centers, which are intended to coincide with the locations for the implementation of the main Enterprise Surveys. The overall number of interviews is pre-determined, and the interviews are distributed between the two urban centers according to criteria such as the level of business activity and each urban center's population. These urban centers are geographically divided to get the sampling areas and Informal Enterprise Surveys are conducted within clearly identified sampling areas. The total number of sampling areas and the geographical areas they contain are chosen such that firms from different sectors have balanced representation.[5] Moreover the placement of sampling areas in each city is determined based on local knowledge regarding the concentration of informal business activity.

The format of both surveys is very similar with a number of overlapping questions. In terms of differences between the two surveys, the first major difference is that of country coverage. Informal Enterprise Surveys do not cover as many countries as covered by Enterprise Surveys. While Enterprise Surveys cover small, medium and large firms, the Informal Enterprise Surveys do not include any large-sized firms and instead consist of MSMEs. Unlike Enterprise Surveys that are designed to provide panel data sets, the Informal Enterprise Surveys are available for just one year for most of the countries in the sample. Lastly, the Enterprise Surveys are designed such that they are representative of the formal private sector in each country. However, Informal Enterprise Surveys may not necessarily be representative at the national level. Given that the real size and structure of informal sectors in developing countries and emerging economies are not well known, it is extremely difficult to get a representative data sample. Despite this caveat, the Informal Enterprise Surveys present a good

---

[3] Defining informality in such a simple way can result in loss of important information about the firms we want to study and understand. For example, firms might be registered for imports and pay import taxes, but not be registered for sales or income taxes. Similarly there can be firms that are registered and pay fees to local market administrators but not registered with other authorities. Nevertheless, the chapter has to follow the definition used by the database utilised for the analysis and readers, while interpreting the results should keep in mind the caveat about this definition.

[4] The Informal Enterprise Surveys are a good source of data on informal firms and deserve credit for making such data readily available for a cross-section of countries. Still, additional efforts are needed to improve the quality and availability of data on informal enterprises. The National Statistics Departments of countries should increase their effort to collect data on the informal sector to gain a better understanding of different interventions that would be most appropriate for the sector.

[5] The sample by design has equal number of firms from services and manufacturing sectors.

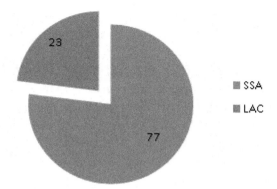

Figure 2. Sample distribution, regions (percent).

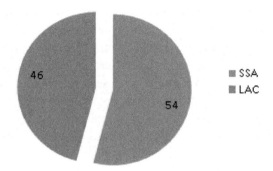

Figure 3. Sample distribution, firm observations (percent).

opportunity to study informal firms and to increase our knowledge and understanding of the barriers they face and the business environment they operate in.

Data for more than 2500 firms from 13 countries in the Sub-Saharan Africa (SSA) and Latin America and Caribbean (LAC) regions is utilized for the analysis.[6] Figure 2 depicts the sample distribution by countries and shows that LAC region represents 23% of the sample (three countries) while SSA region represents 77% of the sample (remaining 10 countries).[7] Even though countries from SSA constitute the majority of the sample, the distribution of firm observations across the two regions is more even with 46% of firms from LAC and 54% from SSA region (Fig. 3). Countries in the sample vary in terms of their levels of income (Fig. 4). Low income countries represent 38% while lower middle and upper middle income groups each represent 31% of the sample. The surveys were conducted in different years for different countries (Fig. 5), and the majority of the data pertains to year 2010.

---

[6] Informal Enterprise Surveys are mostly available for countries from SSA and LAC regions and therefore the analysis done in the chapter concentrates on these regions only.

[7] Countries in the sample are Angola, Argentina, Botswana, Burkina Faso, Cameroon, Cape Verde, Democratic Republic of Congo, Guatemala, Madagascar, Mali, Mauritius, Peru, and Rwanda.

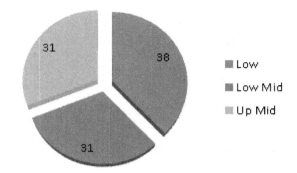

Figure 4. Sample distribution, income groups (percent).

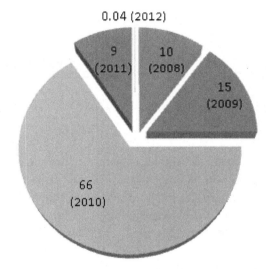

Figure 5. Sample distribution, years (percent).

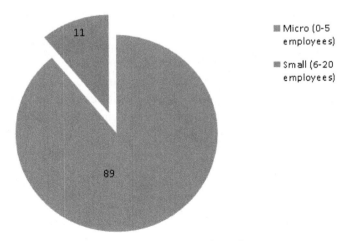

Figure 6. Sample distribution, firm size (percent).

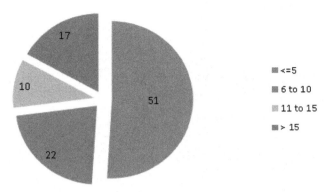

Figure 7. Sample distribution, firm age (percent).

Micro-sized firms defined as those with five employees or less, account for 89% of the firms in the sample (Fig. 6). While with approximately 300 observations, small-sized firms constitute the remaining 11% of the sample. Looking at firm distribution by age, Fig. 7 shows that at 51%, the majority of the firms in the sample are less than or equal to five years of age.

3. Features of Informal Firms

Before presenting the analysis that looks at some of the main characteristics of informal sector firms, the section examines how different firm characteristics are associated with their perception of access to finance as the main obstacle they face. Figure 8 shows how firms with different sizes, age, location, and desire to register all rank lack of access as a major problem.

The figure shows that as firms expand in size, the number of firms citing access to finance as a major constraint increases from 36% to 46%. On the other hand, as firms age, this percentage falls. More specifically, around 39% of firms that are 10-years old or less cite lack of access to finance as an obstacle compared to 32% of firms that are more than 10 years of age. Next, the figure shows how firms in different regions vary in their perception of access to finance as a major constraint.[8] A greater proportion of firms in the SSA region (47%) identify access to finance as a major obstacle. For the LAC region, this number is around 25%. Lastly, firms are categorized according to their desire to get registered. The figure shows that in comparison to firms with no desire to register (32%), a higher proportion of firms cite lack of access as a constraint among the group that wants to register (47%).

---

[8] Despite some similarities, the LAC and SSA environments for informal sectors are significantly different. Factors that can improve business conditions and inclusion for informal firms will be substantially different in the two regions. Same can be said about each specific country in the sample. However the objective of the chapter is to provide readers with an overall picture of financial inclusion of informal firms and has attempted to take into account regional and country level differences in the analysis presented later.

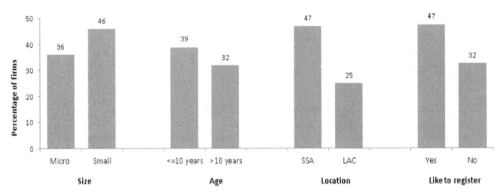

Figure 8. Lack of access to finance as an obstacle affecting operations of informal firms (percent).
Note: The bars represent percentage of firms in the sample that identify lack of access to finance as a major obstacle.
Source: Informal Enterprise Surveys for 13 countries covering micro (0–5 employees) and small (6–20 employees) firms. The bars represent the percentage of firms identifying lack of access to finance as a major obstacle to business.

We now present an analysis that looks at some of the features of informal firms across countries. Even though the sample at hand is not entirely representative of the informal sectors in the respective economies, it is important to examine some of the basic characteristics of informal firms to get a better sense of how they look.

Table 1 provides a summary of features of informal firms in the sample. The first panel looks at some of the more general firm characteristics. As already highlighted in the previous section, the majority of informal firms are micro-sized (89%), employing not more than five people. Also, most of them are 10 years of age or younger (74% of the sample). In terms of level of education, around 6% of firm owners have no education, implying that most of the owners have some level of education or vocational training. Around 8% of firm owners have a job with an established formal sector business.[9]

The next panel highlights the level of use of finance by informal firms. Around 23% of firms identify having a bank account to run their business, while only 11% claim having a loan.[10] Not surprisingly, the majority of informal firms use internal funds, families or moneylenders for financing purposes. This amounts to 80% working capital financing and 84% investment financing from these sources.

The last panel of the table highlights what informal firms think about formalization of their business. Around 4% of firms in the sample started their business as registered

---

[9] Unfortunately the surveys do not provide any information regarding the status of their job with formal sector business. We do not know if they work informally with the formal business or whether they work as formal employees.
[10] Even though the chapter equates financial inclusion with the use of bank accounts and loans, these two financial products can be quite different. For example, countries might require firms to open bank account as part of "starting a business" (see footnote 12 for country examples), so having a bank account may not necessarily translate into financial inclusion *per se*.

Table 1. Features of informal firms.

General charateristics	Firms (%)
Size: Micro (0–5 employees)	89
Age: 10 years or less	74
Level of education of largest owner: No Education	6
Largest owner has a job in a formal business	8
Use of finance	
Use of accounts	23
Use of loans	11
Working capital finance: Internal funds, family and money lenders	80
Investment finance: Internal funds, family and money lenders	84
Business registration	
Registered at startup	4
Like to register	59
Main reason for not registering: Taxes	26
Most important benefit from registering: Access to finance	52

Source: Informal Enterprise Surveys for 13 countries covering micro (0–5 employees) and small (6–20 employees) firms.

firms, while a majority at 59% states that they would like to register. The main reason identified by highest number of firms (26%) for not registering is tax payments. The majority of firms at 52% think that the biggest benefit they can get by registering is better access to finance.[11]

In short, on average informal firms are micro-sized, are less than 11 years of age and the majority of firm owners have some form of educational or vocational training. Very few firm owners have jobs in the formal business, implying that their informal business is their main source of income. Firms report very low use of loans and bank accounts and a significant majority of firms in the sample finance their day-to-day operations and longer term financing through sources other than financial institutions (internal funds, moneylenders, family, and friends). Only a handful of firms started out as registered firms, while a majority would like to register but do not do so as it will require them to pay taxes and they state that relatively easier access to finance would be the most important benefit they could obtain from registering.

---

[11] Despite the fact that informal firms think that registering will increase their access to finance, there is some evidence from impact evaluation studies that suggests otherwise. For example in Sri Lanka, de Mel *et al.* (2012) find firms which formalise are not any more likely to get a business bank account or a business loan. In Bolivia, McKenzie and Sakho (2010) find no impact on the likelihood of a bank loan after tax registration. However, in comparing results obtained from case studies with those obtained from a cross-section of countries, one should keep in mind that results from impact evaluation studies are country specific and reasons explaining these results might also be country specific. For example, for the Bolivian case study, the authors note that banks, while deciding to grant credit, do not care whether firms are registered for tax purposes and show more concern for whether firms have a municipal license.

Table 2. Features of informal firms — by size.

General charateristics	Micro firms (%)	Small firms (%)
Age: 10 years or less	74	75
Level of education of largest owner: No Education	6	7
Largest owner has a job in a formal budness	7	14
Use of finance		
Use of accounts	19	53
Use of loans	11	11
Working capital finance: Internal funds, family and money lenders	81	70
Investment finance: Internal funds, family and money lenders	86	76
Business registration		
Registered at startup	3	6
Like to register	54	72
Main reason for not registering	26 (Taxes)	29 (Information)
Most important benefit from registering: Access to finance	50	58

Source: Informal Enterprise Surveys for 13 countries covering micro (0–5 employees) and small (6–20 employees) firms.

Next, we present analysis that studies how the main characteristics of informal firms vary by their size, their regional location and their willingness to register. Table 2 shows that on average both micro and small firms are 10 years or less. The proportion of firm owners with some form of education is also very similar across micro and small firms. These firms differ in terms of the percentage of owners with a job in the formal sector. The table shows that in comparison to micro firms, owners of small firms are twice as likely to have formal sector jobs. Firms also show variation in their use of finance, with small firms reporting significantly higher use of accounts and relatively low use of internal funds, families or moneylenders for financing their operations. The only exception is in the use of loans, which does not vary by firm size. Firms also vary in terms of business registration. A relatively higher proportion of small firms start their business as registered enterprises, would like to register, but do not do so due to lack of information on registration requirements and procedures, and identify easier access to finance as the most important benefit they can obtain from getting registered. Micro firms also identify access to finance as the main benefit of registration. However, unlike small firms that do not register due to lack of information, micro firms prefer not to register due to tax payments.

Table 3 depicts the variation across firms based on their regional location and shows that in comparison to SSA a higher proportion of firms in the LAC region are micro sized. The number of firms that are less than 11 years of age is not very different across regions, though the LAC region has a slightly lower percentage of young firms. Similarly, the proportion of firm owners that have no education does not vary too much

Table 3. Salient features of informal firms — by region.

General charateristics	LAC firms (%)	SSA firms (%)
Size: Micro [0–5 employees]	98	81
Age: 10 years or less	72	76
Level of education of largest owner: No Education	5	8
Largest owner has a job in a formal business	4	12
Use of finance		
Use of accounts	6	38
Use of loans	14	8
Working capital finance: Internal funds, family and money lenders	87	75
Investment finance: Internal funds, family and money lenders	88	82
Business registration		
Registered at startup	4	3
Like to register	—	59
Main reason for not registering: Taxes	—	26
Most important benefit from registering: Access to finance	—	52

Source: Informal Enterprise Surveys for 13 countries covering micro (0–5 employees) and small (6–20 employees) firms. Empty cells in the last panel of the table are due to non-availability of information.

across regions, though LAC has a slightly lower percentage of firm owners with no education or training of any sort. Interestingly, in comparison to the LAC region, firm owners in SSA are three times as likely to have a job in the formal sector. Use of accounts is higher for firms in the SSA region, while firms in the LAC region report higher use of loans.[12] The LAC region also shows higher use of internal funds, families or moneylenders for their operations. An almost similar proportion of firms in both regions start out as registered enterprises. The remaining aspects of business registration cannot be compared across regions due to non-availability of data for the LAC region.

Table 4 divides firms into two groups based on their willingness to register or become formal.[13] A comparison between the two groups shows that there are relatively fewer micro sized firms in the group that wants to register. Firms across the two groups do not vary too much in terms of their age. Even though the group that has a desire to become formal shows a slightly higher proportion of owners with no education, it also has more firm owners with a job in the formal sector. The group also shows a higher use of accounts and lower reliance on internal funds, family or moneylenders for financing their day-to-day operations. The use of loans and internal funds, family or

---

[12] Among countries included in the sample, Angola, Argentina, Burkina Faso, Cameroon, Cape Verde, Guatemala and Madagascar require a bank account to be opened prior to registration for the paid-in minimum capital requirement (see Doing Business Data at http://www.doingbusiness.org). This might explain the higher ratio of account use seen in SSA.
[13] Results on comparison of firms by age (firms <= 10 years versus firms > 10 years) are not presented as firms show very similar kind of patterns across different age groups.

Table 4. Features of informal firms — by willingness to register.

General charateristics	Want to register (%)	Do not want to register (%)
Size: Micro (0–5 employees)	69	83
Age: 10 years or less	78	76
Level of education of largest owner: No Education	11	8
Largest owner has a job in a formal business	18	10
Use of finance		
Use of accounts	47	24
Use of loans	7	6
Working capital finance: Internal funds, family and money lenders	71	76
Investrnent finance: Internal funds, family and money lenders	85	85
Business registration		
Registered at startup	1	6
Main reason for not registering	32 (Information)	42 (No benefit)
Most important benefit from registering: Access to finance	58	49

Source: Informal Enterprise Surveys for 13 countries covering micro (0–5 employees) and small (6–20 employees) firms.

moneylenders as a source of financing investments is quite similar across the two groups. A lower proportion of firms with a desire to formalize start out as registered firms, they identify difficulty of obtaining information related to registration as the main reason for not registering, and the majority of firms are of the view that easier access to finance is the biggest benefit they can get from formalizing. Firms in the other group that do not want to register also report access to finance as the major benefit of registration. However, these firms do not want to register as their owners think that registration would not benefit their business.

4. Use of Finance: Formal versus Informal Firms

This section first presents some basic bivariate analysis to document the differences in use of finance, financing patterns and reasons for not applying for loans between formal and informal firms. The section then presents multivariate regression analysis that builds upon and strengthens the conclusions obtained from the bivariate analysis. This analysis verifies whether differences in the use of finance by firms based on their registration status hold once various firm level and country level characteristics are controlled for.[14]

---

[14] The analysis in this section shows a positive correlation between formalization and financial inclusion and besides confirming our a priori knowledge, the results obtained quantify for the first time differences between the use of finance among formal and informal firms for a cross-sectional sample of countries.

Data pertaining to formal firms is obtained from the Enterprise Surveys. To make the comparison between formal and informal firms more aligned and meaningful, only small-sized firms from the 13 countries in the original sample are used from the Enterprise Surveys. This results in a sample of approximately 1500 formal firms. Similarly the sample on informal firms is also restricted to small-sized firms. Also for each country in the sample, we make sure that the year in which surveys for both formal and informal firms were conducted is similar.

4.1. *Bivariate analysis*

Looking at the use of bank accounts by firms, Fig. 9 shows that on average 53% of informal firms have bank accounts to run their business compared with 86% of firms in the formal sector. These percentages highlight a significant difference in the use of bank accounts between registered and non-registered firms. Figure 9 shows a similar picture for use of loans by firms in the formal and informal sector.[15] Only 12% of firms in the informal sector have loans compared to 47% formal sector firms.

Looking at various sources firms use for financing their day-to-day operations, Fig. 10 shows that majority of firms — 70% informal and 63% formal — rely on their retained earnings, their families and friends or on moneylenders for financing. Trade credit is the second most frequently used source with 23% of informal and 24% of

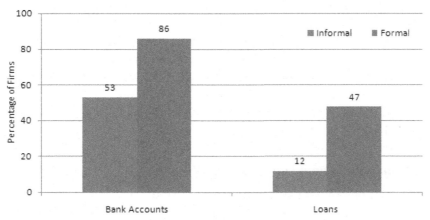

Figure 9. Firms with bank accounts and loans.
Note: The bars represent percentage of firms in the sample that claim to have a bank account and a loan.
Source: Author's calculations based on data from Enterprise Surveys and Informal Enterprise Surveys.

---

[15] For formal sector, loans include loan and/or an overdraft facility from a financial institution. Loans for informal firms refer to loan from any of the following source: Bank, moneylenders, MFIs, and trade credit.

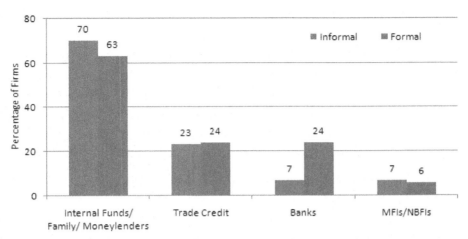

Figure 10. Source of financing working capital (percent).
Note: The bars represent percentage of firms in the sample that identify using a given source for financing their working capital.
Source: Author's calculations based on data from Enterprise Surveys and Informal Enterprise Surveys.

formal firms relying on it. Bank financing is the next option firms opt for, however only 7% of informal firms use this option. This is not surprising given that informal firms lack the required documentation to qualify for a bank loan. In the formal sector 24% of firms rely on banks to finance their working capital. Lastly, 7% of informal firms use microfinance institutions (MFIs) and 6% of formal firms use non-bank financial institutions (NBFIs) for their day-to-day financing. Figure 11, which

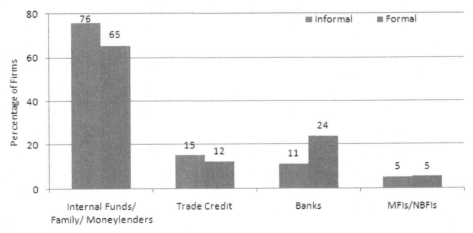

Figure 11. Source of financing investments (percent).
Note: The bars represent the percentage of firms in the sample that identify using a given source for financing their investment.
Source: Author's calculations based on data from Enterprise Surveys and Informal Enterprise Surveys.

highlights sources of financing for investments, reveals a very similar picture. Around 76% of informal firms and 65% of formal firms identify using their retained earnings, their families and friends or moneylenders for financing investments. The next option used by informal firms is trade credit (15% of firms) and by formal firms are banks (24% of firms). MFIs by informal firms (5% of firms) and NBFIs by formal firms (5% of firms) are the least used means of financing investments.

Figures 10 and 11 show trade credit to be an important source of financing for informal firms and whether it is working capital or investment financing, informal firms use this option as frequently as firms in the formal sector. On the other hand, banks are not as common a source of financing among informal firms and among all the given sources of financing, bank financing shows the highest difference between formal and informal firms. Comparing bank and MFI financing among informal firms, the figures show that both of these sources are equally important for working capital financing for informal firms, while for investment financing banks are more widely used.

The top three reasons firms do not apply for loans include, complex application procedures, unfavourable/too high interest rates and high guarantees/collateral requirements (Fig. 12). In the informal sector, around 18% of firms report difficult application procedures, 17% indicate high interest rates and 16% indicate lack of guarantees as the reason for not applying for a loan. Complexity of the application being more of a concern than the price and collateral requirement for informal firms could be due to the fact that these firms tend to lack documentation and other required legal papers needed for a loan application. For formal firms' high interest rates is the most important reason for not applying for a loan (17% of firms). High collateral

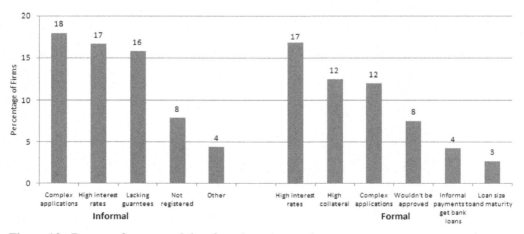

Figure 12. Reasons for not applying for a loan (percent).
Note: The bars show the percentage of firms identifying a given reason for not applying for a loan.
Source: Author's calculations based on data from Enterprise Surveys and Informal Enterprise Surveys.

requirements (12.5%) and complex applications (12%) are also highlighted as significant impediments to applying for a loan.

4.2. *Multivariate analysis*

For the multivariate analysis the following specification is used:

$$FI_{ic} = a_c + b_1 Registered_{ic} + b_2 F_{ic} + b_3 X_{ic} + e_{ic},$$

where FI is an indicator of financial inclusion for firm i in country c. FI indicators are binary variables and are proxied by (i) firms with bank accounts (equals 1 if firm has an account and 0 otherwise), (ii) firms with loans (equals 1 if firm has a loan and 0 otherwise) and (iii) different sources firms use for financing working capital (equals 1 if firm uses a given source and 0 otherwise). *Registered*, is a dummy variable which equals 1 if firm i in country c is registered and 0 otherwise. Firm and country level control variables are represented by F and X. Besides registered dummy variable, other firm level controls include: *age*, which is the logarithm of firm age; *female owner*, equals 1 if firm's largest owner is a female and 0 otherwise and *manufacturing*, equals 1 if firm works in the manufacturing sector and 0 if it is part of the services sector. Country level variables include private credit to GDP and financial freedom as proxies of financial sector development and contract viability, law and order, and property rights to proxy for quality of legal framework.[16] The regressions also control for a regional dummy, LAC which equals 1 if firm is located in LAC region and 0 if it is in the SSA region. Country fixed effects are captured by a_c. Table A.1 in the appendix presents detailed definition and sources of variables used in the analysis.

Regression results are reported in Table 5. The way results are presented is that in each column the coefficients of firm level variables and regional dummy variable correspond to a regression which controls for country dummies and no country level variable. The results reported for each country level variable (private credit to GDP, financial freedom, contract viability, law and order, and property rights) represent a separate regression that controls for a specific country level variable and no country dummies. Since all the dependent variables are binary in nature, a probit model is estimated and marginal effects are reported.

Results in Table 5 confirm the results of the bivariate analysis and show that registered firms have higher financial inclusion, both in terms of bank accounts and loans. In particular, first two columns of Table 5 show that registered firms are 54% more likely to have bank accounts and 32% more likely to have loans.[17] These results hold even after controlling for firm level characteristics like gender of the owner, age and activity of firms

---

[16] Country level variables controlling for institutional quality and financial freedom, which are based on assessments of "industry experts" may not necessarily include viewpoint of the informal sector.

[17] To check the robustness of results for accounts as a dependent variable, separate regressions were estimated for a sample excluding countries that have paid-in minimum capital requirement (see footnote 12). The results obtained are very similar to those shown in Table 2 and hence are not reported. They are available from the author upon request.

Table 5. Formal versus informal firms: Use of finance and financing patterns.
Bank account equals 1 if firm has an account with a bank and 0 otherwise. Loan equals 1 if firm
has a loan and 0 otherwise. The outcome variables under sources of financing equal 1 if firm
uses them as a source of financing and 0 otherwise. Sample consists of small-sized firms from
13 countries. Probit model is used for estimation.

	Bank account	Loan	Sources of financing working capital		
			Internal/Family/MLs	Banks	Trade credit
Registered	**0.54*****	**0.32*****	**−0.13*****	**0.15*****	**−0.09***
	(10.71)	(5.64)	(−2.98)	(3.67)	(−1.73)
Female owner/	**0.01**	**0.04**	**0.02**	**0.02**	**−0.01**
decision maker	(0.75)	(1.56)	(0.80)	(0.87)	(−0.55)
Manufacturing	**−0.0001**	**−0.06****	**−0.08*****	**−0.005**	**0.04***
	(−0.04)	(−2.20)	(−2.63)	(−0.23)	(1.72)
Ln age	**−0.02****	**0.02**	0.002	**0.01**	**0.03***
	(−1.97)	(1.13)	(0.10)	(0.48)	(1.86)
LAC region	**−0.51*****	**0.26*****	**−0.10*****	0.05	**0.22****
	(−5.73)	(2.67)	(−2.75)	(0.72)	(2.21)
Private credit to GDP	**−0.0009**	**0.003*****	**−0.00002**	**0.002*****	**−0.003*****
	(−1.21)	(3.32)	(−0.03)	(2.99)	(−3.48)
Financial freedom	**−0.001**	**0.004*****	**−0.003*****	**0.005*****	**−0.0006**
	(−1.60)	(4.31)	(−2.84)	(6.11)	(−0.67)
Contract viability/	**−0.14*****	**−0.03**	**−0.01**	0.02	**−0.04***
expropriation	(−7.39)	(−1.41)	(−0.23)	(1.33)	(−1.91)
Law and order	0.13***	**0.11*****	**−0.06*****	**0.13*****	0.0007
	(8.30)	(5.15)	(−3.19)	(7.79)	(0.04)
Property rights	**−0.001**	**0.004*****	**−0.001**	**0.004*****	**−0.002***
	(−1.55)	(3.28)	(−0.83)	(4.33)	(−1.73)
Observations	1926	1922	1714	1895	1894
Pseudo *R2*	0.21	0.19	0.08	0.10	0.12

Note: Marginal effects from probit regressions. Robust *z*-statistics in parentheses. Statistical significance
levels: ***$p < 0.01$, **$p < 0.05$, *$p < 0.10$. Data sources and definitions can be found in the appendix,
Table A.1.

and country level factors like the level of financial development and quality of legal
framework. Last three columns of Table 5 show how formal and informal firms differ in
terms of their working capital financing. Results show that in comparison to informal
firms, on average registered firms rely less on internal funds, families and friends and on
moneylenders for financing their working capital. Use of banks for financing is positively
and significantly higher for registered firms. However use of trade credit is lower for
registered firms in comparison to firms in the informal sector. In particular, results
reported show that registered firms are 13% less likely to use internal funds, families and
friends and moneylenders for financing, 15% more likely to have bank financing and 9%
less likely to use trade credit as a source of financing.

Among country level variables, development of financial sector, proxied by private credit to GDP shows a positive correlation with firms having loans and using banks as a source of financing while it is negatively associated with the use of trade credit. Financial freedom is positively associated with firms having bank accounts and loans. It is also positively associated with the use of banks for financing working capital, while it shows a negative association with the use of internal funds, families or moneylenders. Among variables used to proxy for strength of the legal framework, law and order shows the most robust results. It is on average positively correlated with the use of bank accounts, loans and bank financing for working capital. It is negatively associated with the use of internal funds/families/moneylenders for working capital financing.

5. Use of Finance by Informal Firms

This section presents a multivariate regression analysis to study the use of finance by informal firms. The sample used includes micro and small-sized firms. The regression analysis controls for different firm level and country level variables, most of which were used in the analysis presented in the previous section. Also, the specification used in the previous section is utilised again for the analysis of informal firms. However, the dummy variable capturing the registration status of firms is excluded.

This gives us the following specification:

$$\text{FI}_{ic} = \alpha_c + \beta_1 F_{ic} + \beta_2 X_{ic} + \varepsilon_{ic},$$

where FI represents indicators of financial inclusion for firm i in country c. These indicators are proxied by (i) firms with bank accounts, (ii) firms with loans and (iii) different sources firms use for financing working capital. The dependent variables are binary in nature and follow the definition provided in the previous section. Firm and country level control variables are represented by F and X. Firm level controls include: *age*, which equals to the logarithm of firm age; *female owner*, equals 1 if firm's largest owner is a female and 0 otherwise and *manufacturing*, equals 1 if firm works in the manufacturing sector and 0 if it belongs to the services sector. Three additional firm level variables are introduced which include *micro*, *owner's education* and *owner's job in formal sector*. Micro captures the size of a firm and equals 1 if firm is micro-sized and 0 if it is small-sized. Owner's education equals 1 if owner of a firm has secondary school, university training or vocational training and 0 otherwise ($=$ no education or primary education). Owner's job equal 1 if firm's owner has a job with an established formal sector business and 0 otherwise. Country level variables used are the same that were used in the previous section and include proxies of financial sector development and quality of legal framework. Regressions also control for a regional dummy, LAC which equals 1 if firm is located in LAC region and 0 if it is in the SSA region. Country fixed effects are captured by a_c. More details about variable definitions and sources can be found in Table A.1 in the appendix.

Table 6 reports regression results for use of bank accounts by firms in the informal sector. Column 1 shows results when country dummies are used as controls and no

Table 6. Use of bank accounts by informal firms.

Bank account equals 1 if firm has an account with a bank and 0 otherwise. Probit model is used for estimation. Sample consists of micro and small-sized firms from 13 countries.

	Use of bank accounts					
	(1)	(2)	(3)	(4)	(5)	(6)
Micro	−0.16***	−0.17***	−0.18***	−0.16***	−0.16***	−0.19***
	(−5.54)	(−5.90)	(−6.56)	(−5.73)	(−5.55)	(−6.60)
Owner's education	0.10***	0.08***	0.08***	0.07***	0.07***	0.08***
	(−4.59)	(−4.31)	(−4.29)	(−3.75)	(−3.92)	(−4.38)
Owner's job in	0.06*	0.08**	0.09***	0.13***	0.12***	0.09**
formal sector	(−1.76)	(−2.34)	(−2.58)	(−3.58)	(−3.34)	(−2.55)
Lng age	0.003	0.002	0.003	0.01	0.003	0.003
	(−0.35)	(−0.21)	(−0.31)	(−0.60)	(−0.28)	(−0.36)
Female owner/	−0.01	−0.01	−0.01	−0.005	−0.0003	−0.01
decision maker	(−0.35)	(−0.81)	(−0.37)	(−0.25)	(−0.02)	(−0.34)
Manufacturing	−0.01	0.004	−0.01	−0.004	0.003	−0.01
	(−0.52)	(−0.20)	(−0.48)	(−0.21)	−0.16	(−0.38)
LAC region	−0.16***	−0.27***	−0.28***	−0.26***	−0.26***	−0.27***
	(−3.51)	(−12.75)	(−14.28)	(−11.69)	(−11.76)	(−13.29)
Private credit to GDP		0.00***				
		(−3.41)				
Financial freedom			0.003***			
			(−4.46)			
Contract viability/				0.05***		
expropriation				(−3.83)		
Law and order					0.02*	
					(−1.87)	
Property rights						0.002***
						(−3.15)
Observations	2027	1816	2027	1701	1701	2027
Pseudo R2	0.21	0.21	0.19	0.22	0.21	0.19

Note: Marginal effects from probit regressions. Robust z-statistics in parentheses. Statistical significance levels: ***$p < 0.01$, **$p < 0.05$, *$p < 0.10$. Data sources and definitions can be found in the appendix, Table A.1.

country level variables are included. For all remaining regressions which separately control for country's level of financial sector development and quality of legal framework, country dummies are not included. All regressions are estimated using probit model and marginal effects are reported. Results show that use of bank accounts is negatively associated with micro-sized firms. Owner's level of education and whether he/she has a job in the formal sector are positively and significantly correlated with firms having a bank account for their business. Level of financial sector development and quality of legal framework also increase the likelihood of firms using bank accounts for their business.

Table 7 shows regression results for use of loans by informal firms. Column 1 shows results when country dummies are used as controls while results shown in the remaining columns exclude country dummies and separately control for country's level of financial sector development and quality of legal framework. Firm size does not seem to be an important factor as far as the use of loans is concerned. Owner's level of education, level of financial sector development and quality of legal framework increase the probability of informal firms having loans.

Table 8 shows regression results for various sources of financing used by informal firms for working capital. The way regression results are presented is that in each

Table 7. Use of loans by informal firms.
Loan equals 1 if a firm has a loan and 0 otherwise. Probit model is used for estimation. Sample consists of micro and small-sized firms from 13 countries.

	Use of loans					
	(1)	(2)	(3)	(4)	(5)	(6)
Micro	−0.06**	−0.03	−0.03	−0.02	−0.02	−0.03
	(−2.24)	(−1.09)	(−1.29)	(−0.87)	(−0.69)	(−1.27)
Owner's education	0.02	0.06***	0.06***	0.06***	0.05***	0.06***
	(1.26)	(3.99)	(3.91)	(3.53)	(2.83)	(4.27)
Owner's job in	0.04	0.01	0.01	0.02	0.02	0.01
formal sector	(1.29)	(0.28)	(0.50)	(0.69)	(0.65)	(0.40)
Ln age	0.01	0.01	0.01*	0.01*	0.01	0.01**
	(1.46)	(1.54)	(1.89)	(1.84)	(1.44)	(2.00)
Female owner/	0.03**	0.03*	0.03**	0.03**	0.03**	0.03**
decision maker	(2.06)	(1.93)	(2.12)	(2.07)	(2.08)	(2.16)
Manufacturing	−0.01	0.0008	0.01	−0.002	0.003	0.01
	(−0.53)	(0.06)	(0.42)	(−0.14)	(0.23)	(0.44)
LAC region	0.08	0.08***	0.06***	0.08***	0.07***	0.08***
	(1.53)	(4.53)	(4.22)	(4.33)	(3.74)	(4.92)
Private credit to GDP		0.001*				
		(1.87)				
Financial freedom			0.002***			
			(4.99)			
Contract viability/				0.04***		
expropriation				(−3.32)		
Law and order					0.03***	
					(3.21)	
Property rights						0.001***
						(3.12)
Observations	2029	1819	2029	1704	1704	2029
Pseudo $R2$	0.09	0.04	0.06	0.04	0.05	0.04

Note: Marginal effects from probit regressions. Robust z-statistics in parentheses. Statistical significance levels: ***$p < 0.01$, **$p < 0.05$, *$p < 0.10$. Data sources and definitions can be found in the appendix, Table A.1.

Table 8. Financing of working capital by informal firms.
The outcome variables equal 1 if firms use them as a source of financing and 0 otherwise. Probit model is used for estimation. Sample consists of micro and small-sized firms from 13 countries.

	Internal/family/MLs (1)	Banks (2)	Trade credit (3)	MFIs (4)
Micro	**0.01**	**−0.07***	−0.03	**−0.03**
	(0.32)	(−3.24)	(−1.27)	(−2.02)
Owner's education	**−0.06***	0.01	0.03*	**0.02***
	(−2.66)	(1.08)	(1.65)	(2.58)
Owner's job in formal sector	**−0.07***	**0.04**	0.04	0.0001
	(−1.93)	(2.08)	(1.06)	(0.01)
Ln age	**−0.02**	0.002	0.01	**0.01**
	(−2.32)	(0.56)	(1.44)	(2.42)
Female owner/decision maker	**0.05**	−0.001	−0.02	0.0004
	(2.34)	(−0.13)	(−1.49)	(0.04)
Manufacturing	**−0.04***	−0.002	0.02	0.01
	(−1.81)	(−0.29)	(1.43)	(0.93)
LAC region	**0.12***	**0.05**	−0.02	0.001
	(5.58)	(2.06)	(−0.36)	(0.10)
Private credit to GDP	**−0.002***	**0.002***	**0.001**	0.0002
	(−2.78)	(5.18)	(2.06)	(0.53)
Financial freedom	**−0.004***	**0.002***	**0.003***	**0.001***
	(−5.52)	(4.86)	(5.26)	(4.35)
Contract viability/expropriation	**−0.05***	**0.02***	**0.04***	**0.03***
	(−3.33)	(2.89)	(3.16)	(4.30)
Law and order	**−0.05***	**0.02***	**0.03***	**0.02***
	(−4.60)	(2.64)	(3.36)	(2.83)
Property rights	**−0.002**	**0.001***	**0.001***	**0.0004***
	(−2.52)	(4.54)	(2.79)	(1.75)
Observations	1877	1926	2020	1806
Pseudo *R*2	0.08	0.08	0.09	0.09

Note: Marginal effects from probit regressions. Robust z-statistics in parentheses. Statistical significance levels: ***$p < 0.01$, **$p < 0.05$, *$p < 0.10$. Data sources and definitions can be found in the appendix, Table A.1.

column the coefficients of firm level variables (micro, education, job at formal sector, age, gender of owner and activity of a firm) and regional dummy variable correspond to a regression which controls for country dummies and no country level variable. The results reported for each country level variable (private credit to GDP, financial freedom, contract viability, law and order, and property rights) represent a separate regression that controls for a specific country level variable and no country dummies.

Column 1 of Table 8 reports results pertaining to use of internal funds, families and moneylenders as a source of working capital financing. Estimates show owners with more education and a job in the formal sector are less likely to rely on these sources. With more developed financial and legal systems, reliance on these sources also decreases. Next, column 2 shows results for bank financing. The likelihood of a firm using bank financing decreases if it is micro-sized, while owner's job in the formal sector and country's level of financial and legal sector are positively associated with using banks for financing. The correlation between trade credit financing and firm level characteristics is not very strong; however, it is positively associated with owner's level of education and financial and legal sector development of a country. MFI financing is also positively associated with level of owner's education and financial and legal sector development of a country while negatively associated with firm size.

6. Conclusion

The objectives of the chapter were three-fold: First, to document salient features of informal firms, their use, of finance and their financing patterns. Second, to compare and quantify the differences that exist in the use of finance by firms in the formal and informal sector. Third, to identify the most significant characteristics of informal firms that are associated with higher financial inclusion. The chapter utilizes data on informal firms collected by World Bank's Enterprise Surveys.

The analysis shows that firms in the informal sector are on average micro-sized and relatively younger, less than 11 years of age. Most of the owners of informal firms have some form of educational or vocational training and a very small proportion have jobs in an established formal business. Use of loans and bank accounts for business by informal firms is very low and a significant majority of firms finance their day-to-day operations and investments through sources other than financial institutions (internal funds, moneylenders, family and friends). Most of the firms would like to register but tend not to opt for it due to tax reasons and state that relatively easier access to finance would be the most important benefit they could obtain from registering.

A comparative analysis between formal and informal small-sized firms shows, not surprisingly, a higher use of bank accounts and loans by registered firms. Firms in the formal sector are 54% more likely to have a bank account and 32% more likely to have a loan. On average, registered firms rely less on internal funds, families and friends and on moneylenders for financing their working capital and their use of bank financing is higher in comparison to informal firms. These results hold even after controlling for various firm level and country level characteristics.

The chapter also shows that firm size, the level of education of the owner and whether the owner has a job in the formal sector are significantly associated with financial inclusion of informal firms. Micro firms vis-à-vis small firms have lower use of bank accounts, rely less on banks and more on microfinance institutions for working capital financing. Size is not significantly associated with the use of loans. Owner's level of education and whether he/she has a job in the formal sector are positively associated with the use of bank accounts and negatively associated with the use of internal funds and financing from family and moneylender for working capital. Higher education levels of owners are also positively associated with the use of loans by informal firms.

The correlations presented in this chapter hold true on average and while interpreting the results one must recognize that informal sector firms are very diverse. Some firms might be part of the informal sector due to necessity, while others operate in this sector because of an opportunistic entrepreneurial activity (see for example Bruhn, 2013). Therefore the way firms operate and how willing their owners may be to become integrated into the formal economic and financial system in the future would differ greatly. Also, the factors that firms consider important in their decision to formalize may vary as well. Recent research has highlighted that registration costs and knowledge of registration procedures are not particularly important for firms while deciding whether to formalize (de Andrade *et al.*, 2013; De Giorgi and Rahman, 2013). It might be true that variable costs associated with becoming formal (such as tax payments) are considered more important by informal firms. Unless firms that are interested in entering the formal sector grow and become profitable enough to cover such costs it would be very difficult for them to formalize. Enhancing financial inclusion of informal firms interested in registering can potentially help them grow and pave their path toward formalization.

Acknowledgments

The opinions expressed in this chapter do not necessarily represent the views of the World Bank, its Executive Directors or the countries they represent. This chapter was prepared as part of the background work for the 2014 Global Financial Development Report. I would like to thank Oya Pinar Ardic Alper, Nancy Claire Benjamin, Miriam Bruhn, Martin Cihak, David McKenzie, Martin Hommes, Anushe Khan, and Claudia Ruiz Ortega for their valuable comments. I would also like to thank Judy Yang and Mohammad Amin who provided very useful insights pertaining to data from the survey of informal firms. The usual disclaimer applies.

Appendix

Table A.1. Definition and sources of variables used in regression analysis.

Variable	Definition	Source
Loan	At this time, does this business have a loan? Variable equals 1 if firm has a loan, 0. otherwise.	World Bank Enterprise/Informal Surveys
Account	Do you have a bank account to run this business? Variable equals 1 if firm has an account, 0 otherwise.	World Bank Enterprise/Informal Surveys

Table A.1. (*Continued*)

Variable	Definition	Source
Banks	Dummy variable equal to 1 if firm financed day-to-day operations using banks, 0 otherwise.	World Bank Enterprise/Informal Surveys
Trade credit	Dummy variable equal to 1 if firm financed day-to-day operations using credit from suppliers or advances from customers, 0 otherwise.	World Bank Enterprise/Informal Surveys
MFIs	Dummy variable equal to 1 if firm financed day-to-day operations using microfinance institution, 0 otherwise.	World Bank Enterprise/Informal Surveys
Internal/family/ money lenders	Dummy variable equal to 1 if firm financed day-to-day operations using internal funds, moneylender or friends and relatives, 0 otherwise.	World Bank Enterprise/Informal Surveys
Registered	Dummy variable equal to 1 if firm is registered, 0 otherwise.	World Bank Enterprise/Informal Surveys
Micro	Dummy variable equal to 1 if firm is micro-sized (0–5 employees), 0 otherwise.	World Bank Enterprise/Informal Surveys
Ln age	Logarithm of age of firm.	World Bank Enterprise/Informal Surveys
Owner's education	Dummy variable equal to 1 if owner of firm has secondary school (complete or not), university training (complete or not) or vocational training and 0 otherwise (= no education or primary school).	World Bank Enterprise/Informal Surveys
Owner's job in formal sector	Dummy variable equal to 1 if the largest owner of firm has a job in a formal registered business and 0 otherwise.	World Bank Enterprise/Informal Surveys
Female owner/ decision maker	Dummy variable equal to 1 if the largest owner or the main decision maker of a firm is female and 0 otherwise.	World Bank Enterprise/Informal Surveys
Manufacturing	Dummy variable equal to 1 if firm's business focus in on manufacturing, 0 otherwise (services)	World Bank Enterprise/Informal Surveys
LAC region	Dummy variable equal to 1 if firm is located in Latin American and Caribbean region, 0 otherwise (located in Africa reigion).	World Bank Enterprise/Informal Surveys
Private credit to GDP	Deposit money banks and other financial institutions claims on the private sector as a percentage of GDP.	Raw data are from the electronic version of the IMF's International Financial Statistics. Claims on Private Sector by deposit money banks and other financial institutions (IFS lines 22d and 42d); GDP in local currency (IFS line 99B..ZF)

(*Continued*)

Table A.1. (*Continued*)

Variable	Definition	Source
Contract viability/ risk of expropriation	The risk of unilateral contract modification or cancellation and, at worst, outright expropriation of foreign owned assets. The risk rating assigned varies from a maximum score of 4 points and a minimum score of 0 points. A score of 4 points equates to very low risk and a score of 0 points to very high risk.	International Country Risk Guide
Law and order	Law and Order are assessed separately, with each sub-component comprising zero to three points. The Law sub-component is an assessment of the strength and impartiality of the legal system, while the Order sub-component is an assessment of popular observance of the law. Thus, a country can enjoy a high rating –3 – in terms of its judicial system, but a low rating – 1 – if it suffers from a very high crime rate of if the law is routinely ignored without effective sanction (for example, widespread illegal strikes).The index varies from 0 to 6 and higher values represent better law and order situation.	International Country Risk Guide
Property rights	Assessment of the ability of individuals to accumulate private property, secured by clear laws that are fully enforced by the state. It measures the degree to which a country's laws protect private property rights and the degree to which its government enforces those laws. It also assesses the likelihood that private property could be expropriated and analyses the independence of the judiciary, the existence of corruption within the judiciary, and the ability of individuals and businesses to enforce contracts. An overall score on a scale of 0 to 100 is given to an economy, with 100 representing the ideal score.	Heritage Foundation
Financial freedom	Measure of banking efficiency as well as a measure of independence from government control and interference in the financial sector. State ownership of banks and other financial institutions such as insurers and capital markets reduces competition and generally lowers the level of available services. An overall score on a scale of 0 to 100 is given to an economy, with 100 representing more freedom.	Heritage Foundation

Table A.1. (*Continued*)

Variable	Definition	Source
	The index scores an economy's financial freedom by looking into the following five broad areas: • The extent of government regulation of financial services; • The degree of state intervention in banks and other financial firms through direct and indirect ownership; • The extent of financial and capital market development; • Government influence on the allocation of credit; and • Openness to foreign competition.	

References

Bruhn, M (2013). A tale of two species: Revisiting the effect of registration reform on informal business owners in Mexico. *Journal of Development Economics*, 103, 275–283.

de Andrade, G Henrique, M Bruhn and D McKenzie (2013). A helping hand or the long arm of the law? Experimental evidence on what governments can do to formalize firms. Policy Research Working Paper No. 6435, World Bank, Washington, DC.

De Giorgi, G and A Rahman (2013). SME's registration evidence from an RCT in Bangladesh. *Economics Letters*, 120, 573–578.

de Mel, S, D McKenzie and C Woodruff (2012). The demand for, and consequences of, formalization among informal firms in Sri Lanka. Policy Research Working Paper No. 5991, World Bank, Washington DC.

de Soto, H (1989). *The Other Path: The Invisible Revolution in the Third World.* New York, Harper and Row.

Dell'Anno, R (2003). Estimating the shadow economy in Italy: A structural equation approach. Discussion Paper No. 2003-07, Department of Economics, University of Aarhus, Denmark.

Dell'Anno, R and F Schneider (2004). The shadow economy of Italy and other OECD countries: What do we know? *Journal of Public Finance and Public Choice*, 21, 97–120.

Djankov, S, R La Porta, F Lopez-de-Silanes and A Shleifer (2002). The regulation of entry. *Quarterly Journal of Economics*, 117, 1–37.

Field, E and M Torero (2006). Do property titles increase credit access among the urban poor? Evidence from a nationwide titling program. Mimeo, Harvard University.

International Finance Corporation (2012). Enterprise Finance Gap Database, World Bank, Washington DC.

International Labor Organisation (2012). *Statistical Update on Employment in the Informal Economy.* Department of Statistics.

Jaramillo, M (2009). Is there demand for formality among informal firms? Evidence from microfirms in downtown Lima, Discussion Paper No. 12/2009, German Development Institute.

Loayza, N, L Serven and N Sugawara (2009). Informality in Latin America and the Caribbean. Policy Research Working Paper No. 4888, World Bank, Washington DC.

McKenzie, D and YS Sakho (2010). Does it pay firms to register for taxes? The impact of formality on firm profitability. *Journal of Development Economics*, 91, 15–24.

Schneider, F, A Buehn and CE Montenegro (2010). Shadow economies all over the world, New Estimates for 162 Countries from 1999 to 2007. Policy Research Working Paper No. 5356, World Bank, Washington DC.

Smith, P (1994). Assessing the size of the underground economy: The statistics Canada perspectives. Canadian Economic Observer, April.

World Bank (2013). Global financial development report 2014: Financial inclusion. World Bank, Washington, DC.

Chapter 6

Promoting SMEs and Enhancing Labor Productivity in Singapore: A Policy Analysis

Khee Giap Tan and Yan Yi Tan

Asia Competitiveness Institute, Lee Kuan Yew School of Public Policy
National University of Singapore, Singapore

Abstract

While Singapore has been doing well in terms of cross-country per capita income comparisons and in terms of overall employment growth, it has been a laggard when it comes to labor productivity and this concern is more serious for small and medium enterprises (SMEs). In this context, this chapter first identifies the sources of gross domestic product (GDP) growth and simulates different scenarios pertaining to the potential GDP which the economy can achieve given the level of required productivity based on some employment-growth assumptions. Further, the chapter reevaluates the performance, challenges and opportunities for SMEs as well as suggests several policy strategies as to how SMEs can synergize and be more competitive moving forward.

Keywords: Singapore; small and medium enterprises (SMEs); labor productivity; competitiveness.

1. Introduction

By most indicators, the Singapore economy has been an enormous success story. In 2013, gross domestic product (GDP) per capita adjusted by purchasing power parity for Singapore stood at US$62,427 placing it as the third highest in the world. This compared favorably to the other three East Asian newly industrialized economies (NIEs) of Hong Kong (US$52,686), Taiwan (US$39,579), and South Korea (US$33,155) which ranked 7th, 19th and 25th, respectively (IMF, 2013).

The Singaporean economy has been and still is enjoying close to full employment since the early 1970s with a broad-based expansion of the economy. Over the past three decades, more jobs were being created than the local workforce could absorb. Hence, by 2012, the foreign workforce in the country peaked at 1.2683 million, of which a quarter were blue collar employees and the remaining three quarters were white collar employees (Singapore Ministry of Manpower, 2014).

While Singapore has been doing well in terms of cross-country per capita income comparisons and in terms of overall employment growth, it has been a laggard when it

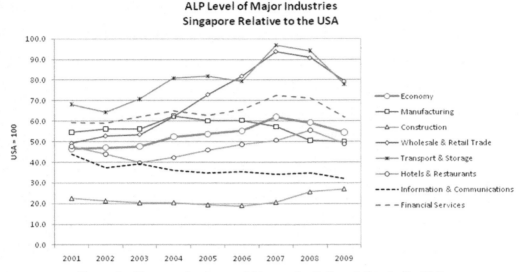

Figure 1. Singapore's average labor productivity relative to the U.S.

comes to labor productivity. For decades, the city state's performance in terms of labor productivity has been a subject of contention, which underlines the need to understand the dynamics of its trends in this rather poor productivity performance. In fact, the average labor productivity of the Singapore economy over the last decade (2001–2009) relative to the United States (U.S.) stands at about 53% (see Fig. 1). The average productivity in sectors such as construction, information and communication, and hotel and restaurants are below the economy's average at 22%, 36% and 47%, respectively.

Four sectors which are subject to international competition, viz. transport and storage, wholesale and retail trade, financial services, trade and manufacturing, tend to have productivity performances which are above the economy's average at 79%, 71%, 64% and 56%, respectively. While productivity growth has been modest in these sectors, it is clear from the data that there is still considerable room for improvement in productivity performances. Further, the concern about modest productivity growth appears to be far more serious for small and medium enterprises (SMEs) than multinational corporations (MNCs) which compete effectively in international markets and tend to be much more efficient and well organized.

Adding to this structural concern has been the fact that Singapore was affected severely by the global financial crisis (GFC) which had a detrimental impact on productivity. Following the GFC, the government swiftly set up the Economic Strategies Committee (ESC) to examine issues at stake, identify problems and make policy recommendations to boost productivity. To be sure, the ESC (2010) suggested the following initiatives to enhance productivity:

> Achieving 2–3% growth per year in productivity — which would raise our productivity by one third over the next 10 years — will

require a major, qualitative transformation of our economy. It cannot be done in one move, and the results will take time to materialize, but we have to start now and vigorously pursue changes in the following key areas: Deepen skills and expertise within every sector of our economy; restructure our economy, to provide more room for rapidly growing and more efficient enterprises; expand abroad and capture new growth activities in order to grow high-value added activities in Singapore (p. 5).

In view of the uphill task in driving productivity, the Singapore Business Federation (SBF) proposed to lower the annual national productivity target from 2% to 3% range to 1–2% range (see Singapore Business Federation, 2012, p. 12). The SBF pointed out that Singapore's economy, having been subject to decades of upgrading, is near the peak of its efficiency and productivity performance and would therefore find it difficult to raise productivity by a significant margin. However, we think such a comment is at variance with facts. In fact, businesses may be too quick to push the panic button, give up too easily in the productivity drive and treat the productivity concept too simply (see Tan and Tan, 2012). Problems of low productivity, especially those of SMEs tend to be structural in nature, with business activities fluctuating over business cycles and having long gestation periods in up-skill programs. Thus productivity enhancements need time to be carried through and cannot be achieved overnight. In fact the national annual productivity target of 2–3% range set by ESC is meant to be achieved over the decade by 2020. So how likely are we to achieve the longer-term annual national productivity target then?

In Sec. 2, we try to conjecture the root causes of poor productivity performance especially since 2000 when the growth of foreign workforce accelerated in the midst of a resilient economy growing close to the potential GDP growth rate of 5.5% between 1998 and 2008. We shall also appraise the core strategies of enhancing international competitiveness through examining the wages-productivity-competitiveness (WPC) nexus. In Sec. 3, we identify the sources of GDP growth and simulate with optimistic, pessimistic and baseline scenarios pertaining to Singapore's potential GDP which the economy can achieve given the level of productivity required, based on three employment-growth assumptions. Considering that low labor productivity in Singapore is a phenomenon particular to SMEs, Sec. 4 re-evaluates the performance, challenges and opportunities for SMEs. We also suggest several policy strategies as to how SMEs can synergize and be more competitive. The final section concludes the chapter.

2. Enhancing International Competitiveness Through Wages-Productivity-Competitiveness (WPC) Nexus

Productivity improvement is paramount to Singapore's future economic competitiveness. This is especially so in light of an ageing population and limited increases to factors of production such as land, capital and labor which Singapore is experiencing. Productivity gains enable an economy to produce more goods and services using the same amount of inputs and are the only route to quality and sustainable economic development in the long-run. It requires the monitoring and improvement of national productivity capabilities in order to ensure higher and sustainable wage growth through strengthening the supply side of the economy.

Lim (2012a) put forward a "Shock Therapy Proposal" (STP) intended to close the widening income gap in Singapore and reduce its dependence on foreign workers, consequently also inducing an enhancement in the productivity of local workforce. His main proposal has been for those earning below US$1500 a month to get a pay rise of 15% in the first year, a further 15% in the second year and another 20% rise in the third year of the restructuring. Over the same period, his plan has called for a wage freeze for those earning above US$15,000 a month. Those people falling in between would get an annual pay rise of around 4–5%. In defending this drastic round of wage restructuring in Singapore, Lim (2012a) argued that the first round of the high wage policy in restructuring the Singapore economy from 1979 to 1981 had been quite successful which formed the basis for this second round of restructuring. However, other analysts have pointed out that the high wage policy could have contributed to the recession in 1985 by pushing wages beyond productivity and resulted in a serious loss of international competitiveness (Singapore Economic Committee, 1986).[1] In response to STP, Lim (2012b) of the National Trade Unions Congress (NTUC) came up with NTUC–National Wages Council (NWC) hybrid which advocates a continued upgrading and matching of skills, as well as redesigning job contents while maintaining the long standing strategy of NWC that wage growth should lag productivity growth.

Singapore's highly open labor market is characterized by "one market-two remuneration extremes" as a result of international competition both at the top tier and at the bottom tier with the middle being further split in between the two with challenging consequences (Goh, 1980). As Fig. 2 shows, ideally Singaporeans would like to move steadily and directly from Quadrant A, exhibiting *low wage-low productivity stalemate* towards the *high wage-high productivity of inclusive competitiveness*, or Quadrant D. The thrust of STP amounts to moving from the current Quadrant A directly to the Quadrant B (*i.e., high wage-low productivity hybrid*) which hopefully would reach Quadrant D. In contrast, the core of the NTUC–NWC Hybrid aims to move from Quadrant A to Quadrant C (*i.e., low wage-high productivity hybrid*) and eventually arrive at Quadrant D.

A case in point is the experience of several crisis-hit European economies which have faced a classic case of loss in competitiveness as in Quadrant B or the high wage-low productivity trap (see Rajan *et al.*, 2014). In a competitive globalized world, this is

---

[1] Empirical work has suggested that while wage increase above productivity has led to a loss in international competitiveness during the early 1980s, the strong exchange rate and the global downturn in the electronics cycle in 1984 as well as the regional slowdown also contributed to the severity of the decline in 1985 (see Singapore Economic Committee, 1986; Tan *et al.*, 2013).

WAGES

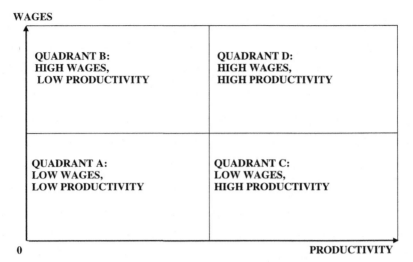

Figure 2. Wages-productvity nexus.

not sustainable as wages are sticky downward with union leaders whose immediate objective tends to be wage maximization rather than job protection.

On the one hand, Quadrant A or the low-wage-low-productivity stalemate Singapore is experiencing currently for some blue collar workforce is another classic case of labor market failure distorted by abundant supply of cheap foreign workforce in a number of industries which minimized incentive for employers to drive productivity. On the other hand, employees are understandably reluctant or unable to put in their best performance given the poor effort-remuneration wage structure. Such a structure has led to productive local workforce tending to shun those industries because *stagnated low wages* are unmatched by the *rising cost of living*.

However, the Quadrant C — as suggested by NTUC–NWC — may not be sufficient either, as upgrading skills tend to take a longer time to materialize. Further, the current manpower policies on foreign workers who are abundant in supply tend to suppress wages of indigenous blue collar workers unless and until a coordinated government effort to fine-tune the inflow on foreign workers by sector happens. Indeed, there is a facilitative role for the government which can be activated to correct labor market failure.

For its part, the Singapore government has understood the need for activist labor market policies selectively. For instance, the Workfare Income Supplement (WIS) Scheme established in 2007 is supposed to encourage indigenous blue collar workers to stay in the job through wage subsidies.[2] Another example would be the Wage Credit Scheme (WCS) established in 2013 with the aim to help employers to mitigate wage costs especially during a weak economy so as to protect jobs.[3] However,

---

[2] See http://mycpf.cpf.gov.sg/Members/Gen-Info/WIS/WIS_Scheme.htm for more details on the WIS scheme.
[3] See http://www.iras.gov.sg/irashome/WCS.aspx for more details on the WCS.

these government initiatives are still unsatisfactory as they have no direct linkages to productivity and have posed a heavy state burden to say the least. Based on Singapore Budget Statement (2013), S$3.6 billion has been allocated for the WCS over a period of three years, while the WIS scheme will cost S$650 million per year. The WIS and WCS programs are much needed by Singaporeans in their late 40s and early 50s who have had only limited opportunities for post-secondary education during the 1970s and 1980s when Singapore possessed limited financial resources. These groups of indigenous workforce, who are mainly employed in the goods producing industries, have been faced with *skill mismatches* and *skill obsolescence* exacerbated by rapid globalization.[4]

Conversely, as Singapore's economy has continued to restructure, over the last decade (2003–2012), value added in goods producing industries has declined from 33% to 29%, while value added in services providing industries has steadily increased from 63% to 69% (Yearbook of Statistics Singapore, 2009, 2013). Since the latter industries are less amenable to automation and other labor-saving technological improvements, Singapore needs a relatively bigger labor force over-time as the economy gravitates towards maturity with both resident and non-resident blue and white collar workers.

Thus, Singapore is faced with the dual conundrum of expanding the workforce by bringing in non-residents to ensure the economy continues to restructure as a means of sustained growth in the global economy, while simultaneously managing the persistent and growing low-wage indigenous workforce.

3. GDP and Average Labor Productivity Growth Projections: 2009–2019

Having discussed Singapore's low average labor productivity growth to date, this section performs a growth accounting exercise in order to project GDP and labor productivity growth for Singapore under some assumptions for the period 2009–2019.

The sources of GDP growth can be summarized by the following accounting decomposition (i):

$$\Delta \ln Y = \bar{\nu}_{K_{ict}} \Delta \ln K_{ict} + \bar{\nu}_{K_{nict}} \Delta \ln K_{nict} + \bar{\nu}_L \Delta \ln H + \bar{\nu}_L \Delta \ln L_Q + \Delta \ln A,$$

K denotes contribution of capital input including ICT capital and non-ICT capital. L denotes contribution of labor input based on hours worked and labor quality differentiation. A is contribution of total factor productivity (TFP) growth.

---

[4] Another proposal to enhance productivity and help lower income workers is that of a minimum wage policy (MWP). Such a policy has gained popularity in many countries in recent times. However, the MWP, once legislated, cannot discriminate against non-Singaporeans. Foreign workers would have to be paid at the minimum wage according to Singapore's cost of living even if their productivity is lower and are prepared to accept a much lower wage. The MWP in fact amounts to equating cost of living between Singapore and those cheaper neighboring countries which would result in potential erosion of government revenues from foreign workers' levies that can be gainfully deployed to improve the well-being of Singaporeans through a further productivity drive.

Sources of labor productivity growth can be categorized by the following growth decomposition (ii):

$$\Delta \ln y = \bar{\nu}_{K_{ict}} \Delta \ln k_{ict} + \bar{\nu}_{K_{nict}} \Delta \ln k_{nict} + \bar{\nu}_L \Delta \ln L_Q + \Delta \ln A.$$

K constitutes contribution of capital deepening including ICT capital and non-ICT capital. L is contribution of labor quality and A denotes contribution of TFP growth (see Jorgenson and Khuong, 2010; Vu, 2013). Thus, policy strategies to promote GDP growth consist of labor productivity growth plus employment expansion. Typically labor productivity should account for over 60% of GDP growth.

In promoting labor productivity growth, we can differentiate between *hard workers* versus *smart workers*, i.e.,:

$$\text{Labor productivity} = \text{VA/EMP} = (\text{VA/OR})*(\text{OR/EMP}).$$

Improvements in value-added (VA) over operating revenue (OR) which focusses on value creation and shift towards higher value-added activities are done by workers who work smarter. Management effort to maximize OR over employment (EMP) requires greater worker perspiration by squeezing hard on dollar per employee.

We conducted simulation exercises by assuming a certain level of employment, labor share, TFP, labor and capital quality growth and econometrically we have simulated three medium-term GDP growth scenarios achievable with various required productivity growth targets. We thus projected GDP and growth for the period 2009–2019 using the following model:

$$\Delta \ln y = \left(\frac{1 - \bar{\nu}_L}{\bar{\nu}_L}\right) \Delta \ln K_Q + \left(\frac{1 - \bar{\nu}_L}{\bar{\nu}_L}\right) \tau + \Delta \ln L_Q + \left(\frac{1}{\bar{\nu}_L}\right) \Delta \ln A.$$

Based on the actual economic performance over the period 1998–2008, we have simulated the associated GDP growth band and productivity target for pessimistic, optimistic and the base case scenarios which we perceive to most likely prevail during the period 2009–2019 as shown in Table 1. By making certain assumptions on employment growth, TFP growth, capital accumulation enhancement, labor and capital

Table 1. Projection of GDP and growth, 2009–2019: Assumptions and results.

	Actual 1998–2008	Pessimistic scenario	Base case	Optimistic scenario	Remarks
Labor share	0.532	0.532^	0.532^	0.532^	^Assumed
Labor quality growth (%)	1.24	1.00^	1.24^	1.50^	^Assumed
Capital accumulation enhancement	0.08	0.08^	0.25^	0.50^	^Assumed
Capital quality growth (%)	0.29	0.18^	0.29^	0.40^	^Assumed
Total factor productivity (TFP) growth (%)	0.51	0.30^	0.51^	0.70^	^Assumed
Employment growth (%)	2.92	1.00	1.50	2.00	^Assumed
Productivity growth (%)	2.52	1.79*	2.67*	3.61*	*Projected
GDP growth (%)	5.45	2.79*	4.17*	5.61*	*Projected

Note: ^Denotes assumptions made and *denotes projected values.

quality growth, we are able to simulate the various productivity growth scenarios which are associated with the corresponding GDP growth projections.

For the period 2009–2019, under the base case scenario, Singapore's GDP growth is expected to average at 4.17% per annum which requires productivity growth of 2.67%. Such outcomes are to be achieved with slower employment growth of 1.5%, much slower than the 2.92% over the 1998–2008. We assumed capital deepening over time from 0.08 to 0.25, *ceteris paribus*.

Under the optimistic scenario, Singapore's average GDP growth over the same period would reach 5.61% which requires productivity growth of 3.61%. Such a performance will be achieved with employment growth of 2%, faster than the base case scenario but slower than the actual growth in 1998–2008. Under this scenario, we assumed higher quality in both labor and capital growth, higher capital accumulation enhancement and TFP. Under the pessimistic scenario, Singapore's average GDP growth over the same period would be 2.8% which requires a lower productivity growth of 1.8% with much slower employment growth of 1% with worsening quality in labor, capital, and TFP.

4. Focus on Small and Medium Enterprises

4.1. *Early bias towards GLCs and MNCs*

Early industrialization policies in Singapore focussed on attracting MNCs to promote economic growth and job creation were dictated by political considerations and economic circumstances when Singapore first gained independence. Hence favorable business and physical environments were created and incentives were being awarded for MNCs. The non-level playing field prevailed for SMEs which were far less competitive and efficient in contrast to MNCs with vast international networking and economies of scale.

The government's attempt in the early stage of nationhood building to recruit the best of the manpower cohort each year into the public services with better remuneration and stable job security was in direct competition with the private sector. This relentless effort to seek out the ablest did creamed off and stifled potential entrepreneurs and to a great extent stifle development of SMEs. Consequently the current batch of successful Singaporean entrepreneurs are relatively less academically qualified or inclined and may not have found good job openings into the elite civil service or with MNCs.

Due to constraints of resources with competing funding for development projects, the government rightly decided to put precious financial resources into developing infrastructural investments such as airports and seaports instead of more universities and polytechnics. From 1960s to 1980s, the relatively fewer vacancies from institutes of higher learning had given rise to a poor education profile, low technical contents and rudimentary management skills for the indigenous labor force.

The Singapore's government-linked companies (GLCs) also intervened to retain and promote industries which are of "strategic interests" such as banking, ports, air and sea liners, since SMEs were perceived to be unlikely to deliver such objectives. However, such well-intended initiatives grew with bureaucratic rules which snow-balled into wholesale dominance of GLCs which further dwarfed the development of SMEs.

However, with the Singaporean economy becoming more open over the decades and total trade amounting to nearly three times of its GDP, coupled with shortening of global business cycles, the vulnerability of the Singaporean economy in terms of volatility in employment generation and external demand has also risen. This has led the government to appreciate the cushioning effect of SMEs in terms of employment in times of economic distress as their workforce tends to be family-based or closely knitted.

4.2. *Recognition of importance of SMEs*

SPRING Singapore (a government agency) suggested that SMEs currently employing 70% of the total Singapore workforce consist of 99.4% of total business entities. SMEs constitute more than 50% of Singapore's value added GDP and that 48% of total SMEs' revenues are derived overseas, reflecting greater internationalization (Straits Times, 2012). The relatively lower productivity or even stagnation of productivity by SMEs (Singapore National Employers Federation, 2010) in comparison to MNCs are likely due to weaknesses in management capability, inefficiency in provision of services and organization of production processes.

The low productivity of SMEs also reflects a certain degree of the non-level playing field in terms of company size since workers are usually reluctant to join SMEs due to limited career prospect unless being compensated with higher remuneration. Fur-thermore, during boom times when things are good, SMEs tend to find themselves short-handed to send employees for productivity training. Similarly, during recessions, when business activities are down, SMEs find themselves being financially constrained to afford staff for skill upgrading hence resulting in a market failure in correcting for productivity mismatch through competition.

Indeed, in recognition of the importance of SMEs, the government-convened ESC came up with a proposal for further economic diversification and resiliency, which actually contained specific strategies on SMEs (ESC, 2010). They include (a) seizing growth opportunities when external environments are favorable so as to ensure sus-tainable budgetary position; (b) developing a vibrant SME sector and globally com-petitive companies as economic restructuring continues; (c) attracting and rooting MNCs and global SMEs for diversification drive and quality employment creation for professionals, managers, executives, and technicians (PMETs); (d) growing knowledge capital to serve as a global information hub and forming a critical mass for innovation, research and development; (e) making Singapore a leading cosmopolitan and liveable city which would ensure her continued relevance and attraction of talents; (f) fostering inclusive growth by growing inclusivity through a renewed social contract and forging national consensus; and (g) ensuring energy resilience and environmental friendliness growth, and finally rationalizing and maximizing value from land as a scarce resource.

In recent annual Budget Statements, more generous funding was made available to support SMEs as part of the explicit policies adopted by the ESC (2010) to identify and nurture 1000 Singapore enterprises with revenues over US$100 million. While the previous official support system to SMEs was far too dispersed to be effective as the SMEs had to deal with many government agencies including statutory boards and ministries, currently all issues pertaining to SMEs including productivity, internationalization of activities and innovation in research and development have been brought under one roof under the umbrella of SPRING Singapore, a statutory board being super-headed to deal with SMEs. Efforts to improve management and leadership upgrading for professional managers, executive and technicians (PMETs) are also being undertaken by the Workforce Development Agency (WDA).

The importance of the Jurong Town Council (JTC) which allocates land and factory landlords cannot be understated as the non-wage components of unit business cost (UBC) such as land cost, rental, fees and charges must be constantly monitored. Businesses tend to treat these costs as given and inevitably there is a squeeze on wage costs. In addition, as the manufacturing share of GDP would no doubt be declining over time, the mission must be revised accordingly to cater to SMEs in services and not just be limited to manufacturing activities.

Beyond survival, in order to ensure that SMEs actually thrive, coordinating efforts amongst government agencies such as International Enterprise (IE) Singapore to help SMEs in international network, marketing and branding are crucial. In addition, having Economic Development Board (EDB) as the middleman to link MNCs and SMEs to invest in a third destination such as Batam in Indonesia and Iskandar in Malaysia are important initiatives.

5. Concluding Remarks

While Singapore's economic performance since the 1970s has been stellar, as the country matures, there are growing concerns of rising income inequality as well as stagnating labor productivity, especially among SMEs. Incremental productivity improvement can be achieved by increasing output per worker and transformational improvement can be achieved by increasing value per output unit. The former approach denotes a red ocean strategy of seeking improvements subject to the physical limitation of a worker as compared to the latter approach which signifies a blue ocean strategy of researching for higher value-added within an output unit.

For promoting growth, one can adopt the transformation approach to boost productivity growth which involves fostering the enabling factors and renewing firm-level strategies. To promote the enabling factors, one can employ human and financial capital so as to stimulate higher value-added activities, support industries with cluster formation and updating information technology. In renewing firm-level strategies, one can introduce higher value-added products and be exposed to higher value technology and penetrate higher end market segments with entrepreneurship and risk taking behavior.

Most would share the concern of the dangers of widening income disparity as well as the plight of the low income earners, whose real wages may have been suppressed or would have been higher if not due to the competitive pressure from the excessive inflow of foreign workers. However, there are many approaches to address these pertinent issues, and the wage restructuring proposal is but one of the many ways of achieving inclusive growth.

It is important to bear in mind that populist public policies, however well intended, could have unintended consequences which in turn could cause market distortions that will be costly and take years if not decades to reverse. The government should resolutely resist the increasing pressure of being pushed toward the slippery road of welfare state which is least sustainable in the longer-run, especially for a small and resource-poor economy such as Singapore. There are various models of welfare state models with dissimilar features (see Puss *et al.*, 2010; Heckman, 2008). However, Singapore is unique and being a small, nimble and highly open economy, the country is unlikely to fit into any of the major four welfare state models, viz. the Nordic, Continental, Mediterranean, or Anglo-Saxon type.

The government must instead continue to pro-actively play the facilitative role of addressing labor market failure through the annual budgetary measures in the form of targeted special transfers to avoid wasting of precious financial resources when subsidising up-skill training programs. With further fine-tuning of the WIS, WCS and the recent introduction of Productivity and Innovation Credit (PIC) Scheme which is to promote production upgrading (see Singapore Annual Budget Statements, 2014), labor market failure and productivity stagnation stalemate can be effectively addressed.

The paramount role of the government must be to ensure continuing economic restructuring, diligently monitor unit business costs, and most of all, to constantly ensure social mobility so as to safeguard against emergence of economic underclass or permanent underclass. We thus have the following four suggestions for consideration which would be executed under the proposed establishment of a high level bi-annual national WPC Taskforce:

(i) Evaluate the social profile and constraints of low wage Singaporeans and the emerging economic underclass.

(ii) Better understand industry-specific manpower issues, business difficulties, labor market requirements, and expectations.

(iii) Explain and educate the public at large on the urgency of productivity drive, international labor market competition, and improved work discipline.

(iv) Ensuring industrial internship as an integral part of the education curriculum for all Singaporeans at tertiary and technical institutions.

References

Economic Strategies Committee (ESC) (2010). High skilled people, innovative economy and distinctive global city. Report of the ESC, February.

Goh, KS (1980). Partners in progress. Delivered at the Pre-U Seminar on Trade Unions in Singapore, at Nanyang University Auditorium, 20 June.

Heckman, J (2008), The viability of the welfare state. Mimeo, World Justice Forum, Vienna, 3 July.

International Monetary Fund (2013). World economic outlook database, October 2013, IMF, Washington DC.

Jorgenson, D and K Vu (2010). Potential growth of the world economy. *Journal of Policy Modelling*, 32, 615–631.

Lim, CY (2012a). Shock therapy II revisited. Address to the Economic Society of Singapore, 9 April.

Lim, SS (2012b). Wage proposal by ex-NWC chief poses future risks: Lim Swee Say. Channel News Asia. Retrieved 21, May 2014, available at http://news.xin.msn.com/en/singapore/article.aspx?cp-documentid=6126330, last accessed on 13 April 2012.

Puss, T, M Viies and R Maldre (2010). EU-12 countries in the context of European social model types. *International Business & Economics Research Journal*, 9, December.

Rajan, RS, KG Tan and KY Tan (2014). *Fiscal Sustainability and Competitiveness in Europe and Asia*. Palgrave Macmillan (Forthcoming).

Singapore Business Federation (2012). Position paper on population, available at http://www.sbf.org.sg/download/docs/sbfinews/pressroom/Position Paper on Population Final2012Dec.pdf.

Singapore Budget Statement (2013). A better Singapore: Quality growth, an inclusive society. Delivered in Singapore Parliament, by Tharman Shanmugaratnam, 25 February 2013.

Singapore Budget Statement (2014). Opportunities for the future, assurance for our seniors. Delivered in Singapore Parliament, by Tharman Shanmugaratnam, 5 March 2014.

Singapore Economic Committee (1986). The Singapore economy: New directions: Report of the economic committee. Ministry of Trade & Industry, Singapore.

Singapore Ministry of Manpower (2014). Foreign workforce numbers. Retrieved 21 May 2014, available at http://www.mom.gov.sg/statistics-publications/others/statistics/Pages/Foreign-WorkforceNumbers.aspx.

Singapore National Employers Federation (2010). SME 21. Retrieved 21 May 2014, available at http://www.sgemployers.com/public/industry/sme21.jsp.

Straits Times (2012). Developing more future-ready SMEs. *The Straits Times*. Singapore, 8 December.

Tan, KG and KY Tan (2012). More productive economy still needed. *The Straits Times*. Singapore, 12 June.

Tan, KG, L Low, KY Tan and L Lim (2013). Annual analysis of competitiveness, development strategies and public policies on ASEAN-10:2000-2010. Pearson Education South Asia.

Vu, K (2013). Information and communication technology (ICT) and Singapore's economic growth. *Information Economics and Policy*, 25, 284–300.

Yearbook of Statistics Singapore (2009). Department of Statistics, Ministry of Trade & Industry, Republic of Singapore, Singapore.

Yearbook of Statistics Singapore (2013). Department of Statistics, Ministry of Trade & Industry, Republic of Singapore, Singapore.

Chapter 7

Determinants of Entrepreneurs' Activities: New Evidence from Cross-Country Data

Doaa M. Salman

Faculty of Management Sciences,
Modern Sciences and Arts University, Egypt

Abstract

This chapter provides an empirical investigation of the main determinants of entrepreneurial activities across three groups of countries over the period 2004–2008, by specifically examining the importance of institutional setting and economic growth on entrepreneurial activities. The classification of countries is based on the Economic Freedom Index and the World Economic Forum (2011) which groups them on the basis of whether they are innovation-driven, efficiency-driven, or factor-driven countries. On the one hand, empirical results find a positive and significant role for economic freedom to accelerate entrepreneurial activities and growth in innovation and efficiency-driven countries characterized by strong institutional systems. On the other hand, the results suggest that in factor-driven countries characterized by relatively less economic freedom and weak institutions, there is a significant negative relationship between economic freedom and entrepreneurial activities.

Keywords: Economic freedom; growth; investment; unemployment; entrepreneurial activities.

1. Introduction

The debate regarding the relationship between economic freedom and entrepreneurial activities (EA) has generated a vast theoretical and empirical literature in recent years. Traditional scholars relate EA to small businesses and they emphasize the role they play in accelerating economic growth. Somewhat more recently, scholars have been more concerned with exploring the differences across countries and the reasons behind these differences (Schmitz, 1989; Grossman and Helpman, 1994; Barro and Sala-i-Martin, 1995). Among other things, the interactions between the entrepreneurship, trade and recent innovative investments have led researchers to explore the role that entrepreneurship plays in stimulating and generating economic growth (Jovanovic, 1982; Audretsch, 1995; Cohen and Klepper, 1996).

While studies have tried to explain the role of EA as an engine of economic growth, only a handful of studies have been undertaken to analyse the differences across countries and over time. Some countries attract entrepreneurs while others prevent them from starting up any business. However, the relationship between entrepreneurship and economic freedom in general and growth in particular has largely been missing in the empirical studies and related literature. This chapter's contribution is based on assessing the impact of institutions in general and economic freedom in particular on EA for a panel of 49 countries spanning 2004–2008. The classification of countries is based on Economic Freedom Index and the World Economic Forum (2011) which groups them on the basis of whether they are innovation-driven, or efficiency-driven, or factor-driven countries.[1]

The aim of this chapter is to provide insights regarding the impact of sound robust institutions in spurring EA. The remainder of the chapter is structured as follows. Section 2 presents the link between EA, economic freedom and growth. Section 3 describes the empirical model and discusses the results. Section 4 concludes with the main findings and proposes a set of policy recommendations for countries targeting to boost EA.

2. Literature Review

The multiple impacts of entrepreneurship on growth, employment, standard of living, innovation and capital accumulation have attracted numerous researchers to explore these links. This section traces the role of the entrepreneurship and how it has evolved over time, giving rise to a variety of theories. It starts by defining entrepreneurship, followed by a brief overview of the theories.

2.1. Defining entrepreneurship and its links to growth

Entrepreneurship is studied in the relevant literature at both the micro-level, i.e., at the level of the individual firm or entrepreneur, and at the macro-level. In 1934, Schumpeter introduced entrepreneurship as an agent of growth, which through the process of innovation, brought about social change and economic development. Furthermore, he distinguished between five manifestations of entrepreneurship, "a new product, a new method of production, a new market, a new source of supply of intermediate goods, and a new organization". Schumpeter's definition therefore equated entrepreneurship with innovation in the small business sense; that is identifying market opportunities and using innovative approaches to exploit them.

Defining entrepreneurship as a small firm might be somewhat misleading as large firms might exhibit entrepreneurial and innovative traits. To that end, an alternative classification emerged based on Wennekers and Thurik (1999) who differentiated between three types of entrepreneurs. The first type are the "Schumpeterian entrepreneurs" who mainly operate in small, independent firms; second are the "Intrapreneurs" who are the innovators and the creative leaders gaining their advantage from

---

[1] Economic freedom index is an indicator provided by Freedom House, organization, Heritage Foundation and the Fraser Institute to monitor worldwide Economic freedom. They have provided for each country a specific rating. A scale from 0 to 100 to evaluate the 10 Economic Freedom factors consist of four main categories; those categories are rule of law, limited government, regulatory efficiency and open markets.

creative destruction; and third are the managerial business owners who focus on the coordination of production and distribution across economic activities.

Later, endogenous growth models highlighted the importance of knowledge as a determinant of economic growth, while the new class of endogenous growth models pioneered by Romer (1990) identified some attributes of entrepreneurship by modeling the process of innovation and deriving the motives for innovation from the microeconomic level.

In parallel with the endogenous growth literature, Porter (1990) provided a modern rendition of Rostow's (1960) stages of growth model by identifying three stages of development: (1) a factor-driven stage, (2) an efficiency-driven stage, and (3) an innovation-driven stage. The factor-driven stage is characterized by high rates of agricultural self-employment. Countries in this stage compete through low-cost efficiencies in the production of commodities or low value-added products. Almost all countries have experienced this stage. To reach the second stage, the efficiency-driven stage, countries must increase their production efficiency and educate the workforce to be able to adapt in the subsequent technological development phase. In the efficiency-stage, countries are characterized by efficient productive practices in large markets that allow firms to exploit economies of scale. In the final stage, countries are characterized by sound economic policies and qualified labor which allow them to deepen the EA and increase entry density through creating more competitive advantages.

In the last two decades, the knowledge and information revolution has renewed theoretical thinking linking entrepreneurship to growth with new theories emerging from the field of industrial evolution or evolutionary economics (Baumol, 1990, 1993; Jovanovic, 1982; Audretsch, 1995). The evolutionary economics literature views entrepreneurs as agents of change who bring new ideas to markets and accelerate growth through a process of competitive firm selection. Wennekers and Thurik (1999) showed that the general innovative role of entrepreneurs included not only newness (implementing inventions), but also new entry (start-ups and entry into new markets).

2.2. Growth and entrepreneurship: Empirical literature

Empirical studies on entrepreneurship and its relationship to economic growth are relatively recent. Most empirical studies focus primarily on a single aspect of entrepreneurship as it is difficult from an operational point of view to fully encompass the totality of EA on growth. Acs *et al.* (1994) report that a majority of Organization for Economic Cooperation and Development (OECD) countries witnessed an increase in the self employment rates during the 1970s and 1980s. Since the 1990s, the rate of business ownership has been rising as a reliable measure. For instance, the entrepreneur is often defined as one who starts his/her own, new and small business at his/her own risk.

Later, in a cross-sectional study of 23 OECD member countries covering the period 1984–1994, Wennekers and Thurik (1999) provided empirical evidence for the role of entrepreneurship (measured by business ownership rates) to be associated with higher rates of employment growth at the country level. Moreover, Carree and Thurik (1999), followed by Audretsch *et al.* (2002) concluded that in OECD countries, there is evidence that higher rates of entrepreneurship accelerate growth rates and lower un-employment.

Audretsch and Fritsch (2002) provide new results from studying 74 (West) German countries during the period 1986 till 1998 and present three key findings. First, they confirm that the start-up rates in the 1980s are not found to be related to employment change. However, in the 1990s, those regions with higher start-up rates experienced higher employment growth. They also find that regions with high start-up rates in the 1980s had high employment growth in the 1990s. There is further evidence of an increase in self-employment in many OECD countries. For example in the United Kingdom, the number of self employed as a portion of the total labor force increased from 7.8% in 1972 to 10.5% in 2000, and in the United States this fraction increased from 8% to 10% in the same period (Van Stel, 2003).

Entrepreneurs are defined as those who initiate activities; however they are individuals or groups of people who aim at initiating economic enterprise in the formal sector under a legal form of business. Entrepreneurship can therefore manifest itself in a number of ways, one of which is innovation. Salgado-Banda (2005) measured innovative entrepreneurship using quality adjusted patent data. He concluded that a positive influence on growth could be asserted for the 22 OECD countries over the period of 1975–1998.

Another set of studies have commonly used business start-up rates as a proxy for measuring entrepreneurship (Klapper and Quesada Delgado, 2007; Naude, 2008). Acs and Armington (2004) used regional data for the United States during 1989 through 1996 to link entrepreneurship to growth using new firm birth rate as a proxy for EA. Results show that higher levels of EA were significantly and positively linked to higher economic growth rates. Their findings suggest that new firms may have a stronger effect in creating new jobs than what was found in previous studies. Creating jobs can be directly linked to economic growth and supporting EA is a powerful force driving innovation, productivity, job creation and economic growth. The effect of EA on economic growth thus depends upon the level of per capita income and economic growth.

In summary, the evidence to date generally points to a significant and positive relationship between new firm formation, economic growth, and employment creation.

2.3. *Determinants of entrepreneurial activities*

There are several potential determinants of entrepreneurship that span a wide range of theories; this wide spectrum of approaches point to the overlapping roles of an entrepreneur. There has been relatively little work on how institutional factors influence EA. Entrepreneurship determinants at the macro level are explained by demand side determinants (named push factors), representing technological developments, the industrial structure of the economy, government regulation, and the stage of development (Wennekers and Thurik, 1999). The supply side determinants (named pull factors), represent demographic characteristics such as population, the income levels, educational attainment, unemployment level, cultural norms, access to finance, and the degree of taxation.

The literature differentiates between the levels of analysis; for instance, at the micro level, the focal point is on the decision-making process by individuals to become self employed (Reynolds *et al.*, 1999; Blanchflower and Oswald, 1998). A number of other studies have also considered the cyclical aspects of self-employment and especially how movements of self-employment are linked with movements in unemployment. Blanchflower and Oswald (1998) found a strong negative relationship between regional unemployment and self-employment for the period 1983–1989 in the UK. A study by Blanchflower (2000) using a panel data of 23 countries for the period of 1966–1996 found that the level of education has a negative effect on the probability of an individual being self-employed. They reasoned that this was because highly educated people may not be willing to be risk-takers. This result is supported by Van der Sluis *et al.* (2005) using a meta-analysis during the period 1980 till 2003. In contrast, Reynolds *et al.* (1999) have outlined why education is vital for entrepreneurship. First, education provides individuals with the necessary skills and qualifications. Second, education creates awareness for career alternatives. Third, education provides knowledge that can be used by individuals to develop opportunities.

Similarly, the impact of unemployment on EA is ambiguous. Storey (1991) attributes this ambiguity to the methodology employed in the studies. He found a positive relation between unemployment and the decision to start a new business in time series studies and a negative relation in cross-sectional or pooled cross-sectional studies during the period 1975 till 1988. Evan and Leighton (1990) provided empirical evidence for the United States and found a relationship between the increased possibility of starting a new business and workers who lost their jobs.

Adding to the previous determinants, income and wealth have been found to have significant impact on EA. For instance, Ilmakunnas *et al.* (1999) used cross-country panel data on 20 OECD countries for 1978, 1983, 1988, and 1993 to test the relation between income disparity and self-employment and provide evidence for a positive relationship.

The foregoing overview suggests several immediate determinants of entrepreneurship. In addition to the previously mentioned determinants, institutions are often perceived as a major determinant of economic growth. North (1990) provided evidence of the explicit relation between economic growth and the entrepreneur in the context of the institutional framework. Accordingly, Baumol (1993) emphasized the institution's role in encouraging productive entrepreneurship, which can be identified as a primary source of economic growth and is responsible for the creation of additional output.

Bjørnskov and Foss (2008) test the relation between entrepreneurship and economic freedom across 29 developed, developing, and transition countries during 2001 using Global Entrepreneurship Monitor data. In addition to finding that the relation between the size of government and EA is negatively correlated, the study also concluded that institutional features, such as size of the government, the degree of administrative complexity, the tax system, the intellectual property rights regime, the level of trust, corruption, and availability of finance capital can affect the level of entrepreneurship in a country.

Bureaucracy costs and regulations could also affect EA, and in a study of OECD countries for the period 2003 and 2004, Fonseca *et al.* (2001) found that fewer individuals become entrepreneurs when the start-up costs are higher. Related empirical studies find that well defined rules and regulations, well-protected rights, sound government, less corruption and an efficient judicial system promote entrepreneurship (Merck *et al.*, 2000; Johnson *et al.*, 2000, 2002; Boettke and Coyne, 2003; Acs and Virgill, 2010).

This chapter attempts to examine the main determinants of EA, especially the effect of economic freedom on EA. This chapter focuses on the main institutional and macroeconomic determinants affecting entrepreneurship using a dynamic panel model for a relatively short time dimension.

3. Empirical Model and Results

3.1. *Data and methodology*

The data used in this chapter are drawn from three different sources and are summarized in Table 1. First, the dependent variable is from the World Bank Group Entrepreneurship Survey (WBGES).[2] The WBGES covers 112 countries during the period between 2004 and 2009 and it provides cross-country data on new business registration and entry density. It is a useful measure to capture the quality of the institutional and regulatory environment facing entrepreneurs in the formal sector.

Following Klapper and Love (2011), the chapter employs the entry density indicator as a proxy for EA. It is calculated as the number of newly registered limited-liability firms in the corresponding year as a percentage of the country's working age population (ages 15–64), normalized by 1000. Table 1 summarizes the variables used in the estimation of the model, with their respective descriptive statistics.

Second, the independent variables are from Heritage Foundation and World Bank indicators which cover the data on macroeconomic and institutional determinants that may affect EA across countries. A country's overall economic freedom score is a

---

[2] Over the last decade, the World Bank has compiled different databases for the study of EA around the world from it WBGES. The data is available at: http://econ.worldbank.org/research/entrepreneurship.

Table 1. Variables with description and source.

Description of the variables used in the regression models		
Variables	Description	Source/database
Dependent		
EA	Entrepreneur activity	New businesses registered are the number of new limited liability corporations registered in the calendar year.	World Bank
Macroeconomic measures		
GDPC	GDP per capita (constant LCU)	GDP per capita is gross domestic product divided by midyear population. GDP at purchaser's prices is the sum of gross value added by all resident producers in the economy plus any product taxes and minus any subsidies not included in the value of the products. Data are in constant local currency.	World development Indicator
UNEMPL	Total (percent of total labor force)	Unemployment refers to the share of the labor force that is without work but available for and seeking employment.	
FDI	Foreign direct investment, net outflows (percent of GDP)	Foreign direct investment are the net inflows of investment to acquire a lasting management interest (10% or more of voting stock) in an enterprise operating in an economy other than that of the investor. It is the sum of equity capital, reinvestment of earnings, other long-term capital, and short-term capital as shown in the balance of payments. This series shows net outflows of investment from the reporting economy to the rest of the world and is divided by GDP.	
EFI	Overall economic freedom index	Economic freedom is the fundamental right of every human to control his or her own labor and property. In an economically free society, individuals are free to work, produce, consume, and invest in any way they please, with that freedom both protected by the state and unconstrained by the state. In economically free societies, governments allow labor, capital and goods to move freely, and refrain from coercion or constraint of liberty beyond the extent necessary to protect and maintain liberty itself.	Heritage Foundation

simple average of its scores on the 10 individual freedom indices from the Heritage Foundation. The economic freedom index (EFI) is individually scored on a scale of 0–100. The 10 indices are grouped into four broad categories: Rule of law (property rights, freedom from corruption); Government size (fiscal freedom, government spending); Regulatory efficiency (business freedom, labor freedom, monetary freedom) and Market openness (trade freedom, investment freedom, financial freedom). In this chapter, the stage of economic development is proxied using GDP per capita.

Several steps are employed in the selection of the sample used in the empirical analysis. As a first step, countries are grouped according to their level of economic freedom forming three groups representing 49 countries during the period 2004–2008. The first group consists of 15 countries that are characterized as being innovation-driven with scores in the EFI above 70%. The second group consists of 19 countries that are efficiency-driven with an EFI score ranging between 55% and 70%. Finally, the third group is a set of 15 factor-driven countries with a score less than 60% implying that they were less free in terms of economic freedom during the same period. The list of all countries is reported in Table 2.

For dynamic panels with a relatively short time dimension, the preferred method is the fixed effects model (FEM), given by Eq. (1). The FEM allows for heterogeneity among subjects by allowing each entity to have its own intercept value. The term "fixed effects" is due to the fact that, although the intercept may differ across subjects, each entity's intercept does not vary over time, i.e., it is time-invariant.

$$\text{LnEA}_{i,t} = \alpha_0 + \alpha_1 \text{LnEFI}_{i,t} + \alpha_2 \text{LnGDPC}_{i,t} + \alpha_3 \text{LnFDI}_{i,t} + \alpha_4 \ln\text{Unemp}_{i,t} + \varepsilon_{i,t}. \quad (1)$$

The subscripts denote the country i and the time period t. EA represents the entry density which proxies EA, EFI represents the rank of economic freedom index,[3] GDPC is the gross domestic product per capita (constant LCU), FDI is the foreign direct investment (FDI), UNEMP is the total unemployment (percent of total labor force) and ε_t is an error term. The dynamic model using the panel generalized method of moments (GMM) — to take care of cross-section heteroscedasticity and contemporaneous correlation — is captured in Eq. (2)

$$\text{LnEA}_{i,t} = \alpha_0 + \alpha_1 \text{EA}_{i,t-1} + \alpha_2 \text{LnEFI}_{i,t} + \alpha_3 \text{LnGDPC}_{i,t}$$
$$+ \alpha_4 \text{LnFDI}_{i,t} + \alpha_5 \ln\text{Unemp}_{i,t} + \varepsilon_{i,t}. \quad (2)$$

3.2. *Empirical results*

Our analysis starts with panel unit root tests followed by the traditional procedures for estimating cross-sectional dependence on the unit root test results. In order to assess the stationarity of the variables employed, this chapter uses four different unit root tests

---

[3] http://www.heritage.org/index/.

Table 2. List of sample countries.

Factor-driven stage countries				Efficiency-driven stage countries				Innovation-driven stage countries			
Country	EFI	Entry Density	GDPC	Country	EFI	Entry Density	GDPC	Country	EFI	Entry Density	GDPC
Algeria	55.72	0.53	4,786	Albania	60.08	0.52	4,108	Belgium	71	3.70	25,100
Azerbaijan	54.18	0.95	5,574	Brazil	60.0	1.91	8,622	Canada	77	6.54	26,102
Belarus	45.92	0.23	2,510	Bulgaria	62.4	4.63	6,798	Cyprus	72	16.55	11,503
Cambodia	57.92	0.13	886	Costa Rica	65.32	11.02	6,582	Denmark	76	4.89	32,320
Egypt	55.48	0.14	1,859	France	61.86	2.78	23,366	Finland	73	2.46	28,790
Guatemala	59.7	0.65	1,892	Hungary	64.72	3.51	5,947	Germany	70	1.12	25,620
India	53.18	0.05	1,042	Israel	63.9	5.29	27,591	Hong Kong	90	10.39	31,515
Indonesia	52.66	0.14	2,187	Italy	63.3	1.81	19,903	Iceland	75	13.01	37,958
Morocco	54.48	0.53	2,827	Jordan	65.02	0.37	3,797	Ireland	82	5.82	30,130
Moldova	57.82	1.40	591	Kazakhstan	56.9	2.33	7,165	Japan	70	1.31	38,563
Pakistan	55.78	0.03	982	Latvia	67.36	4.62	6,056	Singapore	88	5.20	36,972
Sri Lanka	59.82	0.30	2,013	Malaysia	62.22	2.64	8,460	Spain	70	4.82	32,799
Suriname	52.8	0.24	2,600	Malta	66.32	9.12	11,172	Sweden	70	3.29	52,730
Tunisia	58.34	0.73	3,023	Mexico	65.62	0.56	9,507	Switzerland	79	2.57	68,555
Uzbekistan	47.4	0.44	966	Panama	64.9	3.70	6,472	United Kingdom	79	9.77	43,146
				Portugal	63.62	3.54	23,716				
				Romania	56.64	5.80	9,497				
				Slovenia	60.1	2.59	27,015				
				Turkey	55.54	0.87	10,380				

including LLC's test, IPS-W-statistic, Augmented Dickey Fuller (ADF)-Fisher Chi-square test, and Phillips and Perron (PP)-Fisher Chi-square tests. The results of these tests are reported in Table 3 indicating that they are stationary at levels especially for the LLC's test at the 1 percent level.

Table 3. Panel unit root test.

Innovation-driven countries	Variables				
	ED	EFI	GDPC	UNEMP	FDI
Method LLC-*t**					
Level	2.577	−1.269	−3.79*	10.01	18.37
First difference	−14.08***	−5.6***	−3.70***	−6.98***	−2.4**
IPS-W-Stat					
Level	4.11	1.51	1.39	6.95	8.42
ADF–Fisher Chi-square					
Level	15.02	30.38	0.003	1.23	0.51
First difference	44.77	56.822*	267.12***	25.65	12.78
PP–Fisher Chi-square					
Level	15.61	1.29	0.001	0.9	0.04
First difference	105.33***	64.84*	44.77	35.09	7.36
Efficiency-driven countries	LOGED	LOGGDPG	LOGCPI	LOGUNEMP	LOGICTGEXP
Method LLC-*t**					
Level	11.08	−1.68*	1.29	7.52	1.73
First difference	−2.34**	−13.23***	−12.18***	−18.93***	−8.25***
IPS-W-Stat					
Level	4.86	8.35	1.33	4.95	1.38
ADF–Fisher Chi-square					
Level	2.39	26.96	13.54	2.28	13.27
First difference	13.514	133.3***	56.73*	70.745***	87.31***
PP–Fisher Chi-square					
Level	2.39	26.96	14.77	0.179	13.27
First difference	8.31	133.3***	92.95***	76.25***	87.31***
Factor-driven countries	LOGED	LOGGDPG	LOGGDPD	LOGUNEMP	LOGICTGEXP
Method-LLC-*t**					
Level	9.87	10.47	3.29	NA	5.3
First difference	5.87***	−3.98***	−23.59***	NA	−3.76***
IPS-W-Stat					
Level	6.44	3.13	4.38	NA	2.69
ADF–Fisher Chi-square					
Level	0.88	5.48	2.69	NA	2.16
First difference	19.93*	−3.01*	78.48**	NA	42.13
PP–Fisher Chi-square					
Level	0.59	5.48	2.19	NA	0.061
First difference	23.93*	−3.01*	84.59**	NA	42.14

Notes: Numbers in () are standardized errors, *, ** and *** indicate 10%, 5% and 1% level of significant, respectively.

The results reveal a positive significant relationship between EA and EFI in the innovation/efficiency-driven stage countries (Table 4). Furthermore, the results also suggest a positive and highly significant relationship between EA and FDI as well as economic growth in the innovation and efficiency-driven countries. The coefficient of EFI in the efficiency-driven countries is 6.37, higher than the coefficient for innovation-driven countries which is 1.04, in turn underlining the importance of a free economic system to attract more entrepreneurs. Another possible explanation for disparities in results lies in the stage of development as innovation-driven countries are at the steady state. These results are also in line with the literature concerning the importance of economic freedom and institutional measures (Wennekers and Thurik, 1999; Wennekers *et al.*, 2002; Bjørnskov and Foss, 2008).

Table 4. Cross-sectional results macro determinants of entrepreneurial activity.

	Fixed effect estimation			System GMM one step		
	Innovation driven stage	Efficiency driven stage	Factor driven stage	Innovation driven stage	Efficiency driven stage	Factor driven stage
EA_{t-1}				0.4095*	0.3221*	0.1757*
				(0.179)	(0.132)	(0.08)
EFI	1.04***	6.37***	−0.063***	4.8499**	0.185*	−7.727**
	−0.004	−0.0002	−0.0023	(1.566)	(1.239)	(2.2)
GDPC	1.22***	10.32***	0.18***	0.454*	0.715*	0.0333
	−0.006	−0.0003	−0.0003	0.141	(0.1542)	(0.03)
FDI	0.027***	0.58***	−0.018***	0.2511**	0.481**	−1.009***
	−0.0002	−0.00001	−0.000007	0.075	(0.1036)	(0.285)
UNEMP	−0.44***	−2.5422***	−0.021***	0.209	−0.0481*	0.667
	−0.002	−0.00009	−0.00031	0.1846	(0.103)	(0.33)
C**	−14.53***	−117.1	0.4	−21.184**	−16.54**	−30.74**
	−0.05	−0.004	−0.0067	(6.916)	(6.143)	(9.107)
H-statistic	53.16***	22.13	13.4	—	—	—
Serial-correlation test				1.6*	0.08*	0.5
Sargan test				68.6**	12.49**	43.64*
Number of instruments				58	14	33
Number of countries	15	19	15	15	19	15
Number of observation	75	95	75	59	75	45

Notes: The first three columns present the result of fixed effects estimation for the three groups of countries while the last three columns present the result of one step system — GMM. The dependent variable is the entry density.

The *H* test is the Hausman one permitting to validate or not fixed effects results. The alternative hypothesis leads to the adoption of fixed effects results. For Sargan test, the null hypothesis indicates that the used instruments are not correlated with the residuals.

Standard errors are reported in parentheses. ***, *, and * indicate significance levels at 1%, 5% and 1%, respectively.

On the other hand, we find a significant negative relationship between EA and EFI in factor-driven countries. This result highlights the importance of economic freedom and sound institutions for this group of countries to affect EA positively, which could in turn explain their weak performance. These countries face many challenges that are rooted in the economic freedom sub indices. Acs *et al.* (2008) suggest that factor-driven stage countries should work towards the efficiency-driven stage by achieving stable institutional and macro-economic environment and by increasing entrepreneurial capacity and enabling individuals and businesses to absorb knowledge spillovers.

Another important result is the highly positive and significant relationship between EA and economic growth in the three groups of countries. But the estimated coefficient is 0.18 in the factor-driven countries recording the lowest coefficient compared to the innovation-driven countries with a coefficient of 1.22 which in turn is less than the efficiency-driven countries with a coefficient of 10.32. This higher coefficient shows that the efficiency-driven countries with a higher startup rate demonstrate higher growth rates. This important role for EA illustrates how it serves as an agent to stimulate the economy and create opportunities. These results support the conclusions of the previous studies as well (Audretsch and Fritsch, 2002; Acs, 1992).

One of the central goals of public policy among all modern economies is to accelerate growth, attract more investments and increase employment. Results suggest positive relation between FDI and EA in innovation and efficiency-driven countries. The estimated coefficient is 0.027 in the innovation-driven countries which is less than the coefficient of 0.58 for the efficiency-driven countries (see Table 4). This higher coefficient shows the ability of efficiency-driven countries to attract more investment and the reason behind this may be related to the fact that innovation-driven countries require huge investment to start businesses depending on research and development, while efficiency-driven countries require less investment. Similar results were found by Klepper and Sleeper (2000) and Agarwal *et al.* (2004).

On the other hand, in factor-driven countries, we find a negative relationship between FDI and EA. Such results provide additional explanations for the weak performance of a group that is characterized by an economic system that is not only relatively less-free but also suffers from inadequate institutions to attract investments, which appear to be very sensitive to prevailing regulations and laws.

Finally, we find a negative relationship between unemployment and EA across the three groups. The estimated coefficient in the efficiency-driven countries is 2.54, 0.44 in the innovation-driven and 0.021 in the factor-driven countries. The empirical results support what has been termed as a "Schumpeter effect" as he argues that EA reduce unemployment which is in contradiction with some of the other literature (for instance, see Storey, 1991; Foti and Vivarelli, 1994).

We also report the dynamic estimation results using system-GMM in Table 4 which are broadly consistent with the results reported earlier.[4] The dynamic lagged dependent variable emerges as being significant for all the groups of countries. Further, the estimation results reported also show that there is a positive relationship between EA and EFI in innovation-driven countries, but this relation is absent for the other groups of countries. More importantly, the results are consistent in showing that growth and FDI have a positive and statistically significant relationship with EA in both efficiency-driven and innovation-driven countries. The relation between the unemployment and EA is significant only in the efficiency-driven countries.

4. Conclusion

EA have multiple impacts and determinants, which have been documented extensively in a number of theoretical and empirical studies in the literature. However, the importance of institutions in explaining EA has not been paid attention to, which has been the main contribution of this chapter. The chapter reports a set of cross-country tests of the determinants of the EA using data from 49 countries for three groups of countries, classified into factor-driven, efficiency-driven, and innovation-driven countries.

The study shows that economic freedom is one of the main determinants of EA and plays a significant role in spurring EA in innovation and efficiency-driven stage countries. The empirical results of the chapter emphasize the important role of free and sound economic system to attract and encourage EA, as evidenced by the negative relationship between EA and economic freedom in factor-driven countries characterized by weak institutions. Further, the positive relationship between FDI and EA in innovation and efficiency-driven countries, as well as the negative relationship between the two variables in factor-driven countries, stresses the importance of sound institutions in factor-driven countries in attracting more investments that would spur EA.

However, in factor-driven economies, small and new firms are not at the fore-front of the innovation process and hence their impact on economic growth is smaller compared to entrepreneurs in the innovation-driven economies. Moreover, the role of EA is lower in factor-driven countries in comparison with innovation-driven countries. In such countries, a sound regulatory system should help them overcome their institutional inadequacies and allow entrepreneurs to be able to execute business processes efficiently. This could in turn attract more investments that could be channelled into research and development activities which in turn could generate positive spillovers for factor-driven economies.

---

[4] The consistency of the GMM estimator depends on the assumption that the error term ε does not exhibit serial correlation and that the instruments used are valid. Following Arellano and Bond (1991), we used Sargan test of restrictions for over-identification, to test the overall validity of the instruments. Analyzing the sample analogs of the moment conditions used in the estimation procedure proved that Sargan test is robust to heteroskedasticity or auto-correlation. The second test examined the no serial correlation assumption of the error terms.

The results also show the positive and significant relation between EA and economic growth across all the three groups of countries. Finally, the empirical results also suggest that there is a clear negative relationship between an increase in EA and the decrease in unemployment rates across the three groups of countries.

Some broad policy implications arise from the study showing the mediating role economic freedom has attracting more EA to foster economic growth. The positive effect of economic freedom suggests that it may be good for governments to enhance the quality of institutions and the competence of entrepreneurs to accelerate growth.

The study is not without its limitations. Notably, the study depends on the WBGES data that covers only a short period of time (2004–2008). Future research could extend the analysis by considering different or longer periods. Further, the results are based on the overall economic freedom index that is constructed based on ten sub-indices. Additional analysis for each index might provide new results of the role of a specific policy.

Acknowledgment

Earlier version published at the ERF 20th International conference. The author is grateful to the editor Ramkishen S. Rajan for comments and for his helpful suggestions and support and to Karim Badr and Engy Rabie for assistance in preparing the document. The author is grateful to the ERF 20th international conference for the feedback and the comments of Prof Ishac Diwan. The views expressed in this chapter are those of the author and do not necessarily represent the MSA University.

References

Acs, ZJ (1992). Small business economics: A global perspective, *Challenge* 35 (November/December), 38–44.

Acs, ZJ and C Armington (2004). Employment growth and entrepreneurial activity in cities. *Regional Studies*, 38, 911–920.

Acs, ZJ, DB Audretsch and D Evans (1994). Why does the self-employment rates across countries and over time? CERP Working Paper No. 871, Center for Economic Policy Research.

Acs, ZJ, D Sameeksha and H Jolanda (2008). Entrepreneurship, economic development and institutions. *Small Business Economics*, 31, 219–234.

Acs, ZJ and N Virgill (2010). Entrepreneurship in developing countries. *Foundations and Trends in Entrepreneurship*, 6, 1–68.

Agarwal R, R Echambadi, F April and M Sarkar (2004). Knowledge transfer through inheritance: Spin-out generation, development and performance. *Academy of Management Journal*, 47, 501–522.

Audretsch, DB (1995). *Innovation and Industry Evolution*. Cambridge: MIT Press.

Audretsch, DB and M Fritsch (2002). Growth regimes over time and space. *Regional Studies*, 36, 113–124.

Audretsch, DB, I Verheul, AR Thurik and S Wennekers (eds.) (2002). *Entrepreneurship: Determinants and Policy in a European-US Comparison*. Boston/Dordrecht: Kluwer Academic Publishers.

Barro, RJ and X Sala-i-Martin (1995). *Economic Growth*. New York: McGraw-Hill.

Baumol, W (1990). Entrepreneurship: Productive, unproductive, and destructive. *Journal of Political Economy*, 98, 893–921.

Baumol, W (1993). *Entrepreneurship, Management, and the Structure of Payoffs*. Cambridge: MIT Press.

Bjørnskov, C and N Foss (2008). Economic freedom and entrepreneurial activity: Some cross-country evidence. *Public Choice*, 134, 307–328.

Blanchflower, DG (2000). Self-employment in OECD countries. *Labour Economics*, 7, 471–505.

Blanchflower, D and A Oswald (1998). What makes an entrepreneur? *Journal of Labour Economics*, 16, 26–60.

Boettke, PJ and CJ Coyne (2003). Entrepreneurship and development. In R Koppl, J Birner and P Kurrild-Klitgaard (Eds.), *Advances in Austrian Economics: Austrian Economics and Entrepreneurial Studies*, Bingley, UK: Emerald Group Publishing Ltd, pp. 67–87.

Carree, MA and AR Thurik (1999), Industrial structure and economic growth. In DB Audretsch and AR Thurik (Eds.), *Innovation, Industry Evolution and Employment*, Cambridge, UK: Cambridge University Press, pp. 86–110.

Cohen, WM and S Klepper (1996). A reprise of size and R&D. *Economic Journal*, 106, 925–951.

Evan, DS and LS Leighton (1990). Small business formation by unemployed and employed workers. *Small Business Economics*, 2, 319–330.

Fonseca, R, P Lopez-Garcia and CA Pissarides (2001). Entrepreneurship, startup and employment. *European Economic Review*, 45, 692–705.

Foti, A and M Vivarelli (1994). An econometric test of the self–employment model: The case of Italy. *Small Business Economics*, 6, 81–94.

Grossman, GM and E Helpman (1994). Endogenous innovation in the theory of growth. *Journal of Economic Perspectives*, 8, 23–44.

Ilmakunnas, P, V Kanniainen and U Lammi (1999). Entrepreneurship, economic risks and risk — Insurance in the welfare state. Discussion paper No. 453, University of Helsinki.

Johnson, S, J McMillan and C Woodruff (2000). Entrepreneurs and the ordering of institutional reform: Poland, Slovakia, Romania, Russia and Ukraine compared. *Economic of Transition*, 8, 1–36.

Johnson, S, J McMillan and C Woodruff (2002). Property rights and finance. *American Economic Review*, 92, 1335–1356.

Jovanovic, B (1982). Selection and the evolution of industry. *Econometrica*, 50, 649–670.

Klapper, L and I Love (2011). The impact of business environment reforms on new firm registration. Policy Research Working Paper No. 5493, World Bank, Washington, DC.

Klapper, L and JM Quesada Delgado (2007). View point: Entrepreneurship — New data on business creation and how to promote it. Note No. 316, The World Bank Group, Washington DC.

Klepper, S and S Sleeper (2000). Entry by spinoffs. Unpublished Manuscript, Carnegie Mellon University.

Merck, R, B Young and W Yu (2000). The information content of stock markets: Why do emerging markets have synchronous stock price movements? *Journal of Financial Economics*, 59, 215–260.

Naude, WA (2008). Entrepreneurship in economic development. Research Paper No. 2008/20, UNU-WIDER, United Nations University.

North, DC (1990). *Institutions, Institutional Change, and Economic Performance*. Cambridge: Cambridge University Press.

Porter, ME (1990). *The Competitive Advantage of Nations*. Free Press, New York.

Reynolds, PD, M Hay, WD Bygrave and SM Camp (1999). Global Entrepreneurship Monitor: 1999 Executive Report, Kauffman Centre for Entrepreneurship Leadership, Missouri.

Romer, PM (1990). Endogenous technological change. *Journal of Political Economy*, 98, 71–102.

Rostow, WW (1960). *The Stages of Economic Growth: A Non-Communist Manifesto*. Cambridge: Cambridge University Press.

Salgado-Banda, H (2005). Entrepreneurship and economic growth: An empirical analysis. Research Paper Banco de Mexico, pp. 1–46.

Schumpeter, JA (1911/1934). *The Theory of Economic Development*. Cambridge: Harvard University Press.

Schmitz, JA Jr. (1989). Imitation, entrepreneurship, and long-run growth. *Journal of Political Economy*, 97, 721–739.

Storey, DJ (1991). The birth of new firms: Does unemployment matter? *Small Business Economics*, 3, 167–178.

Van Stel, AJ (2003). COMPENDIA 2000.2: A harmonized data set of business ownership rates in 23 OECD countries. EIM Research Report 200302, Zoetermeer, Netherlands, EIM.

Van der Sluis, J, M van praag and W Vijverberg (2005). Entrepreneurship deflection and performance: A meta-analysis of the impact of education in developing economies. *World Bank Economic Review*, 2, 225–261.

Wennekers, S and R Thurik (1999). Linking entrepreneurship and economic growth. *Small Business Economics*, 13, 27–55.

Wennekers S, LM Uhlaner and R Thurik (2002). Entrepreneurship and its conditions: A macro perspective. *International Journal of Entrepreneurship Education*, 1, 25–68.

Index

Printed in the United States
By Bookmasters